The Ball G

The Ball Game Biz

An Introduction to the Economics of Professional Team Sports

DAVID GEORGE SURDAM

McFarland & Company, Inc., Publishers
Jefferson, North Carolina, and London

LIBRARY OF CONGRESS CATALOGUING-IN-PUBLICATION DATA

Surdam, David G. (David George)
    The ball game biz : an introduction to the economics of
professional team sports / David George Surdam.
        p.   cm.
    Includes bibliographical references and index.

    ISBN 978-0-7864-6057-1
    softcover : 50# alkaline paper ∞

    1. Baseball — Economic aspects — United States.   2. Major
League Baseball (Organization) — Finance.   I. Title.
GV880.S87   2010
    796.357'640973 — dc22   2010029786

British Library cataloguing data are available

Cover images ©2010 Shutterstock

Manufactured in the United States of America

*McFarland & Company, Inc., Publishers
    Box 611, Jefferson, North Carolina 28640
    www.mcfarlandpub.com*

Table of Contents

Preface and Acknowledgments   1
Introduction   5

1. Why Economists Are Not Like Most People   7
2. Sports Numeracy   37
3. Game Theory Applied to Sports   57
4. Demand for Games and Profitability   83
5. Competitive Balance, Player Movement, and the
   Reserve Clause   109
6. Will Revenue Sharing Enhance Parity?   131
7. Why Professional Athletes Make Big Bucks   139
8. Discrimination in the World of Sports   152
9. Keeping Out the Riff-Raff   162

Conclusion   179
Chapter Notes   183
Bibliography   189
Index   193

Preface and Acknowledgments

Professional team sports hold many attractions for economists. The industry provides an array of opportunities for economists to test their theories. Because of the many applications of economic principles to professional team sports, economists are increasingly offering courses in sports economics. I suspect that other professors raise an eyebrow at seeing sports economics courses offered in the course catalog. They may suspect that the subject is just another fluff course designed for athletes on scholarships. Students, too, may have misconceptions about the course. They may think it will be a variation of sports talk radio, where opinions are offered freely and facts are rarely presented. The professor teaching sports economics must dispel such beliefs early in the course. Sports economics can and should be as rigorous as other courses in economics.

Learning economics is a challenge for many students. They have to mull over abstract ideas. They should also learn how to gather and apply data in order to test economic theories. Studying professional team sports is a good vehicle for learning economics. Applying economic principles to professional team sports helps students understand economic principles while they attain a greater understanding of professional team sports.

I hope to reach two other groups of readers: sportswriters and sports fans. Much of which follows will contradict the so-called conventional wisdom. To be fair, I have some advantages over sportswriters. Sportswriters have to file regular reports under tight time constraints, while I can concoct this treatise at my leisure. In addition, most sportswriters are not trained in statistical analysis, nor are many of them familiar with formal game theory. I should pay homage to the late Leonard Koppett. His writings inspired me as a teenager. While he was not a trained statistician, he

1

frequently offered cogent analysis of sports issues. He certainly was a pioneer in thinking abstractly about sports. While several sportswriters have trod in his footsteps, none has filled them. I hope that they, as well as the general reader, will gain some insights from what follows.

I will focus upon the three professional ball games: baseball, football, and basketball. I will use historical examples to demonstrate the economic principles involved, so readers will get both an understanding of economics and knowledge of professional team sports' history.

My long-standing interest in sports began when I watched my brother play varsity basketball. While I was a mediocre participant — as Will Rogers might have stated in a scouting report on my baseball-playing ability, "He never met a groundball he didn't boot" — I loved the history and the numbers associated with sports.

Strat-O-Matic Baseball was a good way to combine my love of sports history and sports statistics. I played Strat-O-Matic Baseball with a group of guys from around the country. Playing Strat-O-Matic Baseball was far superior to, though more time-consuming than, fantasy baseball. The game is quite realistic, especially with regard to fielding prowess, and offers valuable insights into the interaction between statistics and building winning teams. I learned to calculate basic probabilities from analyzing the game. I am indebted to the game's creator, Harold Richman, both for creating a fun way to spend hours and for patiently answering my queries.

When I was a mathematics undergraduate at the University of Oregon's Robert D. Clark Honors College, my professors encouraged me to examine baseball run production using regression analysis. Professors Paul Speckman and Richard Koch, along with the late Edward Diller, devoted much time and offered a great deal of encouragement to me, as I struggled to understand the complexity of regression analysis and the frustrations of working with the university's mainframe computer. I found that submitting batches of computer punch cards with their exacting syntax a Sisyphean process. The advent of personal computers and software has been a boon for statistical analysts.

Richard Adams, my high school teacher who has been a lifelong friend, encouraged my interest in sports in his physics class. Kevin Quinn provided encouragement throughout this project. Janine Goodwin meticulously edited an earlier version of the manuscript. Professor Louis Cain of Loyola University of Chicago suggested that I switch fields from Civil War economic history to sports economics, a suggestion that has proven fruitful. My peers at the University of Northern Iowa Economics Department have supported my endeavors in sports economics.

As always, when the publication process neared completion, I had the delightful experience of working with Sarah Statz Cords on the index. As with my previous work, she compiled a strong index. Farzad Moussavi, Dean of the College of Business Administration, and Fred Abraham, head of the economics department, at the University of Northern Iowa generously approved funding the index expense and provided encouragement and support for the manuscript.

Introduction

For many readers, the idea of going to a ball game with an economist ranks somewhere below having your kid sibling tag along with you to a sandlot game. After all, according to ancient wisdom, an economist is someone who didn't have the personality to be an accountant. Indeed, I demonstrated a real knack for accounting and probably should have exercised my comparative advantage by becoming a CPA, but I did not want to fulfill my senior class prophecy and instead became something exciting (but not too exciting, so lion tamer was excluded), getting my Ph.D. in economics.

Economics permeates professional team sports. If a team raises its ticket prices, what will be the effect upon gate receipts? When the property rights to a player's labor changes from the reserve clause to free agency, does this affect the player's salary? Does free agency affect a league's competitive balance? Will building a new stadium invigorate the local economy?

The widespread statistical information on productivity is appealing to economists. Economists study whether players are paid based on their productivity. Unfortunately, the plethora of playing statistics is not matched by a surfeit of financial information. If it were, we could say even more about the economics of sports. In addition, the strategic interaction between teams makes the games readily adaptable to "game theory" analysis. Game theory, pioneered by John von Neuman and John Nash (the latter of whom is renowned for both a Nobel Prize and a big Hollywood treatment, *A Beautiful Mind*), analyzes strategic interaction. The foremost proponents of the science employ heavy-duty mathematics instead of the X's and O's used by coaching geniuses. Economists can, therefore, bring a "triple threat" to analyzing sports: economics, statistics and probability, and game theory.

The reader will learn several basic economic principles in the first chapter. From there I will introduce some basic probability and statistics. Sports fans enjoy debating player and team statistics, and some knowledge of fundamentals of probability and statistics will enhance their understanding. The third chapter covers the relatively novel field of game theory. Game theory is a heavily mathematical field, but the basic insights can easily be explained. Game theory analyzes strategic interaction between two or more contesting parties. Economists often apply game theory in explaining how large firms determine pricing and output decisions when there are rival firms. The remainder of the book applies these basic principles to historical situations in professional team sports. While past events rarely recur exactly, studying history provides useful perspective on persistent challenges facing humans.

While I am a strong believer in the value of understanding the history of professional team sports, there is an economic insight that may temper one's enthusiasm. Nobel Prize winner Robert Lucas revolutionized the way economists think about the economy's response to various government policies. He noted that while understanding past business and consumer behavior is critical, these parties will quickly adjust to any changes in the rules of the economy (such as a governmental policy change). Hence, knowing how owners behaved in the past provides clues to their future behavior, but if the rules of the game have been changed, an observer must factor in the likelihood that owners will adjust their behavior. In sports terms, knowing how professional coaches behaved in the NBA during the 1960s might provide useful evidence in predicting how they might behave in the 1970s. However, the subsequent introduction of the three-point shot would alter coaches' behavior and might force us to alter our predictions.

By studying these examples, I hope the reader will gain a deeper understanding of how professional team sports operate. From this deeper understanding, I also hope the reader will begin to apply the principles to other non-sports topics encountered in the news. Economic literacy is a desirable trait.

CHAPTER 1

Why Economists Are Not Like Most People

Many people take at least one economics course during their undergraduate studies. For some, the subject remains as arcane after they take the final exam as it did before they entered the classroom. While the use of mathematics can clarify many economics principles, the widespread phobia surrounding mathematics and numbers keeps people from gaining knowledge they could otherwise obtain from using the techniques of economics.

Economists like to think that economics is a science. We do strive to develop interesting models with testable hypotheses. While the person on the street may be properly skeptical of economists' ability to divine the path of the economy, our ability to predict the effects of policy changes is pretty strong. Only a minority, probably a small minority, of economists actively seek to predict "what the economy is going to do." Presumably such an ability would afford the savvy economist an opportunity to reap financial benefits in the futures or stock markets. Economists are quite capable of predicting the general effects of, say, an increase in the minimum wage, a change in the tax laws, and many other changes. We can do this, even though, unlike the hard sciences such as physics, chemistry, and biology, we can only rarely run experiments. A growing field in economics is "experimental economics," where researchers enlist undergraduate student volunteers to play simple games. These experiments do provide insights, but, alas, they are quite limited. It would be highly unethical, for instance, to gauge the effects of having generous health insurance versus having no health insurance by creating pools of people and assigning some full insurance while denying any insurance to the other people. This experiment would certainly provide much useful information on the effects of health insurance. Thanks to less scrupulous legislators, experiments of this nature do occur. Economists can treat these legislative changes as "experiments." Favorable tax treatment of insurance premiums paid through an employer is an example. Another example is if the state of Oregon boosts the tax rates on corporations doing business within the state, economists can study the effects. Testable hypotheses would be that there will be more people with health care in the first case and there will be fewer corporations doing business in Oregon in the second. These effects do not occur in isolation, though, as other changes in the economy are happening concurrently and may make it difficult to discern the exact effects of the changes in rules and tax rates. These legislative changes, as well as societal changes, are the best data economists have in testing hypothesis.

The economist's favorite professional hobby is creating economic models. An economic model is a bare-bones depiction of reality. Economists make assumptions that focus on the most salient points in order to make the model usable.[1] People often criticize economists for their "unrealistic" assumptions, but this criticism is misplaced. The icons posted on bathroom doors are a great example of a successful model. Often there's a triangular figure for women and a rectangular one for men (aside from the words "Men" and "Women," which has the drawback of potential confusion; sometimes the "Wo" is obscured and an unwary hurried male can inadvertently enter the wrong room). No one has any friends who resemble these icons, or at least I hope they don't. The icons, though, have an enviable record for prediction. Even the dullest or most inebriated person can ascertain which door to enter and not experience social embarrassment. Economists trade simplicity for ease of use in their models. Adding more complexity comes at the cost of less ease of use. Naturally economists must consider the benefits and costs of more realism.

Many models are created, but few are chosen. How do economists choose between models? John Maynard Keynes' model of the overall (macro) economy remains an elegant model, but Edmund Phelps and Milton Friedman pointed out that Keynes' model did not generate predictions that closely corresponded with reality. The economic conditions of the 1970s disputed Keynes' idea of a trade-off, at least in the short run, between inflation and unemployment. The reader should not cry for Professor Keynes. As advances in mathematics percolated down to economists, his defenders have refurbished the original model. His detractors have, in turn, been forced to revise their criticisms and models. Slowly and frustratingly, economists are developing new insights into how the macroeconomy functions.

Most people have mistaken impressions of economics. To Marxists, economics is a form of apologetics used by lackeys of the running dogs of capitalism. Yet, once you understand what economics is, you will realize that all of us, capitalists and socialists, are bound by economic thinking.

A second notion is that economics is difficult. I'm here to tell you that economics is not rocket science. There are cases of physicists becoming top-notch economists, but I am not aware of any cases in which economists have become top physicists. In any event, economics should be readily understandable. How can I make such a claim? Because I know you're already practicing economic thinking; you just don't know it. You have a powerful incentive to do so. All of us subconsciously use economic principles. A good economics class should reinforce and clarify intuition and common sense.

The Basic Characteristic of Economic Problems

The economic way of thinking revolves around scarcity. Economists often raise the question, "What's it going to cost?" Such a question is relevant only in a world plagued by scarcity. Naturally, such candor does not make us welcome at, say, parties or town hall meetings. Of course, economists are also keenly interested in what benefits might result from a given action. Still, I think our concentration upon costs helps justify the sobriquet "The Dismal Science" in the minds of many people.

What is economics? Here is a formal definition: Economics examines how to deploy scarce resources among alternative uses to best achieve a goal or goals.

In a world without scarcity, there would be no economics, much less a need to study the subject. In a world without scarcity, I'd be out of a job, but I wouldn't care. I wouldn't need to write this book to earn money for rent, for I would live in a world in which the only scarcity would be scarcity itself.

Since everyone, capitalist and socialist alike, faces scarcity, all of us must think about how to deploy our scarce resources among alternative uses in order to best achieve our goals. Notice that nothing is said about people being omniscient or particularly moral. Economists have little to say about what people's goals should be. A Marxist may well have different goals than a capitalist, but both have to be careful, very careful indeed, in allocating their scarce resources in order to best achieve their goals.

All of us face some variety of scarcity, whether it is of income, wealth, health, knowledge, energy, popularity, or even, to be New Age about it, love.

As a child, my Dad often lamented that our family did not have a gold mine in the backyard, where we could simply pick up a nugget or two before heading into town on a shopping trip. Had we possessed such a magical mine, we wouldn't have had to worry much about the figures on the price tags. But, of course, such a mine did not exist. No one has unlimited wealth, but if someone did, I would surely want to be their friend or, better yet, their nephew.

Bill Gates is tremendously wealthy. The constraints upon his wealth are far looser than those acting upon the typical American. He could walk into a fancy department store such as Neiman-Marcus and pretty much buy everything on the shelves. He could afford more shoes than Imelda Marcos in the heyday of her frantic shopping. Still, at some point, Bill Gates has to ask the same question facing the rest of us, "Can I afford this?" Can Bill Gates afford to buy a small state, such as Delaware? Perhaps his tens of billions could buy a small state, but he certainly could not afford to purchase California. In the sports world, George Steinbrenner and the New York Yankees are rich, rich, rich compared to the Kansas City Royals, but even George must eventually ask, "Can I afford another All-Star?"

While Bill Gates' advantage in wealth far transcends our wealth holdings, he faces roughly similar constraints upon his time. There are only twenty-four hours in Bill's day. Although he can afford the best health care, which might add, on average, a few months to his longevity, he faces the same roughly "four score and seven" life expectancy that the rest of us do. Bill can, however, use his wealth to lengthen his days indirectly. He can hire someone to carry out the garbage, vacuum the floor, scrub the tub, and mow the lawn, thereby freeing his time for more enjoyable activities.

What about knowledge? Mr. Gates is obviously an intelligent man. Yet, there are many readers who could successfully challenge him in a *Jeopardy!* match.

Does Bill Gates enjoy more love than most people? Perhaps. But it is more likely that even Bill muses, "I wish more people loved me."

Thus, Bill Gates faces scarcity just as the rest of us do. Because of the constraints facing him, he has to be careful in allocating his resources to attain his goals. Every dollar spent on acquiring Delaware could be used to improve his business, build a truly palatial mansion, fund the arts, or help the needy. Every hour he spends watching *Gilligan's Island* reruns on television — granted, a fancy, wide-screen, high-definition television — means one less hour devoted to walking around his estate, making a business deal, sleeping, or a myriad of other endeavors.

Because scarce resources used for one endeavor usually cannot be used concurrently for another endeavor, there is an opportunity cost associated with any particular use. Those ten dollars you spend on lunch have an opportunity cost: What is the best alternative use for them?

When you were a student, every hour spent studying mathematics was one less hour that you could devote to chemistry, sleeping, or goofing around with friends. The hour spent studying mathematics has an opportunity cost, and that cost is the best alternative use for the hour.

To reinforce this important concept, I borrow a parable. Economic writer Henry Hazlitt re-fashioned a French parable into a tale regarding a broken window. I'll quickly paraphrase the story. Some punk kid throws a rock through a baker's window. As people gather around the storefront, a few people reflect that the incident, while morally reprehensible, will at least improve the economy.[2] "The baker will have to buy a window from the glazier, raising Gross Domestic Product (GDP)." People nod their heads in agreement.

However, such thinking, while superficially plausible, is fallacious. For the $1,000 it costs the baker to buy a replacement window, he could have raised the GDP by purchasing a new computer to keep track of inventory. Had the punk not struck, the baker would have had the original window and the computer. Now he has only a replacement window. The people in the crowd have failed to recall the opportunity cost of the new window.

Such fuzzy thinking permeates society. About two decades ago, the Mississippi River flooded several towns. Lloyd Bentsen, who was the vice president at the time, surveyed the damage and remarked that the rebuilding effort would bolster the economy. I'm sure the flooded residents were ecstatic to do their part for the U.S. economy. Bentsen is a sharp person, so my example demonstrates how easy it is to fall into such a faulty line of reasoning. We used to hear a variation of the argument back when Japan, Inc. was seemingly poised to threaten U.S. economic dominance. Some commentators suggested that Japan and Germany became such formidable industrial rivals because their factories had been bombed during World War II, so they had to rebuild. In the process of rebuilding, they had recourse to the latest technology, so their factories were better than the aging American factories. If this were true, then why not bomb Pittsburgh, Gary, and other industrial cities? (We'd move the people out first, of course.) Then our industrialists could rebuild with better, more modern factories. This suggestion is, of course, risible. In order to rebuild their factories, Japanese and German people had to forego a lot of consumption. It's difficult to truly argue that they were better off with the bombed-out factories, not to mention the large number of civilian casualties caused by the bombing.

So, in order to practice good economic thinking, you must become adept at identifying the relevant opportunity costs and benefits. I can assure you that if you succeed in doing so, your economic analysis may well be superior to much of the nattering that is done in the media by so-called economists. (Many people call themselves economists, and there's no law against impersonating one. After all, economics is one of the rare professions without a licensing or certifying examination.)

Let me repeat a crucial ramification of opportunity costs. Because deploying resources entails opportunity costs, you have to be careful in using your resources.

A simple thought experiment demonstrates the importance of being careful. Suppose I receive a prestigious research grant to be used in studying consumer behavior. I could give one thousand people $100 each to be spent in a local convenience store. You are one of those fortunate people. You can spend the $100 on anything you want, but you must spend the money.

As we track your decisions via hidden camera, some competing tactics become apparent. You could walk up and down the aisles and pick up items at random. Of course, such a strategy would likely result in disappointment. When you returned home and removed the items from the bag, you'd discover that you had purchased cat food for your non-existent cat. You might find a personal hygiene product designed for the opposite gender. There might be some Brussels sprouts or another unsavory vegetable that you detest.

No, most of you would not purchase items randomly. Most of you would carefully compare how much you like the item. "Wow, some chocolate-encrusted cereal would be great for breakfast." Then you'd look at the price. "But not for seven dollars a box." For each item, you'd explicitly or subconsciously weigh the subjective pleasure or usefulness you'd get compared with its cost. If an item gave you more pleasure than it cost, you would consider tossing into your shopping cart. The expression, "It's a good buy," exemplifies this process.

There's another important point to be made about our experiment. In most cases, you know your preferences and goals better than anyone else does. If I ask you whether you'd be willing to have a friend or family member spend the $100 at the convenience store on your behalf, I suspect you'd nix the idea. Why? Your friends or loved ones may not know your preferences well enough to do a good job. Certainly all of us have received unwanted birthday gifts, gifts that the giver did a poor job selecting. In addition, you have a strong incentive to spend the $100 wisely, since it's your pleasure and benefit that are at stake. Your personal shopper might lack knowledge of your preferences or the incentive to adhere to that knowledge.

When we think of opportunity costs, we usually think in terms of dollars. Often people consider the cash price only. Certainly the cash price is the easiest to identify. However, there are other costs involved. Consider the following example.

University of Chicago economists are fond of the phrase, "There's no such thing as a free lunch." You can imagine them ending a joke at the faculty club with the punch line, amidst much laughter. In 1993, the university celebrated its centennial. University officials erected food booths around campus and invited people to pick up a free box lunch. Peering down upon the quadrangles, do you suppose the august economics professors were shaking their heads and admitting the inaccuracy of their favorite phrase?

No, indeed. In your mind's eye, what do you see around the food booths where the free box lunches are being distributed? Long lines. Yes, students had to wait in line. How long would you wait in line for a box lunch consisting of a sandwich, a bag of chips, a cookie, and an apple? It might have retailed for $5.00 in 1993. Would you wait ten minutes? Twenty minutes? An hour? You would probably be willing to wait up to five dollars worth of your time. While the box lunches did not have a cash cost, there was a time cost. The economics professors could renew their faith in the shibboleth.

We can extend our thinking about costs by asking ourselves what type of students would be most likely to stand in line. Would they be undergraduates? Graduate students? Students in professional programs such as law, business, or medicine? Presumably students in the professional schools would be the least likely to wait in line, as they might place a higher value on their time.

For people in paying jobs, a proxy for the value of your time might be the earnings you would forego, based on your hourly wage (you can adjust it for take-home pay, net after taxes).

Here's another general cost. If you enjoy golf, you might want to reconsider an invitation from former President Gerald Ford. Twice during his presidency, he hit an errant golf ball that struck someone; at least that was the rumor promulgated by contemporary comics. Regardless of whether President Ford did so (and, to be fair, he was a good enough athlete to play football for the University of Michigan), the anecdote serves to raise the point that golf, like most activities, entails some risk. Aside from getting hit by an errant golf ball, there are the risks of being struck by lightning or being involved in a golf cart accident. If you like downhill skiing, the risk of breaking a leg used to be quite high. I need not say much about the perils of sky-diving, except that as a university class, it's the one you don't want to flunk. A good statistician could probably give you a estimate of the expected dollar loss from medical bills and time away from work attached to a given activity.

Golf also serves to demonstrate another cost. If you are in a foursome with your boss and a couple of important clients, wearing your loud Hawaiian shirt is likely to diminish you in their eyes. You'll suffer what I call a prestige cost.

Here's another example of a prestige cost. Suppose you are having a group of friends over to watch the Super Bowl. Everyone antes up money for some beer. You go to the grocery store and notice some white cans with black letters: "BEER." You examine the small print, "Manufactured by Butz Beer for distribution by the XYZ Grocery Store." You've read in consumer magazines that Butz often produces beer for what is known as "generic labels." It's the same beer, it just goes to a different spigot in the factory. You think to yourself, "I should buy this beer, since the gang likes Butz." (After all, the ad jingle says, "Butz is good fer yer guts.") The next question echoes the old Toyota ad, "What will you do with all the money you save?" You can now buy chips and pretzels.

The night of the Super Bowl arrives, you greet your friends and direct them to a table laden with beer, chips, and pretzels. However, your ears are soon burning, as the buzz around the room is about, "What a cheap-skate [your name here] is for buying generic beer," among other less savory epithets. You are incurring a loss of prestige. Why? You dash into the middle of the room with the dog-eared, consumer report article, announcing, "It's the same beer! And I was able to get you chips and pretzels, too." Will anyone laud you for your shopping acumen? Probably not.

Why won't they? Are your friends snobs? Not necessarily. One possible reason to prefer the name brand version of Butz is precisely that the company's name is readily identifiable. They have a reputation to protect, as no beer company hopes to stay in business on a one-shot basis (okay, poor liquor pun). However, your friends might be snobs. People are often willing to pay extra for comparable quality if only the right name is on the label. The difference between, say, Ralph Lauren and Alf Loren is huge. If we are clever, we can attach a dollar amount to the prestige cost of an activity.

The final form of cost is pain cost. In the health care field, there are different levels of pain and discomfort associated with various treatments. The pain and discomfort costs associated with mammograms and prostate tests discourage many people from getting regular screenings.

By considering all the kinds of opportunity costs, we can get a more precise idea of the overall opportunity cost of an activity. For producers, an important lesson is that they are not competing solely on the basis of dollar or cash cost. If they were, we'd live in a world of Kmart and other discount merchants. However, consumers appreciate convenience, quality, prestige, and other factors. Producers can compete across a variety of factors.

We can see these facets of costs and benefits by comparing attending a ball game in person with watching it on television. Television became a competitor for attending games in person during the late 1940s. TV offered a cheaper cash cost for each game; no time wasted getting to the park; and no risk of getting hit by a foul ball. On the other hand, watching a game on television probably lacked the excitement and prestige of attending in person, and television screens were tiny for many years, affording a hard-to-see picture.

You may have noticed that benefits and costs often include subjective as well as objective factors. People appear to be more fearful of flying on a commercial jet liner than driving to the local grocery store, although the latter activity is, in reality, more risky. Perhaps it's the feeling that they are not in control of the jetliner that worries them. On an objective level, the commercial jet pilots are the cream of the pilot crop, highly trained and monitored. Unlike the majority of drivers who consistently claim in surveys that they are "above average," suggesting some mass delusion or an example of the Lake Woebegon effect, commercial passenger jet pilots really are above average. Still, people appear to feel more comfortable with the steering wheel in their own hands. A second reason for the heightened fear of flying is the horror factor. Most automobile accidents are over in a blink of an eye, while you sometimes read accounts of people jotting down notes to loved ones as the plane spirals down, down, down. In addition, there may be many more fatalities in a major airline crash compared with even a bus crash. The reality is that American commercial jetliners have enviable safety records, and I suspect they may be the safest place to be, not only of any transportation mode but in terms of mundane activities such as using the stairs or taking a bath.

Because of these subjective aspects of benefits and costs, a government bureaucrat is likely to have difficulty ascertaining how much the public truly values a service. For example, in the context of sports, how much do residents of a given city value a new stadium? At least the private sector producer has sales figures to guide her.

Is there a simple rule in determining how to allocate your scarce resources? Without getting overly technical, to best achieve your goals or your happiness, you need to keep purchasing an item as long as the additional benefits (subjective and objective) exceed or equal its (subjective and objective) additional costs. The additional benefit from consuming an additional unit of an item is the marginal benefit of that additional unit. The additional cost from purchasing another unit of an item is the marginal cost of that additional unit. Your rule should be, therefore, to buy the next unit of an item as long as its marginal benefit exceeds or equals its marginal cost. Economists call this marginal analysis. Marginal benefits generally tend to diminish at some point: Each additional unit of a commodity provides smaller incremental increases in pleasure or utility. Marginal costs frequently begin to increase at some point.

There might be increasing marginal benefit for some levels of consumption. Consider a fan collecting baseball cards. As she gets close to having an entire set, the last few cards may provide more marginal benefit than some earlier cards. The final card that completes her collection may have a particularly high marginal benefit. She probably receives sharply diminishing marginal benefit from additional redundant cards.

To make this clearer, consider a sports mogul. She is considering how many seats to build into her new stadium. For simplicity, let us assume that each additional seat costs $1,000 to build and to maintain. She's already planned for 45,000 seats. "If I add another seat, I'm likely to increase total revenue over the lifetime of the stadium by $1,200. It only costs me $1,000 to add another seat, so this is a good move."[3] She builds the 45,001st seat. She continues in this manner until a seat brings in just as much additional revenue as it costs to build and maintain ($1,000). Then she stops. If she builds more seats, the additional revenue expended would fall below the cost of the seats, so she would be worse off building any more seats.

Scarcity is fundamental to economics. Scarcity underlies the basic decision rule: marginal benefit equals marginal cost.

The Beauty of Price Determination: Supply and Demand

How are prices determined? In some societies, the government dictates prices. In the United States, most prices are determined by the market via supply and demand.

Scarcity underlies both supply and demand. Because of scarcity, the more an item costs (assuming that every other relevant factor stays the same), the less people buy of it. There is an inverse or teeter-totter relationship between price and the quantity demanded. Economists call this the law of demand. There are strong reasons to believe in the law of demand. As something increases in price, eventually some people simply cannot afford to buy it. It is even more likely that when an item increases in price, alternative items become more attractive. If the Chicago Bears increase their ticket prices, Chicago residents may decide they would rather attend a baseball or basketball game, or go to a movie, than attend a Bears game.

The ability to substitute cushions the effect of a price increase. Of course, the amount of "cushioning" depends upon the number and closeness of substitutes. If you are a diabetic, an increase in the price of insulin is difficult to avoid. There aren't many suitable substitutes, so your response in terms of quantity purchased is likely to be small. Conversely, if the price of Burpsi-Cola increases, you might find Pepsi-Cola or Coca-Cola suitable substitutes. Facing an increase in the price of Burpsi-Cola, you are likely to have a strong response and significantly cut your consumption of that cola while increasing consumption of rival colas. Even if you don't like the other colas, you have other beverages that may suffice in lieu of Burpsi-Cola.

After a consumer decides how much of a commodity to purchase at a specific price, the quantity demanded becomes part of her demand curve. An individual's demand for Burpsi-Cola shows how much of it she is willing to buy at any given price, holding all other relevant factors fixed. As we've seen, she's likely to buy less as the price increases.

In addition to the price of Burpsi-Cola, there are many other factors affecting how much is demanded, including the prices of related goods (such as substitutes and complements), incomes, expectations of future prices, tastes and preferences, and taxes or subsidies. We call these demand shifters because they are factors that shift demand. The prices of goods that can be substituted for Burpsi-Cola affect its demand. We've already discussed how the demands for Burpsi-Cola and Coca-Cola are intertwined. If the price of Coca-Cola increases because of a reduction in the supply, people may substitute Burpsi-Cola, increasing its demand. An increase in demand for Burpsi-Cola means that, at any given price, more Burpsi-Cola is demanded than before.

Sometimes you consume goods in tandem. Beer and pretzels are an example. In England, I suppose we would use the example of beer and skittles. Anyway, two goods that are consumed in tandem are called complements. If the demand for pretzels falls, then you'll reduce your demand for beer. Right and left shoes, Laurel and Hardy, baseball games and hot dogs, and bread and butter are other complementary tandems.

If you received an increase in income, you would undoubtedly increase your consumption of many commodities. However, you would decrease your consumption of some commodities. If, when your income increases, you consume more of a commodity, that commodity is a normal good. If, instead, you consume less of a commodity, that commodity is termed an inferior good. The terminology is unfortunate, since many "inferior" goods provide reasonable quality for the money. Macaroni and cheese in a box, rides on mass transit, and generic beer are inferior goods for most Americans. When you are a struggling college student, macaroni and cheese in a box may provide a filling, somewhat nutritious meal for less than a dollar. After you get a real job upon graduation, presumably you will buy fewer boxes of macaroni and cheese. You might begin buying mac and cheese from a deli. In the sports context, bleacher seats, aside from those in Wrigley Field, are probably inferior goods. Many baseball owners even stated this explicitly: As fans' incomes rise, they move to reserved and box seats.

A commodity can be a normal good for certain income ranges and then become inferior goods. At high enough income levels, even box seats can become inferior goods. Wealthy fans might opt for skyboxes or suites, or, for the truly well-heeled, private performances. In the past, wealthy Latin American dictators were known to hire groups of ballplayers to play a few games.

Consumers' expectations of future prices can affect their current demand. Years ago, Johnny Carson apparently made a joke about an impending toilet paper shortage. Fearing the shortage and attendant higher prices, people went to the supermarket and stocked up. The joke was on them. Still, if you anticipate higher prices in the future, your current demand will increase. Conversely, if you think prices are going to fall in the future, you will defer purchasing today and your current demand will fall.

Consumers' demand for a product can be affected by taxes or subsidies. For much of the twentieth century, there was an entertainment tax on tickets for movies and sporting events. Since the consumer is unlikely to care much about who gets the money they pay for a ticket, a 10 percent tax on a baseball ticket is initially the same as increasing the dollar price of attending the game by 10 percent. The demand for baseball games should eventually fall, as should the ticket price. The customers pay the lowered ticket price plus the 10 percent tax. The overall price of ballgames increases, while the quantity demanded falls. Note that the team receives less revenue, as it reaps a lower ticket price coupled with fewer patrons.

Corporate taxes have a different effect. Corporations buy many season tickets for entertainment purposes. A corporation facing, say, a 30 percent rate of taxation on profits figures that buying a $300 season ticket really means $210 in net payment, since $90 would have been paid out in corporate tax. In a sense, the corporation receives a "subsidy" on the price of a baseball ticket. During the 1950s, when corporate tax rates were significantly higher, tickets to sporting events were quite attractive. Some observers noted that the New York teams, with the city's huge base of corporate offices, had a big advantage over the Washington Senators, with that team's small corporate base, when it came to season ticket sales.

When Congress and the Internal Revenue Service began enforcing adherence to rules pertaining to entertaining clients, Major League Baseball owners worried that such scrutiny might adversely affect corporate demand for baseball tickets. As it turned out, the nature of season tickets was actually an advantage, so there was little effect. If corporate income tax rates fall, the "subsidy" would fall, and we could expect corporate demand for season tickets to decrease.

While the demand for a product can change due to the changing preferences or tastes of consumers, economists should be wary of attributing a change in the market price to these factors. One should first ascertain whether there were changes in the other underlying factors. Only if we can eliminate the likelihood of such changes or if there is a clear, compelling reason to expect tastes to change, should an economist resort to the "change in preference" explanation. I provide two amusing examples of definite changes in preferences, both from the early 1960s.

If you watch movies from the 1940s and 1950s or see photos of ballplayers wearing civilian clothes, you will notice that men usually wore hats during those decades. At his inauguration, President Kennedy did not wear a hat. In an attempt to "be like JFK," many men stopped wearing hats, so the demand for hats fell.

After the movie *Psycho* premiered with its famous shower scene, sales of shower doors soared. Apparently people who watched the movie decided that a shower door was safer than a shower curtain: It afforded a nanosecond more warning that a knife-wielding, mother-fixated, homicidal maniac was in the bathroom. So, the demand for shower doors increased.

These situations, as amusing as they are, are not necessarily commonplace.

Each individual consumer will have a demand for a commodity, based on that person's attempts to maximize his or her subjective pleasure or utility with regard to the commodity's price and other relevant information. By adding up all of the consumers' individual demands for the commodity, you can derive the market demand. The market demand almost always demonstrates an inverse relationship between the commodity's price and the quantity demanded, holding other factors fixed. We note that in some contexts, the demand curve might represent producers' willingness to buy raw materials or labor, but the inverse relationship between price and quantity demand still holds.

Another crucial aspect of demand is how responsive the quantity demanded is to changes in price. Owners might ask themselves, "I know an increase in ticket prices will reduce the number of seats sold, but will the diminution be relatively large or relatively small?" Economists have developed a concept, the price elasticity of demand, to discuss such responsiveness. In old economic textbooks, authors used an elastic band, like stretching the waistband of a pair of underpants. If the quantity demanded changes a relatively large amount in response to a given change in price, the demand is price elastic. You can think of an old pair of underwear, where the elastic can be stretched to a great extent. On the other hand, if the quantity demanded changes by only a relatively small amount in response to a given change in price, the demand is price inelastic. You can think of a new pair of underwear whose elastic band doesn't change much.

The concept of elasticity is essentially a proportional measure. Given a one percent change in price, what is the percent decrease in quantity demanded? You can use the concept for many pairs of variables: income and quantity demanded; the price of coffee and the quantity demanded of cream; and the number of hours studied and your score on a test. As simple as the concept is, I suspect it creates the most fear and loathing of all the concepts taught in principles of economics. Why? Because in teaching students to calculate the "arc price elasticity of demand," a goofy formula is used:

$$\frac{[(Q_2-Q_1)/((Q_2+Q_1)/2)]}{[(P_2-P_1)/((P_2+P_1)/2)]}$$

Did your eyes glaze over as you pondered that seemingly imponderable equation? The price elasticity of demand is one occasion upon which knowledge of a little calculus goes a long way. Fortunately, you won't be tested today on calculating the price elasticity of demand.

We can define inelastic demand to be a situation in which a 1 percent increase in price generates a decrease of less than 1 percent in quantity demanded, or where a 1 percent decrease in price generates an increase of less than 1 percent in quantity demanded. In other words, there's a relatively small response to the change in price. Elastic demand is a situation in which a 1 percent increase in price generates a greater than 1 percent decrease in quantity demanded, or where a 1 percent decrease in price generates a greater than 1 percent increase in quantity demanded. There's a relatively large response to the change in price. At some point, demand may be unitary elastic: a 1 percent change in price generates a 1 percent change in quantity. For most commodities, the price elasticity of demand changes across prices. At higher prices, demand tends to be elastic, while for lower prices, demand is more likely to be inelastic. For large changes in price, then, you are likely to face changing elasticity of demand.

There are two extreme types of elasticity of demand. If demand is perfectly elastic, then consumers are highly responsive to prices. Such a case arises if there are perfect substitutes available (such as Farmer Jones' wheat compared with Farmer Smith's wheat just down the road). A company that tried to raise its price will lose all of its customers to rival companies producing the same product. If demand is perfectly inelastic, then consumers are not responsive at all to price changes. No matter what the price is, the quantity demanded remains constant. People sometimes think that a drug addict has perfectly inelastic demand. To satisfy his craving, he will pay any price. Due to scarcity, though, such a situation cannot exist. At high enough prices, the addict eventually runs out of money and must reduce her intake of the drug.

Aside from generating examination questions to torment students, of what earthly use is the concept of price elasticity of demand? Economists frequently use price elasticity in conjunction with total revenue or total expenditure (they are the same amount, depending upon your perspective). Suppose you are a ticket sales manager. You know that total revenue equals price times quantity: Total Revenue = Price × Quantity. You know, too, that price and quantity demanded have a teeter-totter relationship, when one goes up the other goes down, thanks to the law of demand. You want to raise total revenue. You have two choices: raise the price or lower the price. It is important to note that we are discussing revenue and not profits. In order to discuss profits, we would have to bring in costs, which we'll ignore for now.

Suppose you choose to raise the price. You know quantity demanded will decrease, but will it decrease a little or a lot? You hope to be able to "get away" with the price increase by losing just a few customers. In other words, you are hoping that your customers have inelastic demand. If you opt to decrease the price, you know that the quantity demanded will increase. Again, will the increase be small or large? If you put something on sale, you are hoping for a large response. We also know that producers who have weekly sales, such as grocery stores, attempt to boost the effect of a price decrease by announcing such sales boldly. Few producers go out of their way to announce price hikes: "Get it now while prices are at an all-time high!" We note that if demand were unitary elastic, there would be no change in total revenue. In fact, if you think about it, total revenue is maximized at the point of unitary elasticity.[4] Because profits represent a relationship between costs and revenue, you generally do not want to maximize total revenue.

The New York Yankees' financial data from 1915 through 1944 and corresponding data on changes in amusement taxes afford experimental evidence on the price elasticity of demand for baseball tickets. To help pay for America's involvement in the Great War (as World War I was known in the 1920s and 1930s), Congress levied a war tax on amusements. The tax was 10 percent on tickets of fifty cents or more. Congress rescinded the tax in mid–1928. When the Depression deepened, Congress again enacted the 10 percent tax starting in June 1932. These changes created an experiment of sorts. Major League Baseball owners simply tacked the 10 percent tax onto existing ticket prices. From the customer's perspective, the tax was a 10 percent increase in price; the removal of the tax was a 9.1 percent decrease in price.[5] With the removal of the tax, if the Yankees' total home receipts increased, the Yankees' owner, Jacob Ruppert, would have evidence that demand was elastic; if gate receipts decreased, the price elasticity of demand would have been inelastic. With the re-enactment of the tax, if the Yankees' total home receipts (that included the tax) decreased, Ruppert would have evidence that demand was elastic; if the gate receipts increased, the price elasticity of demand would have been inelastic. Gate receipts per game rose after the removal of the tax in 1928 and fell after the reinstatement of the tax in 1932. These changes in gate receipts suggested that demand was elastic. However, the findings suggesting elastic demand, though, are confounded by other events. The 1928 pennant race was tightly contested, while the 1932 pennant race was a blowout. The tight pennant race of 1928 may have amplified the increase in gate receipts. The increased overall ticket price due to the tax imposition in 1932 might have simply exacerbated fan ennui in the face of the Yankees' runaway.

We can generate another useful prediction. As you've seen, you can increase revenue by raising price in the face of inelastic demand. By doing so, you've done two useful things: You've raised revenue and reduced costs, since costs tend to decrease as the quantity gets smaller. Your profits benefit from both effects. Therefore, you should not price the tickets in the inelastic region of demand, with one exception that we'll discuss later.

Because of the rising costs associated with increasing quantity, lowering your price has offsetting effects on profits if you are initially in the elastic region of demand. Lowering price when you face elastic demand increases revenue, but it also increases costs. At some point, costs increase faster than revenue; economists point out that in order to maximize profits, you want to be where marginal benefits in terms of additional revenue (marginal revenue) equal additional costs (marginal costs). Therefore, most producers will operate in the region of elastic demand.

There is an exception to pricing in the elastic region of demand. Most owners of sports teams sell concessions, parking, and other merchandise. If these auxiliary revenues are lucrative enough, the owner may find it beneficial to get more people into the stadium, even if it means lowering ticket prices into the inelastic region of demand. Such a possibility might explain why some studies estimating elasticity of demand of sporting events find inelastic demand.

What factors affect the price elasticity of demand at a point in time?

Two crucial aspects are the number and availability of close substitutes and the effect of changes in income upon demand.

Burpsi-Cola has several close substitutes: Pepsi-Cola, Coca-Cola, generic cola, other carbonated beverages, and other beverages in general. There are many ways to slake thirst while avoiding inebriation. The price elasticity of Burpsi-Cola is, therefore, likely to be very high. A 1 percent increase in the price of Burpsi-Cola is likely to generate a relatively large decrease in quantity sold. On the other hand, appendectomies have an inelastic demand. If you are suffering from appendicitis, you are not likely to haggle over the price of the operation you need. If the hospital announces a "Blue-light special on appendectomies in aisle five," you are unlikely to flock to aisle five and demand to have your appendix removed just because the surgery is on sale.

In reality, most people cannot tell the difference between colas in blindfold taste tests. If you don't believe me, you could check out various marketing journals. Better yet, invite several of your friends over and play the Pepsi/Coke taste test game. Blindfold each other and see whether you can ascertain which is which. I think Pepsi has a sweeter taste, but I blew the test — in front of a classroom of students, no less. If consumers truly cannot taste the difference, the products are perfect substitutes for each other. This would be the epitome, the acme, of competition. No cola company could charge more than the market price without losing its entire market share. In an industry with perfect substitutes, no one firm has any ability to raise price, nor does it have an incentive to undercut the market price, as it would incur reduced profits if it did so.

Why do people demonstrate brand loyalty? Because the companies work very, very hard to differentiate their brand from its rivals. If Pepsi can succeed in convincing you that Pepsi is different and presumably better than Coke, then Pepsi will have price-setting power.

Each year hundreds of Ivy League undergraduates earn business degrees. In order to get a starting salary above the market salary, each one has to create product differentiation. I tell my students that they must create differentiation, but I also caution them to make sure they create positive differentiation. They can attempt to get good grades, chair various committees, perform service work, or do special research projects. Their efforts are put forth in the hope of standing out and thereby being able to command some price-setting power.

Professional sports teams have struggled to create price-setting power. Leagues have attempted to differentiate themselves on the basis of absolute quality: Only the best play big league baseball. Leagues can create territorial rights for participating teams. If you get an NFL franchise for Missoula, Montana, you can rest 99.9 percent assured that the league will not plant another franchise in Missoula. If you are the only NFL team in town, you don't have to worry that a close professional football substitute will become available. These leagues' efforts to differentiate themselves combined with territorial protection to create price-setting power for individual teams, power that they guard jealously.

Let's discuss supply. Each individual producer has a willingness to supply a quantity of a commodity for any given price, based upon his or her desire to maximize profits or some other goal. Are owners of professional sports teams profit maximizers? An owner can't deviate too far from profit maximization, as they may go bust or other people will try and take over. Connie Mack and Clark Griffith had few assets outside of their baseball teams. While both men liked to win and were willing to forego some profits in order to win, they could not afford to sacrifice much profit in doing so. The Michael Douglas character Gordon Gekko, in Oliver Stone's *Wall Street*, personified takeover artists (or bandits, depending on your viewpoint). In the famous "Greed is Good" scene, Gekko is trying to wrest control of a family owned business. He tells the stockholders that he will streamline the company by getting rid of the numerous vice presidents. An owner of a sports team that runs a slovenly enterprise can be sure to be approached by an eager investor seeking to do better (or circled by vultures seeking to feast on the carcass).

Typically, a firm's supply curve is largely determined by its marginal cost, which is the change in total costs associated with producing an additional unit of output. By adding up all of the individual producers' willingness to supply quantities at any given price, we get the market supply curve. The price is a reward for producing, so the higher the price, the greater the quantity the producers will supply. Again we note that in some contexts, the supply curve might represent workers' willingness to supply their labor or other suppliers' willingness to supply raw materials.

Just as there are demand shifters, there are also supply shifters. The prices of inputs, technology, alternative uses of resources, expectations of future prices, and taxes and subsidies are the main supply shifters.

If the price of sugar increases due to bad weather, the cost of producing cola increases and the supply of cola decreases. At any given price, producers are no longer willing to produce the original amount of cola and will reduce their output.

Resources often have multiple uses. A farmer might be able to grow corn instead of wheat on his farmland. A team owner who also owns a stadium must consider the alternative uses for it. Owners of professional hockey teams decided to operate basketball teams in order to keep their stadiums occupied during the winter. If hockey became less popular, one could imagine owners increasing the number of basketball games.

At this point, I think it is important to emphasize that the underlying motive behind both the demand and supply curves is maximization of pleasure, utility, or profits. Consumers and producers are trying to do the best they can for themselves. Even non-profit organizations have goals that they are trying to attain. In a sense, then, the opprobrium attached to profit-maximizers could just as well be applied to utility-maximizing consumers.

Let's see how prices are determined in a freely operating market. The market supply and demand interact to determine the market-clearing price. Think of a group of buyers and sellers. At $2 per 20-ounce bottle of soda, there may be many willing sellers and relatively few willing buyers. Since there are more sellers than buyers, the sellers begin to reduce price in order to induce reluctant buyers to buy. At a price of $0.25 per 20-ounce bottle, there are many willing buyers and relatively few willing sellers. The buyers begin to offer more money to induce reluctant sellers to provide more soda. At some point, say, $0.75, everyone who wishes to buy a soda finds someone willing to sell. Everyone who wishes to sell at $0.75 finds a buyer. No one willing to buy at $0.75 goes home empty-handed. No one willing to sell at $0.75 goes home with unwanted inventory. The market literally clears. There is no unwanted inventory or unmet demand. Economists call this the "market-clearing" or "equilibrium" price.

We have quickly discussed demand and supply. Let us now discuss what happens when one shifts. Suppose the current equilibrium price of soda is $0.75. If the price of sugar increases, the cost of producing soda increases. The supply of soda decreases. When the supply of soda decreases, there are now fewer sellers willing to accept $0.75 than there are buyers. The buyers bid up the price of soda until a new market equilibrium is established. The end result of the decrease in supply is a decrease in the quantity consumed and an increase in the price. Producers are able to "pass on" some, but usually not all, of the increase in their costs. If the demand were perfectly inelastic, then they could pass on all of the increase in their costs, but, as we have seen, this is a highly unlikely situation.

The beauty of the price mechanism is that it coordinates the wants of consumers with the output of producers without a planner and without conscious design. In markets without a freely adjusting price, large inventories of unwanted goods or long lines of unsatisfied customers occur frequently. Inventories and queues of customers use up resources, including warehouse space or time spent standing in line. The market-clearing price is efficient.

The market-clearing price for a commodity is doubly efficient as, under reasonable conditions, no one can be made better off by re-arranging the allocation or price of the commodity without making someone else worse off. All of the mutually beneficial trades have been exhausted. The efficiency of the market is its greatest virtue and one that should not be tampered with lightly.

Let's examine the idea of efficiency more closely. There's probably no word dearer to the heart of an economist than "efficiency." What do we mean?

The first thing to understand is that voluntary trade is mutually beneficial. If you walk into the neighborhood ballpark and buy a three-dollar ticket to a high school football game, then you must prefer attending the game to the three pieces of green paper with a dead president's portrait printed on them. The owner of the ballpark presumably prefers the three dollars to an empty seat. Both the consumer and the producer have gained by making the trade. Voluntary trade is a positive-sum, "win-win," situation: Both parties gain. Many people think that trades are zero-sum games, where what one person gains is exactly offset by the other party's expense. This thinking is incorrect. John D. Rockefeller, Andrew Carnegie, and Bill Gates did not become rich by impoverishing consumers. These men became rich by supplying consumers with what they wanted at prices they were willing to pay.

Paramount in this story, though, is the voluntary nature of the trade. We are specifically ruling out a mugging. You may have heard of an old Jack Benny routine. Benny is being held up by a mugger: "Yer money or yer life!" Benny looks at the mugger. The mugger, becoming impatient, repeats the question, "What's it gonna be, Jack? Yer money or yer life?" Benny, a reputed tightwad, replies with his deadpan delivery, "I'm thinking, I'm *thinking*." Some people might argue that the transaction is still voluntary in the sense that Benny has a choice, but we'll demur.

Usually only a government, whether local, state, or federal, can impose involuntary transactions. For instance, motorcycle riders in most states must buy and wear helmets. We can presume that riders who chose not to voluntarily purchase a helmet did not believe that the helmet provided enough subjective and objective usefulness or pleasure to justify the price. And who can blame them, as riding free with your hair flowing in the wind is one of the great romantic metaphors for Baby Boomers? However, citizens have decided that too many motorcycle riders have been injured and have incurred appallingly large medical bills, thereby draining society's resources. Hence, they enacted mandatory-helmet laws. In the professional team sports context, even though stadium financing is at least indirectly determined democratically, many citizens probably don't want to finance a stadium, even indirectly.

Demand and supply reveal extra information that enables us to quantify the gains from trade. They reveal consumers' willingness to pay for an additional unit, as well as the producers' willingness to supply another unit. Suppose you have two small children. You've read that milk builds healthy bodies, although some studies suggest that African- and Asian-American children may not get as much benefit. You go to the store thinking, "Buffy and Billy need milk for strong bones. I'd be willing to pay $10 for the first gallon, if I had to." Fortunately for you, the market price for milk is $3.00. You get to purchase something you subjectively value at $10 for a measly $3.00. You are better off by $7.00 by buying the first gallon of milk. You then think, "A second gallon of milk this week might be useful, as I enjoy an occasional glass, and then we wouldn't run out. I'd be willing to pay $5 for a second gallon." We note that your willingness to pay for additional units falls as you deploy the milk to less-valued uses. Again, you only have to pay $3.00 for a gallon of milk. You are better off by an additional $2 by buying the second gallon. This continues until the subjective benefit of the next gallon of milk just equals the cost, $3.00. Then you buy that gallon but don't buy any additional gallons. The total benefit of buying the gallons of milk is the difference between what you would have been willing to pay versus what you have to pay. By obeying our rule of buying until the marginal benefit equals the marginal cost, you have maximized your benefit. You earn a surplus. A similar argument holds for producers, who were willing to sell gallons of milk for less than the $3 purchase price but received that price. The producers' surplus is the difference between what they would have accepted and the $3 they can receive and is related to but slightly different than their profits. You are, of course, more familiar with the idea of producer profit, but the idea of consumers making a surplus from voluntary transactions may appear foreign.

Under commonly occurring conditions and assuming no one made a mistake, the market price in a competitive market, where no firm or consumer has any direct effect upon the price, results in maximizing the combined surplus to consumers and producers and is thus efficient. The result says nothing about the distribution of surplus between consumers and producers, so economic efficiency is not about equity. As a rule of thumb, deviating from the competitive market price usually results in inefficiency.

Exceptions to Market Efficiency: Monopoly Power and Externalities

So far, we've been discussing the virtues of a freely operating market, where no consumers or producers have price-setting power.

In the professional team sports world, leagues protect teams' territorial rights within a radius of fifty to seventy-five miles, distances far greater than that between a nation's shores and international waters. By doing so, the leagues insure that there are no close substitutes, no other professional teams in the same league or same sport, for most of the teams. The reduced competition allows teams to have discretion over their ticket prices: It gives them price-setting power. In a purely competitive market, the interaction of supply and demand would dictate price. Territorial rights confer a form of monopoly power for teams and give them discretion over price.

As you've probably surmised, monopolists typically charge more than firms in a competitive market do. In addition, monopolists usually sell fewer units. Some mutually beneficial trades do not occur, so the market will not be efficient under monopoly. There is also a question of equity: Should producers reap higher prices at the expense of consumers? The answer is not obvious. If I asked, "How many of you would like to be a monopolist?" I suspect most of you would raise your hand. Now it's one thing if you become a monopolist because your product is superior or you have figured out how to produce it more cheaply than your rivals: the John D. Rockefeller strategy. It is another thing to become a monopolist because you've created barriers to entry: the professional team sports' strategy.[6] Certainly under a completely free market in professional sports, teams often came and went before fans could blink their eyes. The National Association of Base Ball Players featured chronic churning of teams during the early 1870s.

If you have price-setting power, you may have the ability to practice price discrimination. Price discrimination occurs when a producer charges different individuals or groups of individuals different prices based on their varying demands. In other contexts, consumers are charged different prices because of cost considerations; this is not price discrimination. I suspect, however, that in some cases the distinction is ambiguous. First-class seats cost much more on airlines than coach-class seats. The price differential could be a result of cost considerations: First class features wider seats, which means smaller passenger capacity, and somewhat better food. I suspect, however, the main basis for the price differential is due to demand differences between, say, business and tourist travelers.

To see how price discrimination might work, suppose you own a movie theater in the greater Chicago area. It's 1998, and you've just received exclusive rights to show *Titanic* with Leonardo DiCaprio in the Chicago area. As you know in retrospect the film was enormously successful, so having a monopoly right to the Chicago territory would have been lucrative. What should your 1998 self do? You could set a single, monopoly price and make economic profits. But why be satisfied with simple monopoly profits? Can you do better?

If you could ascertain each customer's reservation price, the maximum he or she would be willing to pay to see the movie, you could do very well, indeed. Economists label this first-degree or perfect price discrimination. In fact, you might even sell the competitive-market quantity and be economically efficient, as all gains from trade would be exhausted and you would have transformed all of the consumer surplus into producer surplus. In this manner, we can see that efficiency has nothing to do with equity. Of course, ascertaining a customer's willingness to pay is time-consuming. If you ran a car lot, you would play twenty questions with a prospective customer in an attempt to pin down how much he or she is willing to pay. Such questioning might result in your getting an extra two or three thousand dollars out of a customer. No wonder car salespeople are so friendly. How long would you be willing to talk with a complete stranger in hopes of getting even two thousand dollars? On the other hand, if you had a pencil monopoly for the city, you probably wouldn't bother to play twenty questions with potential customers over the price of pencils; the possible gains are literally not worth your time. To ascertain a customer's willingness to pay, the best thing to do would be to hire an empath, such as Deanna Troi from *Star Trek: The Next Generation*. "Captain, I sense great urgency. Charge him $40 to see *Titanic*." Of course, empaths don't exist, and besides, they'd be a pain in the neck on a date as you couldn't hide your feelings.

Perfect price discrimination is the Holy Grail for monopolists, and one group of producers came reasonably close to succeeding for a time. Because of the voluminous financial information voluntarily supplied by parents of applicants to colleges, institutes of higher education can practice price discrimination to a very high degree. The financial information ostensibly determines financial aid, but a cynical economist might describe the process as price discrimination based on willingness to pay. Not satisfied with their already advantageous situation, the Ivy League schools got together and fixed financial aid packages so that a bright student would incur the same out-of-pocket expenses at any of the Ivy League schools. Miraculous coincidence? No, it was just a case of plain, old-fashioned price-fixing. The Justice Department put an end to the practice.

Let's return to our story about *Titanic* ticket prices. Since you couldn't find an empath, what should you do? You figure that there are some groups of people, such as old codgers, who don't give a fig about Leonardo's matinee idol persona and are willing to pay an amount between a marginal cost of, say, $5 and your monopoly price of $15. You could charge old codgers $8 and all others $15. By doing so, you'd attract a few more codgers and still get a price above the competitive market price. Notice that you are discriminating on the basis of different demand for the movie. The additional cost of admitting an old codger probably isn't any different than that of admitting a teenage girl.

Why stop now? You also know that on average, teenage girls have the greatest willingness to pay for this movie and are willing to pay over $20 to see Leonardo. You charge women under twenty-one years old $20 to see the movie. Everyone else pays $15 (except old codgers, of course).

The beauty of your scheme is that your ticket-takers don't have to play twenty questions, "How much do you like Leonardo? Do you *really, really* like Leonardo?" They can tell at a glance or, at most, a quick look at an I.D., who is a young woman, an old codger, or neither of the above. While the sorting mechanism is crude in the sense that you lose some young female customers who are unwilling to pay $20 and you undercharge some old codgers who might have been willing to fork out $15 in order to re-live the sinking, its virtue is its simplicity.

Sports teams charge different ticket prices. Again, part of this may be due to cost considerations. Seats in a suite have higher costs than seats in the bleachers. Some of the differential is based on the actual desirability of the seats in terms of their location within the stadium. Variable ticket pricing attempts to get more revenue from the most attractive games. Some of the variation in ticket prices is undoubtedly price discrimination based upon different demand by groups such as women (Ladies' Days) or children. Eventually, teams even began having Seniors' Days. Again, it is unlikely that the additional cost of admitting women, children, or seniors differs from admitting young men.

Again, none of the foregoing implies that the market is equitable in the distribution of resources. Although the market may allocate players efficiently between the New York Yankees and Kansas City Royals, there is no need to assume that the result is equitable. If the Yankees practice perfect price discrimination, they will be economically efficient, but readers may question whether such an occurrence would be equitable. Defining equity can be difficult. Equity is similar to art in that it is found only in the eye of the beholder.

We turn to another crucial economic concept. If there are third-party effects, denoted as externalities, the market may not be efficient. An externality occurs when benefits or costs affect a third party who was not involved in the original transaction. A classic negative externality occurs if I buy steel from a mill located on a river. The mill dumps waste into the river that injures a resort downstream. The effect on the resort is an externality. A positive externality occurs if having a professional sports team in your city inspires youngsters in your neighborhood to play sports and not to loiter in front of your store or gives you a good feeling when the team wins. The team cannot charge those casual fans who simply like to live in a city of champions but don't pay admission to any games. These fans are "free-riding." The problem with externalities is that either too much (in the case of a negative externality) or too little (in the case of a positive externality) is produced. A typical solution for externalities has been for the government to either subsidize a positive externality or tax a negative externality. There are market-based solutions, though, that can ameliorate externalities, while governments often have difficulties in assessing or levying the correct subsidy or tax.

We have seen that supply and demand determine prices. The free market generally has two virtues: coordinating consumers and producers' decisions to buy and sell and being efficient. These virtues occur, unless there are externalities and price-setting (monopoly) power.

Profits and Keeping Score in the Business World

In a freely operating market, firms are free to enter and free to exit. The ability to enter and exit is another form of competition. Years ago, the NBC television show *Friends* debuted. As you may recall, the show centered on six young, single people living in New York City and doing practically nothing except sitting in a coffee house or in their apartment. The show immediately vaulted to the top of the ratings and earned the network handsome profits, especially since it appealed to the right demographics: people aged between twenty and forty-four. Other networks took notice, and by the next season, each one had its rip-off of *Friends*. Imitation is, indeed, the sincerest form of flattery. Of course, most of the *Friends* knock-offs were pale imitations, and the saturation of the market for such shows was quickly reached. Some did not last an entire season, although *Drew Carey* and *Caroline in the City* persisted for several seasons. You'll notice that the latter show was NBC's own knock-off of its *Friends*. A successful sports league often faces the formation of new leagues unless the incumbent league can create barriers to entry.

If firms can easily enter and exit a market, then the market supply curve responds to profits and losses. Over time, if an industry is profitable, we would expect envious firms to enter and drive the price down to the level at which they make normal rates of return. In such a market, the long-term level of economic profits should be zero. If firms incur losses, some of them will exit the industry. The market supply decreases and price increases until remaining firms break even and earn zero economic profits.

The concept of zero economic profits can be difficult to accept at first. After all, why bother if you are just going to break even? An economic profit of zero means you are doing just as well in the endeavor as you would have in your best alternative. It is important to understand that economic profits take into account all economic costs, which may differ from accounting costs. This is an important distinction.

Economic costs include implicit valuation of your time and a normal market rate of return. Suppose you were born with the proverbial silver spoon. You have $500 million lying around. You could buy an NBA team with the money and be like Mark Cuban, leading cheers, haranguing referees, and high-fiving your employees. Since you are a hands-on boss, you quit your job evicting helpless widows from your many apartment complexes. You used to make $5 million annually doing so. You could earn 6 percent by investing your money in the stock market.

At the end of the season, your accountant shows you these figures:

Revenues		$300,000,000
Less		
Player payrolls	$150,000,000	
Other expenses	$130,000,000	
Total Expenses		$280,000,000
Net Income		**$20,000,000**

"Congratulations! You made money." The $20 million net income is what you would report to Uncle Sam. An economist, though, would demur. After all, you incurred two opportunity costs not shown above. First, you could have invested the $500 million in the stock market and received $30 million in dividends and capital gains (the 6 percent return). Second, you could have earned $5 million in your previous job. Instead of making $20 million in accounting profits, an economist would argue that you lost $15 million. Your $15 million economic loss means that you are $15 million worse off than you would be had you pursued your best alternative uses of your capital and time.

Now before you conclude that buying the basketball team was a lousy deal, I need to emphasize a point. You may well get much more subjective pleasure from owning the team than you would have received from evicting helpless widows and perusing the Dow Jones. That pleasure may be worth $15 million to you. However, the economist's reckoning gives you a more accurate measure of what's going on. "In order to enjoy being an NBA owner, I'm foregoing $15 million." Only you can decide whether it's $15 million well spent.

There's nothing wrong with earning zero economic profits. As we've seen, most firms in competitive industries eventually do so. Then again, there's nothing particularly right about earning zero economic profits. If you could bar entry into your currently profitable industry, then the good times could persist. Owners of professional sports teams, then, have a real incentive to keep out interlopers. We'll discuss this topic at length in Chapter Nine. For now, suffice it to say that economic profits inspire envy; envy triggers entry; and entry drives economic profits to zero.

Nothing in the previous discussion about profit implies accounting shenanigans or chicanery. We're not discussing the stupid accounting tricks that destroyed several prominent firms during the last decade. The accountant for your basketball team was scrupulous. I'm also not suggesting that accountants are stupid and economists are smart. Accountants and economists address different questions. An accountant is using generally accepted accounting rules and laws to determine profits under a legal definition. An economist is asking, "Are you better off or worse off?" In other words, should you buy the basketball team or should you opt for your best alternative?

We'll see how ambiguous interpreting profit figures can be in Chapter Four.

The Role of Time

There's one last concept to learn. Although it is not strictly a matter of economics, the concept of present value, which is used often in finance, is useful in thinking about player contracts and other situations in which money is paid over periods of years.

Present value deals with the fact that a dollar paid today is not the same as a dollar paid a year from now. If you receive a dollar today, you can invest that dollar and earn interest. Hence, a dollar today is not equivalent to a dollar received (or paid) in the future. In order to make the dollars paid over time "equivalent," one must discount future dollars by the foregone interest. Without getting too technical, a dollar received ten years from now foregoes ten years' worth of interest and is worth only a moderate fraction of a dollar received today.

Why is this important? Management and players toss around millions of dollars in player salaries. During the heyday of the American Basketball Association (if such association can be said to have had a heyday), prominent players received million-dollar contracts. Such contracts gained widespread publicity. A look at the fine print, however, revealed a different story. In some cases, players were to receive their money over a ten- or twenty-year period. Although the team would literally pay a million dollars over the life of the contract, the contract was worth quite a bit less in present dollars.

To understand this better, think of those mega-dollar lotteries. "The winner will receive $100,000,000!" claims the excited local television reporter. Yes, the state running the lottery will pay the winner $100,000,000, but typically the payments will be spread out over twenty years. If you want all of the money up front, they usually offer you roughly $53,000,000 (which is approximately the present value of $100,000,000 paid in twenty annual installments with an 8 percent rate of interest). The present value is the relevant amount not the $100,000,000. Normally, a business that pulled a similar stunt that the state government pulls would face civil penalties. Consumer advocates would scream loud and long. They remain strangely quiet when it is a government that is practicing deception.

Present value is important in understanding claims about "greedy" pharmaceuticals and prescription drugs. You often hear pundits wring their hands about how Drugs-R-Us makes obscene profits off some prescription drug. Let's consider Cancer-B-Gone, a drug that battles pesky carcinogens.

Drugs-R-Us spent millions of dollars to develop this drug. The research costs are incurred upfront. Years will pass before the firm can patent the drug and get Federal Food and Drug Administration approval to sell it. The company also incurs marketing costs in informing physicians and patients of the drug's availability and efficacy. Drugs-R-Us' revenues will occur several years later, so the revenues should be discounted according to the present value calculation. Even if it is true that Cancer-B-Gone earns a handsome profit, Drugs-R-Us had several drugs that proved unsuccessful, either in terms of efficacy or of meeting physician's and patient's approval. Cancer-B-Gone, then, has to earn enough profit to cover the losses incurred on the unsuccessful drugs. Looking at Cancer-B-Gone's unadjusted profit figures can be highly misleading. In any event, if pharmaceutical companies are making obscene profits, then the reader should ask why other firms don't enter the market; firms love obscene profits.

Aside from player contracts, present value is also useful in understanding the finances of building a stadium. The stadium's construction costs must be paid up front, while the revenues accrue over a lengthy period of time. The revenues, then, must be converted into present value.

We've had a whirlwind tour through basic economics. When you turn the page, you'll enter the realm of numbers, probability theory, and statistics.

CHAPTER 2

Sports Numeracy

Americans appear to be more afraid of numbers than people in other countries. Discomfort about numbers and mathematics leaves many people vulnerable to fallacious arguments. In this chapter, I hope to illuminate some useful concepts in a user-friendly manner. If this was a 1950s-style educational film, I would entitle it "Your Friend: Numeracy."

Those Long Odds

We begin with some simple examples of probability theory.

The Boston Red Sox looked dead and ready for burial in October 2004, but the New York Yankees forgot to bring shovels. The Sox were down three games to none in the American League Championship Series. It was impossible to win four in a row ... wasn't it? Pundits reveled in saying, "No team down three games to none has ever come back to win a series."

While the Yankees had a slightly better overall record than the Red Sox during the regular season, the Sox had won the head-to-head matchup. Let's try a thought experiment. Suppose the two teams were evenly matched. In other words, suppose the probability of the Red Sox winning any game with New York was 50 percent (for convenience, we are ignoring home-field advantage). This would be analogous to a toss of a fair coin.

Winning the next game would be a 50–50 proposition. Winning the next two games would be similar to throwing tails twice in two tosses. Such an occurrence happens once every four tries on average. Winning three in a row (tossing three tails in a row) would happen once every eight tosses. Finally, winning four in a row would happen once every sixteen tosses.

The next obvious question would be to ask, "How many times has a team been down three games to none?" As we've seen, if the two teams were equal, then once every sixteen times, on average, we'd see such a comeback.

I'd point out, too, that a one-in-sixteen occurrence is hardly miraculous. In most contexts, you would not accept a one-in-sixteen chance of dying: "Drive the new Dare-Mobile, explodes once every sixteen times you turn the ignition on." No airline could turn a profit if its flights crashed once every sixteen times. The odds, while long, are not really that far out of the ordinary.

Why hadn't we seen a team come back from a three-game deficit? Two possibilities offer themselves. First, the Red Sox, like most teams which find themselves down three-to-zero, might have been slightly inferior to the Yankees; after all, they did finish the season a few games behind them. However, in head-to-head competition at the championship level, it's unlikely that one team would have even a 60 percent to 40 percent advantage in any particular game.

For the purpose of illustration, suppose that the Yankees could be expected to win three games out of every five with the Red Sox. The odds of winning two games in a row then become 4-in-25 or 16 percent. This is a marked drop from the 25 percent probability of winning two in a row if the two teams were, in fact, equally likely to win. Winning three games in a row becomes only an 8-in-125 shot, or 6.4 percent. Finally, winning four games in a row now has a 2.56 percent probability, or a 1-in-39 shot. While this is longer than the 1-in-16 shot described above, it's still not so unusual that you'd want to bet your life on such an outcome. No Yankee fan would seriously bet, "If the Sox come back, I'll forfeit my life."[1] The odds against the Red Sox were almost tenfold better than those facing your local high school's star player making it to the pros.[2]

The second possibility is that the odds lengthen because of demoralization. After all, the actual players are not Strat-O-Matic Baseball card versions of themselves, and in real life, past events affect present events. People often think if three heads appear in a row, then a tail "is due," but this is nonsense. The coins have no memory of the previous tosses, so on every toss the odds remain 50–50. However, nonsensical beliefs make owners of Las Vegas casinos rich. In any case, ballplayers are not coins. Being down three games to none must have some effects, even for the most confident player. Most people would assume that the losing players would become less confident or less aggressive, thereby decreasing their probability of winning the next game.

We could turn this argument around, as the team holding the three-to-none advantage might also become less aggressive. After all, they can afford some mistakes. They may find it difficult to maintain the killer instinct. If they proceed to lose a couple of games, the commentators remark on how the momentum has shifted and the pressure is now on the heretofore winning team not to "choke."

We've now entered the realm of psychology, and I'll say no more about the mental aspects.

A third point is that the number of times a team has been down three games to none in a championship series is relatively small, so the absence of a comeback from this position is not unusual.

For now, though, we simply note that recovering from a three-to-zero deficit, while difficult, is, on paper at least, not as astounding as to be labeled a miracle.

The pundits also delighted in discussing that the events through Game 3 of the 2004 American League Championship Series were not unique for the Sox. Fans and sportswriters revel in superstition. The famous "Curse of the Bambino" and "Curse of the Billy Goat" appeared to be alive and well all the way through game three. The Boston Red Sox apparently exorcised the curse by winning eight straight games against the New York Yankees and St. Louis Cardinals. Prior to their World Series victory, the Sox had not won a series since 1918, an era encompassing four World Series losses, two of which were to St. Louis, and some excruciating playoff losses. Nevertheless, the "Curse of the Bambino" did not seize the public's imagination until the mid–1970s. There's no evidence that Mr. Bambino himself, Babe Ruth, ever uttered a curse against the team, raising the philosophical question, "If no one hears a curse in a forest, or in a crowded ballpark, can there be a curse?" Before the sale of Babe Ruth, the Red Sox had won five World Series in a row: Was this the "luck of the Bambino"? Of course, he wasn't around for two of those Series.[3]

The other afflicted baseball team, the Chicago Cubs, appeared to have been well-cursed years before the Billy Goat incident, having lost their previous six World Series appearances before their final appearance in 1945. The goat and his owner were just kicking the Cubs when the team was already down. By losing the 1945 World Series, the Cubs set a record that would soon be matched by the "Boys of Summer" Brooklyn Dodgers: losing in seven consecutive World Series appearances. I don't recall any curse haunting the Bums, although apparently people prayed throughout Brooklyn churches during a Gil Hodges slump. It's not even clear what the Billy

Goat curse delineated: Whether it meant the Cubs would not reach the World Series, or the Cubs would not win the World Series. Since the Cubs' record in the years since 1945 has been laughably inept, given the team's wealth, the true goats in the front office were probably happy to have a quadruped assume the blame.

The Cubs and Red Sox are pikers when it comes to being accursed. Were the Los Angeles Lakers cursed after leaving Minneapolis, where they were the toast of the fledgling NBA? After all, the Lakers lost their next eight NBA Championship Series, far surpassing the agony of the Red Sox and even the Cubs. Was there a curse of the recently deceased George Mikan? "If you leave the Twin Cities, I curse thee." What about the poor Buffalo Bills, who lost Super Bowls in four consecutive years? When you think about it, the Bills had to be a wonderful football team to appear in four straight Super Bowls. As far as I know, no other team has. The Denver Broncos and Minnesota Vikings also lost four non-consecutive Super Bowls, although the Broncos later bounced back and won two. Did John Elway find an exorcist? Most observers simply attributed the Broncos' failures to an inadequate cast surrounding Elway.

No, a truly accursed team is one saddled with an inept or penurious owner, or, even worse, an inept *and* penurious owner. The St. Louis Browns made their only World Series appearance during World War II. Apparently fewer of their players got drafted into the military than the Tigers or Yankees. Did Browns fans walk around bemoaning some cute curse? I think not.

As you've guessed, I am skeptical about curses. While losing six or seven evenly contested Series in a row is a one-in-64 or 128 occurrence, it may well have been that the Red Sox were the weaker team in at least three of their Series appearances, shortening the odds surrounding their misery. The Cubs, too, had the misfortune of running into the 1929 Philadelphia Athletics and 1932 New York Yankees, two exceptionally strong teams.

Anyway, I suppose belief in curses is harmless fun, and, if I ever run an inept franchise, you can damn betcha I'll concoct some sort of curse to explain the sad fate of my team.

We can extend our discussion of winning four in a row to the "hot hand" in sports. Suppose your favorite NBA star normally hits 50 percent of his field goals. (For simplicity's sake, we'll ignore three-point shots.) You can see that if all conditions are equal, hitting four shots in a row is a one-in-sixteen occurrence. It's rare, but not that rare. You might begin to get excited after six in a row. The same is true for NFL quarterbacks and pass completions. In fact, since most NFL quarterbacks complete closer to 60 percent of their passes, the probability of completing four passes in a row is almost 13 percent. Conversely, for a good major league hitter who is batting .300, getting four hits in a row occurs with a 0.8 percent probability.

Vinnie "Microwave" Johnson was known as a "streak" shooter. He usually shot less than 50 percent from the field. When he heated up, he really heated up, hence the nickname. Supposedly he'd either come off the Seattle Supersonics bench and hit several shots in a row, or, more likely, miss several shots in a row.

A statistician observing Vinnie might want to examine his record shot by shot. If his shooting is truly random, with odds of 50–50, then the odds of hitting a shot after making his last one should still be 50 percent. If, after many, many shots, the statistician discovered that Vinnie hit, say, 56 percent of his shots immediately after making a successful shot, then we might have something worth discussing. In fact, two researchers discovered that players on the Philadelphia 76ers during the 1980s were *less* likely to hit a shot after making a basket than after a missed shot.[4]

Another consideration of the "hot hand" theory is that defenses should adjust. If Vinnie truly warmed up, then the opposing coach should guard him more closely, driving down the Microwave's probability of hitting any given shot. Of course, if the defensive team is devoting more attention to Vinnie, then his teammates should be able to get better shots, raising the likelihood of their hitting shots.

All of which leads me to an amusing bar bet. Do you want to win back the purchase price of this book? Tell your friend to either flip a coin one hundred times or to make up a list of one hundred coin flips and record the outcomes. Give your friend even money and bet him that you can discern whether he actually flipped the coin or made up the list (make sure to have an impartial third party verify your friend's action). You should be able to win money off this bet.

How can I be so sure? Well, if your friend makes up the coin tosses, it's likely that he'll be "sophisticated" and think, "I will not include any long strings of heads or tails." Thus, if there are no strings of four or more heads (or tails) in a row, you can feel relatively assured that he made it up. We've seen that four-in-a-row occurs once every sixteen times on average, so in one hundred tosses, you're likely to have a few such strings. Even a string of five in a row occurs on average once every thirty-two times, so it's also likely.

Let's apply probability theory to another question. How do we know whether one team is superior to another? The professional sports leagues play widely varying numbers of games to determine seedings for playoffs. Each team in the National Football League plays 16 games, while Major League Baseball has a 162-game schedule. Professional basketball has an 82-game schedule.

The supposed virtue of the regular season is that luck should "even out" across the extensive number of games, especially in basketball and baseball. Allow me to rant: These leagues then jettison this virtue in favor of short playoff series, where a lucky bounce can loom large. I'm done with my rant. I feel much better.

However, even a 162-game series does not necessarily demonstrate the best team. Suppose you invite nine of your friends over for an exciting night of coin-flipping. A single toss of a fair coin determines the outcome of a game. You will play 162 games (home team gets to toss the coin, and wins if the coin comes up heads). Of course, you'd expect to win 81 games on average.

Oh, the excitement is palpable as the season unfolds. Since everyone is using a fair coin, you'd expect a tight pennant race. You would still find a spread of several games. If you won with, say, eighty-seven victories, could you claim to be a superior coin tosser? Of course not.

Here we see the normal distribution at work. The distribution of wins would resemble a "bell curve," a concept most of you are familiar with in conjunction with a classroom's distribution of grades.

Employing the statistical concept of standard deviation, we can generate league standings that have distributions of win-loss records not far removed from actual standings between teams of varying abilities. For the 162-game baseball season, the standard deviation is 6.36 games. In other words, almost one-third of the major league teams would be outside a range of seventy-five and eighty-seven wins. The spread associated with two standard deviations would be sixty-eight and ninety-four wins, very close to most races. Roughly 95.5 percent of teams should be within two standard deviations of the mean. For a sixteen-game football schedule, one standard deviation is two games, so two-thirds of the NFL teams should fall between six and ten wins. For two standard deviations, the range would be four to twelve wins.

Returning to the coin-flipping league, if we alter our story slightly and one of you has the knack of flipping a coin so heads comes up 55 percent of the time (a home-field advantage, so to speak), you still wouldn't be guaranteed to win the pennant. Suppose you are the only one with such a knack. You'd still expect to win 40.5 of the eighty-one "road" games, and you'd expect to win 44.55 of the "home" games. But even with this edge, there's a non-trivial probability that you would not win the pennant.

Of course, the potential "distortion" is magnified in a short series. An inferior team can win a three, five, or seven-game series a surprisingly high proportion of the time. Suppose the New York Vets are heavily favored over the Kalamazoo Kazoos. The Vets would win 60 percent of the games with the Kazoos if they played many, many games. In a three-game series, though, the Kazoos have a 35.2 percent probability of winning. The Kazoos have a 31.7 percent chance of winning a five-game series and a 29 percent chance of winning a seven-game series. Thus, upsets should be fairly common in short series. For drama and raising hopes, short series are wonderful. For determining the "true champion," they introduce too much noise.

To use statistical jargon, short series have a high probability of a Type I error: rejecting a true hypothesis that the Vets are the superior team and falsely anointing the wrong team as superior. Since a sporting match is not a life or death matter (yes, even for Red Sox fans), we can live with such a high degree of error. In many contexts, though, we would not accept such a shoddy way of determining quality. A medical test that gave almost one-third false positives would be almost useless.

In baseball, artificial scheduling is another reason a short series is not a good determinant of a team's superiority. Baseball is unique in that several top performers, the starting pitchers, may not see action in any particular game. The traditional World Series arrangement was two games on the first weekend, followed by a travel day; games three through five on Tuesday through Thursday, then another travel day; and remaining games, if needed, on Saturday and Sunday. This built in at least one extra day of rest. Hence, in the days of four-man starting pitching rotations, a pitcher could start games one, four, and seven, or three-sevenths of the games. Over the course of a season, a starter might hurl one-fourth of the games. In addition, the second starter could pitch two of seven games, instead of the usual two of eight. Indeed, the fourth and fifth starters need never start a game in the old World Series setup.

Even with the additional rounds of playoffs, the fourth and fifth starters' importance recedes relative to the regular season. In a sense, a team with a deep starting rotation forfeits part of its advantage. When Arizona had Randy Johnson and Curt Schilling, the thinking was that the two of them could start at least four and possibly five games in a World

Series, giving the Diamondbacks an enhanced advantage. The Atlanta Braves with four quality starters did not reap as large an advantage from this strength in a short series as they did during the regular season.

The next time your favorite sports pundit anoints a team to be superior, be wary. Be very wary.

Playoffs use small numbers of games to determine who advances and who goes home. We now turn to situations with larger sample sizes but no greater level of general understanding. You often hear broadcasters say, "Joe Doe owns pitcher John Roe. He's hitting .400 off of him." Now the most extreme version of this story has Doe going two-for-five off of Roe, but usually there are at least thirty at-bats of experience. By now, you can probably predict how this story turns out. One lucky hit in thirty at-bats represents .033.

Suppose you are a .250 hitter. What is the likelihood of hitting exactly .400 after thirty at-bats off an average pitcher? The answer is just less than 3 percent. It is possible to have a higher batting average than .400, so the probability of hitting at least .400 off any average pitcher is better than 3 percent. Thus, by sheer chance, our mediocre hitter will "own" some pitchers. Just as with Vinnie Johnson and the hot hand, you would want to see whether the subsequent frequency of getting a hit off the pitchers you own is higher than for those you don't own. A hitter may become more comfortable psychologically batting against pitchers with whom he's had success in his limited experience, but whether the psychological gain is real and significant is difficult to ascertain. To make decisions based on limited at-bats seems foolish to me.

Even after 600 at-bats, a .300 hitter could have a surprisingly large standard deviation in his batting average. On average, he would have collected 180 hits, but the standard deviation is 6.14 hits. The range of batting averages associated with one standard deviation is .290 to .310. About one-third of the time, he'd fall outside that range.

This goes back to a point made earlier about Strat-O-Matic Baseball versus real life: In Strat you know the true probabilities, whereas in real life, you can only estimate them. This is an insight that is forgotten at your own risk.

Lies, Damn Lies, and Statistics

Benjamin Disraeli, or perhaps Mark Twain, claimed that there were three types of lies: white lies, damned lies, and statistics. An old statistical saw goes, "If you torture the numbers long enough, they'll talk." Many people believe that you can "prove" anything with numbers. "Figures don't lie, but liars figure."

The essence of sports is to outscore your opponent. As Howard Cosell might have pontificated in his nasal drawl, "A team manifests its superiority by achieving a plurality on the scoreboard. Right, Dandy Don?" Poor Don Meredith would have been too busy sorting through the highfalutin' words and would have only responded, "Huh? Howard."

Why am I making so much of such an obvious fact? Well, sportswriters and the public appear to have lost sight of this reality. The simplest way to think about why a team wins is to look at its runs versus runs allowed or points versus points allowed. Baseball statisticians have noted the strong correlation between such differences and a team's winning percentage. Of course, this should be the obvious place to start. If runs or points are reasonably randomly distributed across a season (that is, if a team does not have an inordinate number of slugfests and shutouts), then the ratio of points to points allowed is a good indicator. A team that breaks even in scoring should play around 0.500, with some variance. A team that wins 60 percent of its games should outscore its rivals, just as a team that loses 60 percent of its games should be outscored.

Bill James pioneered what is called the "Pythagorean Theorem" for baseball based on the run-to-runs allowed ratio. He took a useful insight and carried it to extremes. Using statistical methods, one can create an equation predicting how many games a team should win based on its runs:runs allowed ratio. Baseball researchers can use equations such as:

$$\text{Win-Loss Pct.} = .5 + \beta \, (\text{Runs} - \text{Runs Allowed})$$

or

$$\text{Win-Loss Pct.} = \beta \, (\text{Runs}/\text{Runs Allowed}).$$

They then let a computer estimate β. The drawback is that β is an estimate. The "actual" β falls within a range around the estimated β. For purposes of estimating how many wins a team "should have," baseball researchers such as James act as though β was the true coefficient. If a team wins more games than is predicted, James ascribes this to the manager's acumen. Rarely do James and other researchers consider the ramifications of the range. First, there is the ever-present variance. A team may have a large number of slaughters, inordinately affecting its runs-to-runs allowed ratio. A team that wins two more games than was predicted may simply fall within the range for β, just as our coin flipper who won eighty-three out of 162 tosses falls within one standard deviation. These estimates are fun to read about, but the reader is cautioned against placing too much weight or money on them. A little statistical sophistication can be harmful to your (financial) health.[5] Second, "coaxing" wins out of a given runs-to-runs allowed ratio is only part of the manager's job. The manager also has to decide which players to put on the field. To take an extreme case, consider Leo Durocher and Willie Mays in 1951. Mays, a rookie, is mired in a slump to start his major league career. He begs Durocher to pull him out of the lineup, but Leo assures him that he is the center-fielder, now and for the rest of the season. You know the result of Leo's decision.

James devised his own system of rating managers.[6] He weighted his system toward winning the World Series and various playoff rounds. We've already seen how much "noise" is involved in short playoffs. Of course, this makes his system incompatible with pre–1969 managers, but most of his system is ad hoc anyway. How do I know this? Because he assigned points arbitrarily: fifty for winning a World Series; twenty-five for winning the playoff determining the pennant; twelve for winning a division (but none for being a wild card); ten points for winning one hundred or more regular-season games; and five points for winning ninety or more games. On what did he base these points? Can you spell a-r-b-i-t-r-a-r-y?

Presumably the best method would be to measure how an "average" major league manager would have fared with the available playing talent and then compare the actual manager's record with it. Of course, given the variance involved in even a 162-game season, one can't be certain whether a manager's "sparkling performance" was the result of sheer dumb luck or true skill. Such difficulties also abound in the non-sports business world. What makes a successful CEO? The ability to look good in a suit? The ability to make the correct decision? If it is the latter, suppose there are only a handful of really crucial decisions to be made during the year. In other words, how could we tell whether the CEO's decision-making is better than flipping a coin? How many decisions do we have to observe before we know the CEO is damn good?

You see this in those crazy "Top Ten Mutual Funds for 2010" articles in business magazines. Ten funds have to have the best rates of return for the year, but they aren't necessarily the product of sharp decision making. You would want to track the fund managers' performance over several years. After all, recall the story of Joseph in the Old Testament. Yeah, sure, his brothers sold him into bondage, but our Joseph was nothing but resilient. He eventually rose in the Egyptian government (showing, perhaps, that the Pharaohs are maligned — at least they promoted on merit). God eventually told Joseph that seven fat years would be followed by seven lean years. Insider trading information doesn't get any better than a message from God.[7] As I advise my Masters of Business Administration students, imagine that Joseph announced this revelation to the Egyptian people. Religious considerations aside, how would you assess his pronouncement? "The grain market is going to crash in seven years!" First, you would ask, "Who is Joseph?" Then, you would ask, "What's his track record as a commodities prognosticator?" You should also ask, "What is his system? Is it based upon sound financial and economic principles?" Indeed, fantasy baseball aficionados who subscribe to those fantasy tip sheets should ask the same.

We'll discuss principal-agent problems later, but owners of professional sports teams hire managers and coaches to be their agents in getting the best performance from the players. Ascertaining how good a job a manager or coach did is difficult under any circumstance. Still, I think Bill James' rating system is profoundly flawed, as is much of his work.

Again, it is the relative ratio, points:points allowed, that is paramount. The next step, then, is to consider what contributes to runs or points. All other numbers are, at best, secondary. Moreover, looking at offensive and defensive statistics in isolation has drawbacks in some sports. Just because a team allows fewer points than average does not necessarily imply that it has a strong defense. In football and, to a lesser degree, basketball, teams with good offenses or teams that play a deliberate style may eat up the clock, giving opponents fewer plays. The defense can look good simply by not having to play as much. Clearly, yardage per play or points per possession might address this issue.

Similarly, teams which lead the league in passing or in passing defense may be reflecting the strength or weakness of their defensive or offensive units. In the former case, a team with a weak defense may find itself behind and be forced to pass more frequently, thus gaining more passing yards (and also incurring more interceptions). Of course the reverse holds, too; a team with a strong offense that puts its opponents in a hole may force the rivals to pass more frequently. The team's pass defense may actually be pretty good, but its total passing yards allowed may look mediocre.

For basketball, the former Boston Celtics coach Red Auerbach made an interesting suggestion years ago. He claimed that Sam Jones' contribution to the team was difficult to measure with conventional statistics. He had someone keep track of the score when Sam entered and exited the game. According to Auerbach, Jones' presence typically helped the Celtics reduce a deficit or increase a lead. By seeing how the score changed during Jones' participation, one could gauge his effectiveness. Unfortunately, Red didn't discuss how other players fared under this formulation. One could also wonder how much such score-keeping would need to be adjusted for the quality of the other team's unit. Suppose Sam played mostly against the reserves instead of the starters. Then his positive contributions might be misleading. "Yeah, he cleans up against the scrubs, but what can he do against the starters?" Conversely, some ratball player such as myself could have a much higher Auerbach rating by playing with, say, Larry Bird, Kevin McHale, Robert Parrish, and Dennis Johnson than I would if I were on a team with any of the Los Angeles Clippers' four best players.

Baseball is famed for its statistics that many fans can quote, season and game. However, some statistics are not very useful.

Many sports statistics are seemingly irrefutable proof of a player's productivity. Of course, a player's interactions not only with opponents but with teammates may affect his statistics. If you want to lead the NBA in rebounding, get yourself on a talented defensive team that holds its rivals to a low field-goal percentage. The defensive team usually corrals a large majority of rebounds, roughly two-thirds. In a presidential forum, two-thirds is a helluva mandate. But it also helps if your own team is a gang that can't shoot straight. In addition, your team's and the rival teams' free-throw shooting abilities may also affect the number of potential rebounds. Apparently a team's proclivity towards shooting three-point shots or forcing its rivals to do so doesn't have much impact on the likelihood of getting rebounds. Finally, make sure you are the baddest dude on your team's block in terms of rebounding. If your team has other strong rebounders, you'll be competing with them for rebounds.

Your shooting percentage may jump if you have great teammates. Bryon Scott was the proverbial fifth wheel on the Los Angeles Lakers. With teammates Kareem Abdul-Jabbar, Magic Johnson, and James Worthy receiving most of the opposing teams' defensive efforts, there was less defensive attention paid to Scott. True, Scott might not have gotten as many shots, but he probably got better shots than he would have gotten if he had played with the Los Angeles Clippers. Before Scott, Gail Goodrich benefited by having Wilt Chamberlain and Jerry West drawing the opponents' best defenders.

Other statistics are affected by the game situation. A relief pitcher entering a game with a runner on third and none out is almost guaranteed to allow the runner to score and possibly blow the save.

During the 2004 American League Championship series, much comment was made about how Mariano Rivera, famed Yankees' reliever, blew a save. If I recall, he blew a save by getting a batter out, albeit on a sacrifice fly that scored a run. All blown saves are not equal. It's hard to fault a reliever for getting a batter out.

Speaking of Mariano Rivera, the nature of "closers" has evolved during the past two decades. Hoyt Wilhelm had a lengthy career as a relief pitcher. He pitched in over one thousand games, but started only fifty-two games. In several of his top years, he hurled more than two innings per appearance. Rollie Fingers averaged at least one and a half innings per outing during his heyday. Dennis Eckersley averaged about one inning per appearance. Today, of course, Mariano Rivera and others consider it a long day at the office when they pitch more than one inning. You can pick up a save for an inning's work. Managers appear loath to employ their valued closer for any inning but the ninth inning. I've often wondered whether the regularity is so important. If you had men on first and third with one out in, say, the seventh, why not bring in your flame-throwing "closer"? Is the psychological aspect so important that the pitcher has to throw only the final inning? Is there proof that these relievers are more effective being used only one inning instead of two innings?

Other statistics achieved and retained prominence because of laziness.

Years ago, many people used the batting average as a primary measure of a hitter's productivity. Around the 1960s and 1970s, researchers began to demonstrate the higher correlation between either on-base percentage or slugging average with runs scored. Both statistics were superior to the traditional batting average. Today, of course, such worthies as Billy Beane, Theo Epstein, and Bill James have raised such beliefs to the status of dogma. Others are slow to relinquish their faith in the batting average.

Suppose you were one of the first baseball general managers to figure this out. You have Steve Garvey on your roster, a .300-hitting first baseman who doesn't draw many walks and might hit twenty homeruns. You figure that John Mayberry, who usually hits .280 but draws many more walks and belts a few more homeruns, is more valuable. I show their 1974 statistics. Garvey was the National League MVP in 1974, and he also had a better reputation with the glove. He was not as prone to striking out as much as Mayberry, but notice the latter's number of walks.

	AB	Bave	OBP	Save	HR	RBI	BB	TPR
Garvey	642	.312	.346	.469	21	111	31	-0.3
Mayberry	427	.234	.359	.424	22	69	77	0.1

Mayberry spent part of 1974 injured. He'd had two previous seasons of high on-base percentages and better slugging averages than Garvey. On a per-at-bat basis, Mayberry's RBI total was close to Garvey's total. A general manager recognizing the importance of on-base percentage and slugging average could see a possible arbitrage opportunity here. Just as a speculator who believes a stock is under-valued or over-valued can make money off an arbitrage opportunity, so can astute general managers. Hence, Billy Beane and Theo Epstein might well leverage their superior information to improve their teams to the detriment of their rivals. In addition, by keeping their mouths shut about the importance of on-base percentage, they might have been able to suppress the salaries of players such as Mayberry: "You only hit .234, ya bum."

In efficient markets, usually characterized by good flows of information, arbitrage opportunities typically disappear quickly. For commodities traders, an ill-timed trip to the washroom might cost them thousands of dollars. In professional sports, it seems to take years for other general managers to realize how important alternative statistics may be. Heck, it took the Yankees and Red Sox years to "discover" how good black players were, as we'll see in Chapter Eight. Hence, a truly astute general manager would keep his mouth shut regarding such arbitrage opportunities. To misuse a Biblical injunction, you truly want to hide your on-base percentage "light" under a bushel basket. In addition, it is disadvantageous to become known as a sharp trader, as other traders will become wary of dealing with you. For these reasons, I hope Billy Beane made a shipload of money off of *Moneyball*, because he appears to have divulged some of the arbitrage opportunities that were available before he published them, such as looking for patient hitters. Ironically, Ed Barrow, the former general manager of the New York Yankees, out-beaned Billy. After 1925, his teams almost always led the league in walks, on-base percentage, and slugging average. You might respond, "Heck, with Babe Ruth and Lou Gehrig, how could you not?" There were years, however, in which the remaining Yankees still collectively drew more walks than most of the other American League teams even after Ruth's and Gehrig's walks were subtracted from the total.

In assessing Garvey and Mayberry, one notes that John did strike out a lot. I'd suggest that a hitter's ability to get wood on the ball is overemphasized. Despite his much larger number of at-bats, Garvey struck out fewer times than Mayberry did. You hear a lot of managers and pundits griping about a slugger's strikeouts. "He should have put the ball in play." Well, it depends. Suppose Garvey was prone to grounding into double plays. Such a penchant would make a manager long for strikeouts. Al Oliver, a contemporary of Garvey and Mayberry, with an even higher batting average, grounded into twenty double plays in 1974, while Mayberry, in fewer at-bats, grounded into just four. If you have base runners, Mayberry's propensity to strikeout may be a blessing in disguise. You might argue that so-and-so would have a higher batting average, if he didn't strike out so much. If two hitters are the same in most ways, the fact that one strikeouts more is not necessarily a detriment. Oliver's sixteen additional at-bats that grounded into double plays effectively erased sixteen base runners, offsetting some of his higher on-base average.

Pundits have recently seized upon the OPS, the sum of on-base percentage and slugging average, as a true measure of a batter's productivity. While OPS is a stronger measure than the batting average, it is a goofy number, literally adding bases to base runners. The on-base percentage indicates how a proficient a hitter is at becoming a base runner, while his slugging average measures how many bases he advances other base runners and himself. Is it any wonder, then, that estimation of the respective weights pretty much rule out the possibility that the two measures are equal. The on-base percentage typically has a coefficient three to four times greater than slugging average, reflecting the dichotomy between base runners and bases advanced. In estimating regression equations, the OPS alone explained less of the variance in run production than did the tandem of on-base percentage and slugging average. There appears to be no statistical basis for using OPS, so there is no reason, save convenience and simplicity, for simply adding the two together.[8]

A similar argument holds for pitchers. The ratio of strikeouts to walks is often touted as a wonderful method of evaluating pitchers. We know that walks are bad (although they are better than yielding the same number of hits). In some contexts, having a flame-throwing hurler is an advantage. If you're facing men on second and third with none out, the ability to strike out hitters is useful. Conversely, men on first and second, none out, and you may long for a pitcher who can induce groundballs. Anyway, some pundits use the strikeouts to walks ratio, with a three-to-one ratio being the demarcation of a good pitcher. But such a ratio covers a wide range of pitchers. On a per-nine-inning basis, a hurler with twelve strikeouts and four walks is probably worse than the one with six strikeouts and two walks. Walks are bad. Hits are worse, but they aren't included in the ratio. A pundit would certainly be better off using Opponents Slugging and Opponents On-Base Average in gauging pitching efficiency, perhaps even more than Earned Run Average. A starting pitcher's ERA may be affected by the quality of the relief squad. Of course, everything should be adjusted for park characteristics. The strikeouts-to-walks ratio may simply reflect good pitching, but good pitching is essentially not allowing many base runners (whether via base hits or base-on-balls) and keeping the ball within the park.

Another area of dubious statistics is "clutch" hitting. A hitter has a subset of his at-bats where there are runners in scoring position. Given our previous discussion, then, you would expect a relatively large variance. How much of clutch hitting is attributable to "luck" becomes a key question. Second, even if clutch hitting existed, I'm not sure it is important. Sure, everyone would like to see their favorite star come through with runners in scoring position, but if a hitter made a disproportionate number of hits when there were no runners on base, perhaps he is "adept" at getting rallies started.

If I were a general manager, I would hire a statistician to crunch the numbers. In baseball, playing conditions differ greatly between ballparks. The configurations of various stadiums affect the ability of right-handed or left-handed hitters to hit homeruns. Atmospheric and lighting conditions also affect hitters and fielders. Humid air may retard the ball's flight, while the thin air of Denver is conducive to homeruns. In football, although the playing fields are identical in size and shape, weather conditions are not. Snow, cold, heat, rain, and wind affect playing conditions. For both sports, we've said nothing about artificial turf or domes.

I would want to see whether there are some players who might be "diamonds in the rough," in the sense that their statistics are depressed because of (individually) adverse conditions. A right-handed slugger — we'll call him Joe Bob Mantle — playing in a park where the left-field wall is 420 feet away instead of, say, 350, is going to hit a lot of long fly balls. His averages are going to appear lousy. There's an arbitrage opportunity here. If my stadium has a left-field wall only 350 feet away, Joe Bob may "blossom." The beauty of crunching numbers is that you can identify players who might be a good fit for the physical aspects of your stadium. If I was scouting for players, I might hire some bright undergraduate to watch recordings of the previous season's games in which Joe Bob is playing at home. The student would chart the number of fly balls Joe Bob hit that were caught, say, 360 feet from home plate. I would then ask my scouts their opinions. The number crunching is a useful adjunct to the eyes and ears of your scouts. In some cases, the number crunching might be more accurate than your scouts' assessments, but in other cases, the scouts might know something that is difficult to quantify. Scouts, as with any professionals, have shibboleths that they obey. Statistical analysis may reveal which shibboleths are erroneous.

In football, coaches and commentators consider turnover ratios decisive, but not all interceptions are created equal. A quarterback facing third and long on the opponent's thirty-five yard line who throws an interception at the five-yard line with no return probably doesn't hurt his team much. It's unlikely that the team would have gotten a field goal, and a punt and ensuing return probably would have advanced the ball beyond the five-yard line. Aside from the "killing momentum" aspect, which may be dubious, there's not much real harm done, certainly less than there would be with the same outcome on first and ten at the opponent's thirty-five yard line. Conversely, a quarterback who is pinned to his team's own one-yard line and who drifts back into the end zone and hurls a pass intercepted at the ten-yard line does hurt the team.

Football announcers, like all of us, wish to appear sophisticated. A couple of decades ago, they began to extol the time of possession as a crucial statistic. The statistic's explanatory power may be limited. I've often thought the best way to win a game would be for your return personnel to break free and score touchdowns on every kickoff and punt return. Sure, your time of possession would be minimal, but in the metric that really counts, you'd rack up a lot of points. The style of play may affect the time of possession. The old, "three yards and a cloud of dust" offense featured in many Big Ten games ate up the clock but didn't necessarily score a lot of points. A successful running team dominates both the clock and the scoreboard. A team prone to falling behind early may resort to frequent passes, with attendant, clock-stopping incompletes. Such a team may lose the time of possession contest as well as the game. The team loses because it couldn't score enough points, not because it didn't dominate the clock. The time of possession may be a ramification of the losing style of play, but it is not the cause. I understand that a good football team wants to run out the clock, when it is ahead. Still, it's the points that win the games, not the time of possession.

Then there are the more general shibboleths. Quarterbacks get over-emphasized by the media. Around Super Bowl Sunday, you begin to hear how Dan Marino never won one, as though the game were a mano-a-mano affair. Recently, Tom Brady was being anointed as one of the greatest quarterbacks of all time, with phrases such as, "He's won three Super Bowls." Brady is, indeed, a fine quarterback, but New England's overall strength has to be a factor, too. Ironically, the following week Brady and the Patriots got creamed.[9] Whatever happened to football being a team game? Of course, even coaches fall for the hype. In selecting Olympic teams, basketball coaches appear to jettison their "Defense wins games" mantra. At least once or twice, coaches had the opportunity to send a clear message that defense and rebounding matter by selecting Dennis Rodman. I know Dennis was volatile, but few players have ever affected a game the way he did. Sure, he wasn't a big-time scorer, but wouldn't it have been fun to see him shut down those fancy shooters from around the world?

Many fans and pundits literally revere sports numbers. However, such numbers are rarely compiled under laboratory conditions. A true measure of a player's ability would hold as much constant as possible. SABR-metricians adjust for ballpark differences, but playing rules change over time. While Roger Maris received much grief over setting his homerun record after 154 games, he received less criticism over the fact that he faced diluted pitching: There were 25 percent more pitchers in the American League in 1961 than in 1960. Although today's fans bemoan steroid use and its "unfair" effects on the record books, I have to believe that facing 25 percent minor-league caliber pitching is a bigger advantage than steroid use (heck, you still have to hit the ball). In addition, *Sports Illustrated* claimed that the ball was "deader" in 1962 than in 1961, so Maris and the other sluggers (except for Harmon Killebrew) who feasted in 1961 never attained those slugging feats again.[10]

In basketball, the three-point shot is presumably affecting scoring records. Would Jerry West and Oscar Robertson have bulked up their scoring totals with a three-point shot? You damn betcha, although it would be easy to over-estimate the effects. Conversely, Robertson achieved his triple-doubles in an era in which there were more rebounds per game. Teams in the early 1960s shot more frequently and compiled lower field goal percentages. There is no doubt that Robertson was a great player, and he is my pick as the guard most likely to have been better than Michael Jordan. However, his number of "Triple-Doubles" was aided by the conditions under which he played.

The National Football League continually tweaks its rules, trying to maintain some balance between offense and defense. Certainly these rule changes affect player statistics.

The search for a "tell-all" statistic continues. Because many people have math phobia, they are fearful and therefore suspicious of statistical/ mathematical formulas. The BCS rankings, using various computer models, are a case in point. No pollster has spent hours watching all of the top forty college football teams in America. The pollster must, therefore, rely upon reputation as well as on experience. Clearly, too, there are incentives for pollsters to vote for certain teams, regardless of their merits. There's a lot of money at stake on the poll outcomes. Hence, hiring some mathematical "geeks" to crunch the numbers in a supposedly neutral fashion is appealing and astute. The computer models may produce different orderings, but this should not upset us unduly. In addition, the orderings cannot tell us with certainty which team will win an upcoming game. After all, there is a non-trivial probability of upsets, just as in the case of the World Series. Ideally, we'd like to have the top two teams play several games to establish superiority, but this is not possible in college football.

Computer models depend upon assumptions and incomplete knowledge. Those "best college" ratings are quite similar to the football polls. Few, if any, college presidents have scrutinized even the top one hundred universities in America, though they are often asked to fill out surveys ranking universities. They fall back on reputation and hearsay. The ratings depend upon the weights assigned to the various categories. Once schools know the weights placed on the categories for the ratings, they can make adjustments. "Selectivity" is particularly egregious. Different schools may have different definitions of whether a student applies, so they can massage their selectivity rate. A similar drawback occurs with those "Top Ten Places to Live" ratings. Much depends upon the weights placed on the categories.

People appear to have a craving for a single number that tells you everything you need to know in evaluating competing products. Even the Total Baseball Rating (TBR) that I've used in my research is dubious, though seductive. I have doubts about the fielding metric used in the ratings.[11] Fielding prowess is notoriously difficult to measure. There's range, and then there's sure-handedness. A fielder with limited range may be effective because he knows how to play the hitters. The player who is out of position and has to run and make a shoestring catch may get on the highlight film, but, really, who is the better fielder? That said, the TBR appears to be as close as we can get to an ideal single statistic in measuring players. Pitchers tend to fall short of the top rungs on the ratings, as do catchers. One drawback is that regular players that are below average accumulate negative ratings (often -10 or more for their careers), while seldom-used players hover around zero. We could reasonably assume that a slightly below-average regular player is often superior to the little-used substitute. The TBR is not useful for assessing these situations. Still, the TBR produces few surprises (Bobby Grich and Ron Santo are two of the players underrated by the public and Hall-of-Fame voters, according to the TBR) and essentially confirms the consensus of the experts.

Enjoy the statistics, revel in them, but don't take all of them too seriously.

CHAPTER 3

Game Theory Applied to Sports

Professional sports leagues in America are cartels. The leagues set rules and schedules and monitor team activities. American sports leagues generally control the entry of new teams. While firms in competitive industries may eventually drive out rivals, teams in sports leagues typically do not desire to drive out rivals in their own leagues. The Yankees have to play somebody, so there is a symbiotic relationship between the Yankees and the Browns. Although the cartel exists to squelch some forms of competition, it allows individual teams to compete for players and to set ticket prices. Game theory can help us understand a cartel's behavior.

Game theory analyzes strategic interaction. The context need not be a "game" but is often a business situation where each party's actions affect a rival party. Professional team sports provide many applications of game theory.

Prisoner's Dilemma and Its Applicability to Team Sports

The teams in sports leagues face strategic interaction in several ways. Game theory principles can be readily applied to these interactions.

Suppose two owners are bidding for the services of Mickey Mantle Bonds ("the greatest that ever played," to borrow a line from *The Natural*). Because of a salary cap, each owner can only offer $10,000,000 in salary. In every meaningful way, the owners and the teams they represent are equally attractive to the player. The player will meet with each owner separately. If the player still finds them equally attractive, he'll flip a coin to decide where he'll play. Each owner knows that the player has a penchant for a rare vintage of Oregon wine produced in Drain, Oregon (yes, there's an actual town with that name and there are vineyards nearby). We'll call the wine Draineaux, as adding a faux–French name hypes the sales. A bottle of Draineaux costs $100,000, and there are only two left. The winery limits sales to one bottle per customer. Bottles of wine do not count against the salary cap.

The first owner, Georg Frankensteinbrenner (be glad you don't have to sign autographs or checks with that surname), owner of the New York Vets, figures, "If I show up bearing a bottle of Draineaux as a sign of respect, Mickey Mantle Bonds will sign with me." For a measly $100,000, it's a cheap way to clinch the deal. Of course, it's unlikely that rival owner, Walter O'Nalley, heir to a potato chip fortune, is any less astute. He's thinking, "If I show up bearing a bottle of Draineaux as a gesture of respect, Mickey Mantle Bonds will sign with me and not that jerk Frankensteinbrenner of the Not-Nice Empire." Both owners show up with bottles. Bonds thanks them and flips the coin. He ends up with the $10,000,000 plus two bottles of Draineaux.

Suppose the two owners meet the day before their appointments with Bonds. "Georg, what's the point of us both intoxicating Bonds with bottles of Draineaux? Might as well keep the $200,000."

"You're right, Walter. Let's shake on it; neither of us will show up with the Draineaux." They shake hands.

This sort of price-fixing occurred at times in American economic history. If we assume that Frankensteinbrenner and O'Nalley are ruthless, rapacious, running-dog capitalists (okay, it's lousy alliteration, but sports fans are used to such) who are bent on getting every edge possible, then we can safely predict each will renege on the deal and show up with the bottle of Draineaux. Naturally, such collusive agreements run afoul of antitrust legislation, so neither owner can appeal to the judicial system, even though the system would be very interested in the shenanigans. No matter how firm the handshake, each has an incentive to renege. In fact, each hopes the other acts "honorably" and adheres to the collusive agreement.

Many people think that capitalists will stop at nothing to increase profits, and would sell Grandma for a mess of pottage if it would improve the bottom line. Economists usually temper their depiction of capitalists, using the more neutral term "profit-maximizer." The conventional wisdom then takes its assumption that capitalists are rapacious, lets them meet for merriment and diversion, and immediately has them conspiring to collude against the public. Even Adam Smith cited the propensity of producers to collude. Still, our scenario remains very similar to the economist's story of profit-maximizing firms. However, the next, and presumably final, step is for the conventional wisdom to end the story by saying, "The conspirators lived happily, and profitably, ever after." Somehow conventional wisdom, though not Adam Smith, has dropped the assumption of rapacity. Why should rapacious behavior immediately end upon the implementation of a collusive agreement? Wouldn't it make more sense to imagine the colluding parties immediately start thinking about improving their position within the cartel? In fact, this is usually what happens. Back in the Gay '90s—1890s, that is—producers attempted to fix prices.

> It was no uncommon thing for a manufacturer to station a salesman outside the building [where the collusive agreement was being negotiated], and, as soon as a price settlement was reached, to stroll casually over to a window and, by fingering the shade in a prearranged way, indicate to him the level agreed on, whereupon the salesman would proceed to undercut the price his employer was even then pledging himself to maintain.[1]

In this anecdote, the ephemeral nature of most collusive agreements is poignantly depicted. The hands of the producers hadn't even cooled from the handshakes before they started cheating on the deal. Most collusive agreements recall Sisyphus and his rock. The siren call of enhanced profits induces attempts to collude and raise prices, but the collusive agreement falls apart when members cheat. They get back together, trade recriminations, and again agree to collude, but with no better results.

Although the public loves to see conspiracies lurking everywhere, the reality is that most collusive agreements to fix prices or otherwise exploit consumers fail because of the producers' individual profit-seeking behavior. Ironically, the "greed" of profit-seeking producers creates protection for consumers.

What Frankensteinbrenner and O'Nalley need is some enforcement mechanism, and I don't mean putting a horse's head in their rival's bed as in *The Godfather*. They can't find recourse in court, so most collusive agreements founder upon the shoals of self-interest. There is one exception. Baseball owners seem to have colluded successfully to tamp down bidding on free agents during the late 1980s. Most economists would first ask, "How did they enforce the agreement?"

Back in the 1940s, owners faced a similar problem with "free agents." The old-style free agent was a seventeen-year-old kid or a college ballplayer who hadn't signed with a professional team. Not satisfied with their enhanced bargaining power over professional players via the reserve clause, owners wanted to stamp out the last vestige of a free market for baseball labor by subjecting amateur players to a one-buyer draft. But I jump ahead of the story.

Since the owners seemingly couldn't help themselves in signing bonus babies, they decided in the late 1940s to define bonus babies as amateurs who received $6,000 or more in signing bonuses. Such bonus babies often had to remain on the big league team's roster, rotting on the bench and displacing veteran journeymen. Some owners sought to violate the spirit of the rule by signing players for bonuses which were in excess of $6,000 but were paid over a period of time; the owners quickly closed that loophole.

Major League Baseball finally got around to eradicating competition for amateur players when they enacted a draft in late 1964. There were two rationales for the draft. The first and more publicized reason was that a reverse-order draft would promote competitive balance. Presumably this was the argument that convinced legislators to countenance an otherwise egregious violation of antitrust laws. In fact, the inception of the amateur draft coincided with the collapse of the Yankees' dynasty. We'll examine the claim that the Yankees' dynasty collapsed because of a draft later; suffice it to say that most economists are dubious about the draft's effects on competitive balance. Competitive balance is the fig leaf covering the owners' naked desire for more profits through cutting player acquisition costs. The second, unpublicized reason for the draft was to create single-buyer power for a youngster's talent. Such single-buyer power should have reduced the bonuses being paid. Richard Reichardt received $200,000 as a signing bonus in 1964, and the horror of that signing helped prompt owners to do something. Instead of having twenty major league teams pursuing the next Reichardt, the major league owners thought it better to have just one suitor.

What took baseball owners so long to implement the draft? While owners publicly mentioned their fears that high bonuses corrupted youngsters and impeded their development, since they often had to remain on the major league roster, owners also feared legal repercussions. Combining a draft with the reserve clause might have triggered Congressional scrutiny and even action. To sign a seventeen-year-old to a professional contract that would bind him for his playing life to the whims of a single baseball team was an audacious violation of his civil liberties. Finally, owners recognized that signing a seventeen-year-old to a contract was legally dubious, because the player could potentially repudiate the contract later. Although a legal commentator expressed the opinion that the public would have scant sympathy for the player, as a boy "who no longer would be able to get a Pontiac convertible for each member of his family, plus a big bonus for himself, is not a particularly appealing plaintiff," the fears persisted.[2]

Congress, indeed, took notice. Even Charlie Finley, not a patron saint of player's rights, recognized the inequity in testifying before the Senate in 1965: "[major league owners] adapted a free agent draft to eliminate the excessive bonus bidding, thereby solving its own problem at the expense of the prospective player."[3]

Earlier, Leslie O'Conner, former assistant to baseball commissioner Kenesaw Mountain Landis, had made an eloquent argument against the draft: "If [Senate Bill] 2391 be enacted, its proponents ought to be congratulated or condemned ... for an atavistic achievement. For that will be a denial of human rights, of labor's rights, and a throw-back of over six hundred years to the despotic first labor laws of England — the *Ordinance of Laborers* and the *Statute of Laborers*."[4] As he explained, the amateur draft denied due process to the drafted players; transferred part of a player's monetary value of his skills via confiscation to the drafting team; denied players their constitutional freedom of contract; and denied baseball team owners their constitutional freedom of contract. On the last argument, one is entitled to feel less sympathy; after all, it was the owners who collectively enacted the draft. Of course, for the owners of wealthy teams, such as the Yankees, Dodgers, and Milwaukee Braves, the draft might have been injurious.

In any other context, such rigging of a labor market for young professionals would trigger public outrage. A reverse-order draft of Certified Public Accountants among the shrinking number of big accounting firms is amusing to contemplate. "Ernst & Young is proud to select Uriah Heep as the number one pick in the 2011 draft. He can balance the books, and he is the master of double-entry accounting. In addition, he is unctuous. Boy, is he unctuous." Since law firms could publicize their "win-loss" records, they are prime candidates for a reverse-order draft. (Here's a friendly tip: if you're up for Murder One, choose a law firm with a winning record in capital-crime cases, adjusted, of course, for strength of cases.) After all, if the Sharkey & Barracuda law firm corrals all of the top lawyers, it could drive out other law firms and create a MONOPOLY. Heaven forbid! Imitating professional sports team owners, law firms could plead that such a draft is necessary, or else "We'll just die."

The inordinate attention paid to the professional football and basketball drafts is doubly silly. Tout sheets are devised months in advance of the proceedings, and sportswriters provide "scouting reports." I imagine that few things are as irritating to a 360-pound lineman as hearing a middle-aged, beer-bellied sportswriter denigrate his 4.6 time in the 40-yard dash or his inability to bench-press three members of the gymnastics squad. Fresh off the streets, where they have been protesting "sweatshops" and their unfair exploitation of labor, many college students troop to the local communal television to root for their classmate's fortunes in the draft. Again, if law firms held a draft, would fellow classmates wonder breathlessly, "Will Perry Mason, with his genius for eliciting courtroom confessions at five minutes before the hour, be the number one pick out of Yell Law School? Will Sharkey & Barracuda trade down in the draft for the proverbial 'lawyer to be named later?'" Although the fledgling law school graduate may make more money than his or her classmates, the rigged market is still exploitive. Instead of sitting about with their beers and foam-rubber "number-one" fingers, Mason's classmates should be protesting vociferously against the reverse-order draft. Of course, few of them bemoaned their quarterback's exploitation by State U. Sure, Tommy Thrower, star quarterback, got free tuition, books, and rooms (list price $40,000 a year, but, then, just as with TV game shows, the prizes are not bought at list price), perhaps a few dates with cheerleaders and a greased palm by alumni, but the basic result holds: Thanks to the NCAA cartel, Tommy is exploited. Sure, his sweatshop is posh — big screen television, carpeting, air-conditioning — but he is still likely to be exploited. Think of how much Patrick Ewing meant to Georgetown. Always a fine school, Georgetown became nationally known thanks to Ewing and his teammates. Patrick was a real bargain at even $40,000 a year (in today's dollars). Don't buy the rationale that universities are non-profit organizations doing good for society. Exploitation is not given virtue even if it is perpetrated for a "good cause."

The introduction of an amateur draft was an overt collusive agreement. Usually collusive agreements are clandestine, and because of the secrecy involved, economists don't have as much information on their formation and maintenance as we would like. There are some industries where collusive attempts are more likely to occur and may be more likely to be maintained. A collusive agreement is more likely to succeed if there are only a few firms in the industry; if the industry is heavily concentrated in the hands of a few relatively large firms; if the firms produce identical goods or services; or if a trade association exists. By nature, professional sports leagues are a form of a trade association. The existence of the trade association is useful because it routinely holds gatherings. Under the cover of yearly conventions, the boys and girls can meet in the backroom and make clandestine agreements. In addition, a trade association or league may be well organized, which may facilitate monitoring and enforcement of agreements.

Adam Smith wrote in *The Wealth of Nations* that, "People of the same trade seldom meet together, even for merriment and diversion, but the conversation ends in a conspiracy against the publick, or in some contrivance to raise prices." Ironically, he does not advocate for an antitrust department to ferret out such shenanigans: "It is impossible indeed to prevent such meetings, by any law which either could be executed, or would be consistent with liberty and justice."[5] Smith probably relied upon the inherent stability of such conspiracies as protection for the public.

Since cartels and collusive agreements are mostly illegal in the United States, they must often resort to extra-legal enforcement, to use the polite term. Peer pressure begins in a benign form, the "gentlemen's agreement," but it can escalate. Southern gentlemen employed peer pressure in the form of night riding: Groups of hooded cotton growers or their thugs would ride to recalcitrant growers' plantations and whip some sense into them. Mint juleps, anyone? Chicago-style gangster enforcement is more direct. Baseball owners won an antitrust exemption in a Supreme court ruling in 1920.

Another way to see how there can be "too much competition" within the league is to assume that owners are both profit-maximizers and sportsmen. While fielding a good team helps generate large crowds, the additional cost of acquiring good players limits how powerful a squad a team can build. Suppose, though, that owners also get a big "high" from winning the championship. After all, your players douse you with champagne, sportswriters sing your praises, and grateful fans genuflect towards you. What person wouldn't enjoy the acclaim? Suppose that most owners would be willing to pay $5,000,000 for the limelight associated with winning a title. The added pleasure of basking in the warmth of a championship is similar to having a cash prize for winning, in addition to the usual profit from attendance and broadcasting.

An owner, then, would go beyond the profit-maximizing quality level in order to acquire the prize. If most or all of the owners expend additional resources to field the championship team, it's unlikely that the original team rankings will change. Again, the owners are collectively worse off by expending resources to get the prize. In essence, this is the same situation as the bidding for Mickey Mantle Bonds.

These two examples are similar to the Prisoner's Dilemma. Like it, they demonstrate that people who act rationally can end up worse off.

The classic Prisoner's Dilemma problem goes as follows. Two petty criminals, Slick and Sluggo, are hauled before the District Attorney (D.A.). The D.A. knows that the two have committed a series of thefts but is not certain she possesses enough evidence to get a conviction on any of the thefts. She needs confessions from them. Each theft will draw its own separate sentence. She separates the two criminals and interrogates them individually. To each she offers the following deal:

Both confess: each gets three years.

Neither confesses: each one gets one year on a vagrancy charge.

One confesses; the other doesn't: confessor gets half a year, non-confessor gets five years.

We set up the payoff matrix:

	SLICK'S STRATEGY	
	Confess	Don't Confess
Confess	(3 , 3)	(0.5 , 5)
SLUGGO'S STRATEGY		
Don't Confess	(5 , 0.5)	(1 , 1)

(Sluggo's payoff, Slick's payoff)

The matrix demonstrates that if Slick confesses while Sluggo does not, then Slick gets half a year and Sluggo gets five years.

The two prisoners make their decision separately. Put yourself in Slick's shoes. Your thoughts go as follows:

"If Sluggo confesses, my best strategy is to confess and get three years instead of not confessing and getting five years.

"If Sluggo doesn't confess, my best strategy is to confess and get half a year instead of not confessing and getting one year."

Regardless of what Sluggo does, Slick's best strategy is to confess, so Slick has what game theorists denote as a "dominant strategy." A dominant strategy occurs when, regardless of the strategy your opponent selects, your best strategy is the same. A player does not always have a dominant strategy. Since the payoff matrix is symmetric, Sluggo also has a dominant strategy, which is to confess. They both confess and each gets three years for this one theft. Notice that if both had kept quiet, each would have received only year. The D.A. has cleverly arranged the payoff matrix so that it was in the best interest of each individual to confess.

The dilemma, of course, is that each individual acted rationally and followed their best strategy, but collectively they ended up worse off. Is there any way for them to both keep their mouths shut? Notice that the D.A. keeps them incommunicado, so they can't overtly collude. But suppose they traded messages at lunch or via fellow prisoners. "Keep yer yap shut, Slick, and I'll keep mine zipped." "Yeah, sure, Sluggo." If each agrees to keep quiet, they have a deal. Once before the D.A., however, each hopes the other adheres to the agreement, while he sings like a canary and gets only half a year. Each has an incentive to renege on the deal, so each confesses and they each get the three years.

They need some sort of enforcement mechanism. Recall that Slick and Sluggo have several other theft charges pending. The situation is a repeated game. Even if the two criminals cannot explicitly discuss their strategies — "I'll get you, you rat, if you squeal," perhaps in the prison yard or wherever prisoners congregate — they may be able to collude tacitly. The two criminals can punish one another for confessing in a previous round by confessing on the next round. There may be a credible retaliation. The two can also signal their willingness to cooperate. The repeated game aspect creates opportunities for the criminal players to affect each other's behavior.

Now there are many different possible strategies. In the opening round, Slick and Sluggo may have been too upset to think about retaliation or cooperation. Let us rewind the tape. Slick and Sluggo, still held incommunicado, are sitting in their cells. Slick may think, "If I squeal, Sluggo is going to be mad. He will probably squeal on the next theft charge." Sluggo may be thinking the same thing. They may both decide independently to keep their mouths shut on the first round, hoping that the other will, too. If one does squeal, the other will retaliate in the second round by squealing. This simple one-time retaliation is known as the Tit-for-Tat strategy. Conversely, one could follow the strategy that he will keep his mouth shut as long as the other does, but if the other prisoner ever confesses he will then retaliate by confessing for the remainder of the games, a stronger but not necessarily wiser form of punishment.

Another interesting question is what happens when both players come to the last theft charge. If they know the game will end with that charge, the threat of retaliation dissipates. In fact, the whole spirit of cooperation can dissipate if both players know that the game is finite. Both criminals may think, "Sluggo (Slick) is going to confess in the last period. Therefore, in the next-to-last period, my threat will not have credibility. I can't retaliate, since we're both going to confess in the last period." Any collusive agreement to keep their mouths shut unravels like a cheap sweater.

In an ongoing business relationship, such as between a manufacturer and the supplier of a raw material, both are under the threat of retaliation as long as the relationship's duration remains ambiguous. The ambiguity concerning the duration of the relationship exerts a restraining effect upon any opportunistic behavior. If the supplier knows the manufacturer is going out of business at the end of the year, though, the supplier may begin to drag his feet when meeting the manufacturer's needs. Conversely, the manufacturer may take his time paying the raw materials supplier. In other words, both may begin to act opportunistically.

If there are more than two participants in the game, such as several owners colluding to keep bidding for free agents down, the story might become more complicated but the general findings from Slick and Sluggo's story hold. If anything, the penalty for being the only honest player in a gang of conspirators may increase. If all the owners agree to restrain bidding for free agents, and you are the only one to adhere, then you may find yourself not signing any free agents as the others all cheat and raise their offers.

The owners need to find an outside enforcer or create rules, such as salary caps, to limit bidding. They could, I suppose, each deposit a large sum of money into a league bank account and pledge to forfeit it if they are caught reneging on the collusive agreement.[6] Overall, I rather doubt that any voluntary collusive agreement can long withstand the individual incentives to cheat.

Owners are not the only group that might benefit from an agreement not to compete. Athletes, too, could benefit. Because the "prize" from being the best is so high, many hear the call to strive to be the best ... but few are chosen.

The large salaries earned by top athletes attract many potential entrants. Normally a surge of people wanting to be ballplayers might keep salaries down, but there are only a few slots for "the best," so salaries remain high. Many are called, few are chosen. Many youngsters dream of being professional athletes. The harsh reality is that few will ever achieve their dream. The dream of becoming an opera singer at the Metropolitan Opera or a solo violinist who plays with top orchestras is probably equally difficult to attain. Such overly optimistic assessments of one's chances to strike it rich in the entertainment field is not new. Adam Smith wrote of the overly enthusiastic young lawyers hoping to become a top barrister:

> To excel in any profession, in which but few arrive at mediocrity, is the most decisive mark of what is called genius or superior talents. The publick admiration which attends upon such distinguished abilities, makes always a part of their reward; a greater or smaller in proportion as it is higher or lower in degree.[7]

He continues:

> The over-weening conceit which the greater part of men have of their own abilities, is an antient evil remarked by the philosophers and moralists of all ages.... The chance of gain is by every man more or less over-valued, and the chance of loss is by most men under-valued, and by scarce any man.... The contempt of risk and the presumptuous hope of success, are in no period of life more active than at the age at which young people chuse their professions. How little the fear of misfortune is then capable of balancing the hope of good luck.[8]

Economists reading this passage can be discomfited by Smith's implicit charge of irrationality, somewhat palliated by the emphasis upon youth. Modern economists Robert Frank and Philip Cook echo Adam's argument. Their book, *The Winner-Take-All Society*, with its front cover blurb reading, "How More and More Americans Compete for Ever Fewer and Bigger Prizes, Encouraging Economic Waste, Income Inequality, and an Impoverished Cultural Life," paints an especially dismal picture of the quest to be "the best."

As an example of the human cost of having too many potential entrants for a very few jobs, the Chicago *Tribune* once ran a lengthy investigative report on the recruiting of junior-high boys by high-school coaches. In almost every case, a parent lamented that until the coaches came calling with their promises of fame and fortune, beginning with free shoes, the boys had been reasonably diligent students. Afterward, with the glare of stardom blinding them, most drifted away from studying. There can be real costs involved with the overzealous pursuit of professional stardom. For some reason, team sports seem to have a deleterious effect upon academic performance, whereas performers in individual sports contests, such as swimming, gymnastics, track and field, or cross-country appear to do better academically; at least the female participants seem to keep studying.

Sports economist Roger Noll estimated that "a fifteen-year-old [who] is a good prospect to be a football player [and make the high school varsity team] ... has about a three percent shot at a college scholarship ... and another one-fourth-of-one-percent shot at an NFL career."[9] Noll estimated that such a player had a present expected value of $11,000. He estimated that the player might devote 2,000 hours, over three years of high school, or an average of $5.50 (roughly minimum wage). Of course, the player may derive pleasure from the effort, but if most of the players are only interested in attaining the top, and devote additional effort and time in the attempt, the overall ranking probably changes little — the natural athletes still out-perform the less-gifted ones — and the added effort is for naught. The prize remains the same, regardless of whether the hundreds of thousands of youths devote extra effort or not. A tacit agreement by all of the youth not to devote added resources to attaining the prize would, therefore, be beneficial. Of course, keeping any youngster from "cheating" and practicing more is impossible.

There is a complicating factor. Not all youth will reckon their costs and benefits of practicing sports the same. The blunt truth about minimum wages is that the burden falls disproportionately upon poorer Americans, especially those living in depressed economic areas. Since the imposition of the minimum wage, black teenage unemployment has typically been much higher than white teenage unemployment. The most recent series of hikes in the minimum wage has been no exception.[10] Before the reader ascribes this to simple racism, it is important to realize that the story is more nuanced. In many poor neighborhoods, the local businesses cannot afford to pay as much as businesses in prosperous neighborhoods. A hike in the minimum wage may force these shoestring businesses to cut more employees than similar businesses elsewhere or to go out of business completely. Black youth face lower entry-level employment opportunities, and this lack is a detriment in the long run. Youth often get basic job skills by working at unskilled, low-wage jobs. They learn to show up on time, treat the customer courteously, follow orders, run business or other machinery, and acquire other basic skills. When these entry level jobs disappear, black teenagers may end up being like the character in those action films who is chasing a helicopter as it leaves the battle zone. As the poor fellow reaches for the rungs, the helicopter rises and pulls the rung out of reach. For black teenagers, then, spending hours practicing sports might make more sense than it would for his white cousin in the suburbs. Access to lower quality schools only exacerbates the skewed opportunity costs, as students in higher quality schools have better future prospects outside of sports.

Shooting baskets, therefore, has a lower opportunity cost for a black, inner-city youth than it does for a white, suburban teenager.[11]

These are examples of Prisons' Dilemma. You can probably think of similar situations in your daily lives. We'll look at other examples in later chapters.

Asymmetric Information and Bidding

Groucho Marx might have been the better Marxist economist when he quipped, "I don't want to belong to any club that will accept people like me as a member."[12] His quip touches on the issue of asymmetric information, a situation that occurs when one party to a proposed transaction has relevant information that the other party does not.

Earlier, we discussed a key result in economics: Voluntary trade is mutually beneficial. However, in cases of asymmetric information, such a result may not hold.

Suppose I hand two people each an envelope. The envelopes may contain $5, $10, $20, $40, $80 or $160. One of the envelopes contains twice as much money as the other envelope. Neither examines their envelope. If both decide to trade, they trade. If one or both refuses to trade, there is no trade.

You may think that trading is beneficial, believing that you have a 50 percent chance of doubling your money versus a 50 percent chance of losing half of your value:

Expected Value = .5(2) + .5(.5) = 1.25

You calculate that you should get a one-quarter increase on average, so you trade. If neither of you knew what your envelope contained, such thinking might be astute. Then again, you may be thinking this offer is too good to be true.

Suppose each of you peeks into your respective envelope. If only you can see what your envelope contains, and if only your potential partner in trade can only see what is in her envelope, the story takes a twist. Suppose your envelope has $160 in it. Obviously, you will refuse to trade. Conversely, if your opponent has $160 in her envelope, she will refuse to trade. If you have $80 in your envelope, you won't be likely to improve by trading, since, if your rival has $160, she won't trade. She'll only trade if she has the $40. If you have the $40 envelope, then you won't trade, knowing that people possessing the $80 envelope won't accept a trade and so on. The process unravels until the only person willing to make an offer is the one holding the $5 envelope (the reader may notice the similar logic used in the Prisoner's Dilemma situation with a known, finite end). Clearly, if your opponent wants to trade, you probably don't want what they have.

This situation occurs frequently. In the famous economic treatment of it, George Akerlof and Janet Yellen used the market for used cars. They used the term, "the market for lemons."[13] The seller knows more about the car than does the potential buyer. If a person has a good used car, he may have difficulty persuading a trading partner to pay a requisite amount, since the buyer may be dubious. People with good cars will become discouraged and withdraw their cars from the market. Eventually, any car that is offered is a "lemon" and not a "cream-puff" (I've never ascertained the reason for the pastry imagery). As with Gresham's Law, in which bad money drives out good money, bad cars drive out good cars.

At some point, asymmetric information may preclude any transactions, even though there are some mutually beneficial transactions to be made. Of course, people do buy and sell used cars. How do you buy a used car? What can buyers do to improve their knowledge of a car's quality? You take it for a test drive, kick the tires, or hire an expert. How does an owner of a cream puff signal to potential buyers that the car is not a lemon? The seller may offer service records and a warranty. If the seller is a dealer, then the buyer may rely upon the seller's reputation. Your Momma was right, your reputation does matter. If you plan to sell many used cars over time, then you do not want to run the risk of misrepresenting lemons as cream puffs. People talk.

Asymmetric information occurs in the market for insurance. People who voluntarily seek health insurance are more likely to perceive themselves as high risk. The company might do well to avoid selling to them. The problem is partially solved by selling group policies.

What does this have to do with professional sports? Well, instead of labeling poor quality goods "lemons," we call them "bums" or "busts." These are players who prove disappointing. An owner usually knows more about her players than does a rival owner. She may know that John Dough exerts a bad influence in the clubhouse or that he has a trick knee.

You own a basketball team and are considering signing a talented high school player. If the player works hard, he can become a productive player. While you can ask his high school coach about his work habits, the past is not a perfect predictor of the future. If you sign the youngster and give him a large bonus, he may slacken his efforts.

How can the youngster signal that he is, indeed, a hard worker? How can he establish credibility? If he is a non-athletic student desiring to impress future employers that he is highly talented and motivated, he could avail himself of one of the expensive top undergraduate programs instead of a cheaper state university. "Many people say they're committed to a career, but going to [a top private] school is a way to prove it. It's an investment worth making only if you're planning to earn it back."[14] The NBA prospect might have to scramble to find a means of demonstrating his commitment. He could agree to a contract that is not guaranteed, trading the guarantee for a higher payoff if he succeeds. Or he could agree to a contract with many bonus clauses based upon performance. However, such a tactic is risky for the player, since he might get hurt.

Two owners contemplating a trade can be stymied by fears of receiving damaged goods. Is a player being offered in a trade injured? Is this why the other team is willing to offer him? Just as potential buyers of used cars can kick the tires or hire a mechanic, a team can hire a physician to check the player. We note, for legal purposes, that kicking a prospective player's legs may entail legal liability leading to damages, so we won't carry the used-car analogy to its extreme.

Arbitration, Winner's Curse, and Bidding for Free Agents

While Major League Baseball players' success in getting binding salary arbitration does not receive the publicity that free agency did, that success was critical in raising salaries.

Players and owners involved in arbitration can employ game theory. A player and his agent typically submit a salary figure, while the owner and his general manager do likewise. Depending upon the setup, an impartial arbitrator then decides which figure best reflects a player's value or imposes some compromise. Neutral arbitrators are typically well paid for their services. Owners and players chart arbitrators' decisions. If an arbitrator appears to be biased, then he/she may have trouble gaining the approval of two prospective parties. Naturally, arbitrators desire to be employed in future arbitrations. If they have discretion, they may frequently opt to "split the difference" between the two salary figures. By doing so, the arbitrator may hope to get a reputation for being fair. A system where the arbitrator must choose one or the other figure creates a different dynamic. Both the player and the owner are likely to temper their figures, as a wildly inflated or deflated salary offer will probably be rejected by the arbitrator.

Bidding for free agents is quite similar to attending an auction. The various bidders have different subjective preferences and different financial abilities to achieve their preferences.

While professional athletes might appear to have objective value in terms of their productivity, that very productivity may be ambiguous. A star quarterback placed on a team with a lousy receiving corps or offensive line may have a different level of productivity than he would if he were placed behind a strong front four or supported by speedy, sure-handed receivers. Alex Rodriguez might mean more to a team without a solid cleanup hitter than he would to a team with many good hitters, like the Yankees.

In addition, as we've seen, a player's performance is stochastic, subject to random fluctuations and variance. This is true first because of statistical variation. Remember our discussion of the .300 hitter with 600 at-bats, whose batting average could vary between .290 and .310 and still be within one standard deviation of his true ability.

Potential bidders are, therefore, likely to have different objective and subjective valuations for a free agent. Although having deep pockets helps, a wealthy team already well-stocked with stars may eschew making a strong bid for another star. A relatively poor team, lacking a marquee player who can both improve the team's win-loss record and have a disproportionate effect on the gate, might splurge and make a strong bid.

Regardless of the team's financial strengths, eventually one of the most optimistic teams will win the bidding. Ideally, the winner bids one dollar more than the second-highest bidder, but, of course, the ideal is rarely achieved. Being optimistic is often a wonderful thing, but in the context of bidding, it can be costly.

An auction where the highest bidder ends up paying the second-highest bid usually generates a truer estimation of a player's value. In addition, if the auction is via sealed bid, bidders frequently are more likely to bid truthfully.

If the league has a rule that the current team owning the rights to a player has the right to match any offer, then a bidding team may act strategically by jacking up the offer, thus forcing the original team to match it. By doing this, the bidding team may knock out the original team from bidding on other players. Of course, if the original team opts not to match the offer, the bidding team must sign the player.

Principal-Agent Problems in Professional Sports

Once you've signed your professional contract, a new issue arises. How can the owner get "110% effort" from you?[15]

Economist Steven Cheung used the following anecdote to establish the nature of the problem:

> Some time ago, a Westerner was traveling by boat up the Yangtze River in China. At a particular narrowing of the river where the water ran fast it was impossible for boats to proceed under their own power. They had to be pulled upstream by teams of coolies, who trudged along the shore with harnesses around their necks. An overseer whipped and beat the coolies in order to elicit more effort from them. The Westerner was horrified by this cruel treatment of the obviously overworked coolies. That is, horrified until it was pointed out that the coolies owned the right to pull boats over this stretch of water. Because each coolie had an incentive to shirk in the team effort of pulling boats upstream, they had *hired* the overseer to monitor their effort and provide "incentives" to work hard.[16]

Let me restate the situation. Suppose Mayor Richard Daley of Chicago gives thirty-one of us the exclusive franchise for architectural boat tours along the Chicago River. These tours, featuring breathtaking views of the Sears Tower, Merchandise Mart, and other wonderful examples of architecture, are quite popular. The franchise is potentially very lucrative.

As economists are fond of saying, "let us also assume" that Al Gore was elected President in 2000, and he promptly outlawed the internal combustion engine. We have to tow our tour boat along the river. We'll split into two groups of fifteen, don our harnesses, and grab the ropes. Once each month, each of us gets to play "tour guide," riding the boat and extolling the marvelous sites. At the end of the day, we'll split the proceeds thirty-one ways.

So far, so good. People like our tours and business is brisk. However, as Spring evolves into Summer, the weather turns hot and muggy. As you're straining and sweating, you're thinking, "It's too darn hot. Well, if I slack off, no one will tell the difference." So, you slack off.

Most of your co-owners are just like you. They are probably all thinking the same thing. Pretty soon, everyone starts to slack off, and the boat comes to a standstill, perhaps in front of the Sears Tower. Our stalwart thirty-first compatriot tries to save the day by digging deep into her knowledge of the Sears Tower to compensate for the boat's stationary position, but, of course, the tour is a disappointment.

At the end of the day, we crowd into our favorite watering hole. Recriminations fly around the table. "You shirked!" We realize that our franchise is worthless unless we solve what economists call a "principal-agent" problem.

In the professional team sports world, owners are the principals. They hire players ("agents") to perform. They hire managers ("agents") to monitor players and to get the utmost production. The trick is to arrange incentives so that the agents have the same agenda as the owner. A player who has signed a long-term guaranteed contract may decide to take it easy on the field. I don't want to exaggerate a player's potential to shirk, as there are countervailing forces, such as personal pride and sheer competitiveness, that motivate a player to his best efforts. Of course, a player's performance is in the public eye, so the level of scrutiny is high. If you are a public school teacher, the principal is, literally, a principal (ultimately, she is also the agent of the school district). You are an agent of the school district and are monitored by the principal. The school district and principal have to arrange incentives so that you will show up and teach in a responsible fashion. Otherwise, you might begin to resemble the teachers depicted in *Ferris Bueller's Day Off* and many other teen comedies: inattentive, demoralized, and lazy.

We return to our tour boat franchise. After the recriminations die down, someone gets a bright idea. "Well, the Bears have finished training camp and cut a bunch of players. Why don't we hire a couple of big guys, arm them with whips (our peer has watched too many galley-ship movies) and give them legal authority to chastise slackers." Among cries of, "Bravo!" and "Hooray!" we authorize her to go to the training camp site and hire a couple of disappointed players, Tad and Igor (facial scars and neck-bolts optional).

The next day, whips in hand, our new overseers begin their work. When you start dragging your feet, you feel the lash's caress. Everyone works hard, and our tour boat franchise appears saved. Notice that this story is amusing because it reverses the typical principal-agent problem: We, the principals, had to hire the whip-wielding football players, the agents, to monitor our behavior.

But wait, our story is not complete. After a couple of days of unending drudgery, enlivened only by our dividing the lucrative pot of money at the end of the day, you begin to think, "Pulling this boat is still a drag. Maybe if I slip an Andrew Jackson ($20 bill) to Igor, he'll ease up with the whip." Again, your compatriots are thinking the same thing. Pretty soon, Tad and Igor each have an extra $300 for the day, and the boat comes to a standstill once again. Our agents are "shirking" or, more specifically, are engaging in malfeasance. We must monitor our agents, and so we return to the classic principal-agent problem. Another problem may arise if Tad and Igor have deep-seated psychological issues that make them ill-equipped to be whip-wielding overseers. If they become "over-zealous" or capricious in their lashings, the incentive structure collapses. We might try and guard against such behavior by employing a battery of psychological tests before hiring them. Whatever we do, our goal is to devise a monitoring system that ensures, as much as possible, that Tad and Igor's interests are coincident with ours.

The issue is the same in professional sports. Except, perhaps, for owners of the Roman Coliseum, sports moguls throughout the ages have had to worry about athletes putting forth maximum effort. The gladiators were presumably motivated by that most basic of incentives: staying alive. Another stringent incentive system might involve holding an athlete's family hostage to encourage maximum effort. In more modern times, battling for one's life or for the fate of hostages is no longer used as an incentive mechanism in professional sports.

Tom Yawkey of the Boston Red Sox was beloved as a generous owner. In his book, *Summer of '49*, David Halberstam recounts a conversation between Tommy Henrich, Yankees outfielder, and Bobby Doerr, Red Sox second baseman. The Bosox were an arguably more talented team than the Yankees, but they often finished second. Doerr asked Henrich why the Yankees usually prevailed. The former Yankee replied, "Because you didn't have to [win the pennant] and we had to. We needed the extra money from the World Series check. That was our extra salary. You guys were all making more money than us because of Yawkey."[17] Reporters also made the same point, describing the Red Sox as playing under country-club circumstances and having their incentives to win blunted. Of course, the Red Sox may have simply been unlucky in losing three pennants by a total of six games between 1948 and 1950.

On the other hand, some management theorists would argue that Tom Yawkey was astute in paying his players more than the Yankees. During the early part of the twentieth century, Henry Ford gained fame by offering a Five-Dollar Day. Five dollars a day was well above the standard for semi-skilled workers such as his auto workers. Ford was not being philanthropic. An old, fallacious theory was that he figured that if he paid his workers well, they'd buy Ford cars. A stronger theory is that by paying handsome wages, he could induce his workers to put forth more effort because the penalty for shirking was higher: The shirker lost a lucrative job. We might interpret Yawkey's generosity as a similar ploy. Players might hustle more in the hopes of staying on the Red Sox rather than being traded to the more frugal Yankees or, even worse, the truly penurious Washington Senators.[18]

Baseball owners agreed to set up a pension fund for players after World War II. While the fund may have been created to foster good will, it could also function as a disciplinary force. The vesting period was several years, so players might have been forced to curtail colorful behavior in order to stay in management's good graces. Indeed, some owners even commented on this aspect of the pension. The pension plan also helped deter players from joining outlaw leagues, such as the Continental League.

What incentives can be built into contracts to help ensure that players exert maximum effort? Explicit incentive clauses are an obvious place to start. The New York Yankees began offering bonuses to players right after World War I. Initially the team offered bonuses to star players if the team finished first, second, or third. In a sense, these bonuses were similar to employee profit-sharing plans. While the star player presumably had some effect on the team's standings, just as an employee might have an effect on the company's profits, the connection was ambiguous. A star player might exert himself and still watch the team crash. It's also possible that the rewards might not be enough to inspire effort. Under a typical profit-sharing plan, such as our tour boat, would the lure of an extra dollar of profit split thirty-one ways be sufficient to inspire an individual to exert more effort?

Apparently these bonuses based on the team's finish did not elicit satisfaction, so the team began offering individual performance bonuses, which were given primarily to starting pitchers for the number of games won. There were also bonuses for remaining on the roster for the entire season and signing bonuses. The team reduced its use of performance bonuses during the Great Depression. The team also used bonuses to elicit "good behavior," with payment based upon a manager's approval. Management may have preferred using bonuses as incentives because bonuses are flexible; a management that gives bonuses is not committed to paying higher salaries. Players appear to have been loath to have their salaries cut, even in the face of deflation. A bonus is by nature a temporary arrangement, so there may have been less resistance to eliminating bonus clauses for subsequent seasons. Occasionally performance bonuses boomeranged, as they allegedly did in the case of the Chicago Black Sox. Eddie Cicotte was disgruntled because management kept him from starting a game where he might have notched a crucial victory and earned a bonus. In retaliation, he helped arrange to "throw" the 1919 World Series. In novelist Mark Harris' *Bang the Drum Slowly*, protagonist pitcher Henry Wiggen, a free spirit, receives bonus payments for each win above fifteen. At one point, some fans and fellow players accuse the manager of not using Wiggen as frequently as he did earlier in the season in order to limit the bonus payments.

Labor economists suggest that another incentive structure is to underpay workers early in their careers but to promise overpayment later, incumbent upon good behavior. Naturally, such tactics redound to management's advantage, as the workers have to rely upon staying in management's good graces as well as being subject to the shared risk of the company folding.[19] For long-standing, stable companies, the tactic may work well. There is evidence that although aging players may eventually face a pay cut, they may well continue to earn salaries above their actual productivity. A variation of such a tactic would be to place a large sum of money in a special account. If the player behaves well throughout his career, he gets the money.

In a real sense, professional sports' reliance upon the reserve clause, at least for the first few seasons of a player's career, creates a salary path similar to that described above. The reserve clause tamps down salaries early in a player's career, but the promise of free agency prods players to perform well in hopes of landing a rich contract. In baseball, arbitration may ameliorate the underpayment the reserve clause causes during the early years of a player's career.

The league might act as a monitor of the principals' (team owners) behavior. A reverse-order draft of new talent can create perverse incentives for teams. It is assumed that players and teams always try their best to win any particular game. On the other hand, consider the Milwaukee Bucks and Phoenix Suns in the late 1960s. If they finished last in their divisions, they could find themselves in a coin flip for Lew Alcindor (later known as Kareem Abdul-Jabbar). Second prize was Neal Walk, and I don't mean Neil "Walk on the Moon" Armstrong. Suppose Milwaukee had to play a rival in its division and the two teams were tied in the standings for last place. Do you think Milwaukee's fans would mind if the coach rested the starters and played the scrubs in an indirect attempt to lose the game? In fact, should anyone mind? Well, I suppose an astute lawyer might sue, claiming that the ballclub defrauded him: "I paid good money to see the Bucks give 100%, and I all got was this lousy chance to be in a coin flip."

To forestall this, the National Basketball Association implemented new systems in which throwing a game has smaller benefits.

Games with Mixed Strategies

Sports broadcasters, who need to fill an incredible amount of airtime, often make inane comments, usually about the allegedly asinine play selection of experienced coaches and managers. "That was a bad play call," they pontificate. Perhaps the play call was bad, but the pundit usually declares it so for the wrong reason. A play that works isn't necessarily the right play, and a play that doesn't work isn't necessarily the wrong play. In most contexts, you should think of ten or a hundred exactly similar situations. Which play is likely to be the most successful over repeated tries? A suicide squeeze bunt may be the correct play, but the execution is difficult. Imperfect execution doesn't negate the wisdom of calling the play.

Beginning tennis or racquetball players are exhorted to play to their opponents' backhand, based on the observation that most players favor their forehands. Such predictability erodes the value of playing to the opponent's backhand. Some poker players, like my Dad, never bluff. If George Surdam bet strongly, you darn well knew he had the goods. Unless you had a superlative hand, you knew you should fold. Unfortunately, that meant he rarely won large pots. The non-bluffing player finds his winnings are reduced. Thus, mixing your strategies may be beneficial. To reap the maximum benefit from mixing strategies, you want to be unpredictable.

Think about a football coach. Some coaches are famous for running the ball on first downs: "three yards and a cloud of dust." They only throw the ball if it is third down and long yardage. These coaches may mix their strategies, adding in some passes with their runs, but the predictability of the mix reduces its effectiveness.

A famous military strategist, Sir Basil Liddell Hart, proposed the "indirect approach" to war. He chided many generals who used the direct approach and attacked the most obvious points. Surprise attack by an indirect route could create psychological turmoil within an enemy army. If the indirect approach or the surprise attack were predictable and anticipated, though, it could lead to a worse disaster than the frontal assault. The football coach whose decision to throw long on third and one is anticipated by his opponent can end up with an interception or a sack and foregoes the relatively high probability of gaining a first down with a run up the middle. Since it is difficult to consistently fool your opponents by "think and counterthink," only a random approach to play selection can create true unpredictability.

Consider the following story from Edgar Allan Poe's "The Purloined Letter." The prototypical detective Dupin is relating how he knew a schoolboy who won all of the marbles in the schoolyard game of "even and odd." One player holds some marbles in his hand. The other player guesses whether there is an even or an odd number of marbles. If he guesses correctly, he wins a marble; if he guesses incorrectly he loses a marble. The schoolboy's feat elicited widespread admiration:

> Of course he had some principle of guessing; and this lay in mere observation and admeasurement of the astuteness of his opponents. For example, an arrant simpleton is his opponent, and, holding up his closed hand, asks, "are they even or odd?" Our schoolboy replies, "odd," and loses; but upon the second trial he wins, for he then says to himself, "the simpleton had them even upon the first trial, and his amount of cunning is just sufficient to make him have them odd upon the second; I will therefore guess odd;"—he guesses odd, and wins. Now, with a simpleton a degree above the first, he would have reasoned thus: "This fellow finds that in the first instance I guessed odd, and, in the second, he will propose to himself, upon the first impulse, a simple variation from even to odd, as did the first simpleton; but then a second thought will suggest that this is too simple a variation, and finally he will decide upon putting it even as before. I will therefore guess even;"—he guesses even, and wins.[20]

Dupin questioned the boy and found that the lad tried to mimic his rivals' thoughts and expressions in order to ascertain whether he was holding an odd or even number of marbles. In an episode of *The Simpsons*, Bart and Lisa decide to resort to "Paper, Scissors, Rock" to resolve a dispute. Bart thinks, "Rock, good old rock." Lisa thinks, "Poor, dependable Bart always chooses rock." She chooses paper, and wins. Bart exclaims, "D'oh!"

We return now to our football coach. Suppose he faces third and long on the opponent's twenty-eight yard line. Most people would choose a pass. Of course, the defense suspects a pass. The following matrix shows a simple strategic interaction, as we're ignoring various types of pass and run plays.

OFFENSIVE COACH

		Run	Pass
Defensive	Blitz	+4	-4
Coach	Run Stop	-2	+8

If the offense selects a pass and the defense blitzes, the result is a loss of four yards, which may take you out of field goal range. Conversely, if the offense had selected a run play and the defense blitzed, the offense would have picked up four yards and would have a reasonable shot at a field goal. To get the first down, the offense needs to pass, but the defense knows this, too. For simplicity, we'll assume the offensive coach only cares about maximizing yards gained and the defensive coach only cares about minimizing yards given up.

If the offense is predictable and always chooses to pass, the team will always lose four yards. If the offense always chooses to run, it always loses two yards. Hence, complete predictability results in a loss. Conversely, if the defense becomes predictable, then the offense can exploit the predictability.

Suppose the offensive coach chooses to mix his play calling. He decides to call pass and run with equal likelihood, tossing a fair coin to determine his call. If the defensive coach understands the offensive coach's procedure, then he has to decide his counter-strategy.

If the defensive coach decides just to blitz, then half the time he gives up four yards and half the time he sacks the quarterback for a four-yard loss. On average, the offense gains no yards. If, instead, the defensive coach employs a run/stop defense, the offense may expect to gain three yards. In the face of the offensive coach's 50–50 play calling, the defensive coach figures the blitz defense is the better choice. However, the story is more complicated if the situation recurs. Once the offensive coach realizes that the defensive coach will respond to the 50–50 run/pass strategy with a blitz, the offensive coach should alter his strategy.

Ultimately, both coaches must employ mixed strategies. Once they determine the optimal mix of strategies based upon the assumption that the other coach is also selecting his optimal mix, then they just roll the die, flip a coin, or employ a random number generator. There is likely to be a mix of defensive and offensive strategies such that neither coach has an incentive to alter his mix. Once the two coaches are set in their mixes, then there is an equilibrium. This is a situation of predictable unpredictability. Each coach may know the likelihood of his rival calling a particular play, but there is no gain from trying to guess the opponent's next call.

In our story, we've simplified the number of plays, the predicted outcome, and other factors. In reality, coaches face variability in any given play's outcome: a handoff might be sloppy, a defensive back might slip, anything might happen. In the Strat-O-Matic Baseball version, we can calculate the probabilities in a way that a real-life coach cannot. Still, the basic point holds. In order to guarantee unpredictability, a coach should only select the proper mix of strategies given the assumption that the other coach is doing the same. Once the mixes are set, coaches resort to a random selection based upon the optimal proportions. Even if a play doesn't work on any particular down, the coach cannot truly be said to have erred in his play selection.

Of course, both coaches are trying throughout the game to discern any pattern on the part of the other coach's play-calling. To guard against predictability (aside from the other coach knowing the odds of your calling a particular play, which he should be able to estimate closely), you have to be random.

An economist and a game theorist would applaud the previous discussion. A coach, of course, would be hesitant to relinquish control of calling any particular play. In addition, he would be reluctant to admit that he was employing a random number generator, whether a lowly die or coin or a sophisticated, computer-generated random number. "I chose the play at random," is likely to get him fired by an owner, who probably does not understand game theory.

For a baseball manager and fans, deciding when to attempt a stolen base is part of the fun. Of course, one should recall that the basic tradeoff is getting a base in return for risking a base runner. Earnshaw Cook and other early statistical analysts suggested that to break even from attempting steals, one needed to be successful in roughly three out of four attempts.[21] In addition, a manager would probably be better served stealing with two outs than with none out. Of course, if the manager became known for never stealing with none out or one out, then opposing managers would adjust. A manager might opt to attempt an occasional steal with none out or one out, just as a successful poker player runs an occasional bluff.

Just how beguiling is individual play calling that attempts to out-guess your rival? Well, no less a game theory expert than Richard Nixon could not help suggesting football plays during the NFL playoffs. According to Henry Kissinger, Nixon always strove to create uncertainty in the minds of Chinese and Russian leaders: "What's that crazy Nixon going to do?" Fresh from calling an end run through Cambodia, Nixon suggested a flanker reverse play to Washington Redskins coach George Allen. Unfortunately for Allen, the play netted a loss of thirteen yards but remember from our previous discussion that there is probably no way to state definitively that it was the wrong play for the situation. If the P.A. speaker blares, "The president is calling the next play," you'd probably be wise to expect something dramatic. Few celebrity play callers would opt for something simple and mundane, such as a plunge off center. How could Allen not run the play? "George, your country and the free world need you, pull that flanker reverse play." Apparently Nixon also suggested plays to Don Shula and Tom Landry; the latter observed drily, "If the play succeeds, he should get a thrill out of it. If it's intercepted, I'll get a thrill out of it."[22] I suppose an owner of a woebegone team could try to raise revenues by selling fans the right to call the next play.

We have seen that sports leagues face competition within their ranks. This competition creates many situations of strategic interaction. The game theory examples discussed above are just the most general examples. Fortunately for the teams in the leagues, the leagues may be able to curb "ruinous competition" by an adroit use of game theory principles. Major League Baseball has an explicit antitrust exemption that allows the organization to enact anti-competitive rules. The National Football League and the National Basketball Association have permission to be exempt from antitrust legislation with respect to negotiating national television contracts and a few other issues. Many other industries can only wish they had similar protection against "too much competition."

CHAPTER 4

Demand for Games and Profitability

Each year millions of fans troop to games in cities such as New York, Chicago, and Los Angeles. Because most newspapers have a daily sports section, fans and pundits alike believe that professional sports teams generate large sums of money. Surely professional sports teams are indispensable to the local economy.

How Important Are Professional Sports Teams to a City's Economy?

Are professional sports teams a significant part of a city's economy? The Yankees take in $250 million $300 million per year. How does this compare with other local businesses?

In 2006, consumer expenditures for admissions to spectator sports, including non-professional sports and professional non-team sports, amounted to $17.2 billion out of a total consumer expenditure of $9,224.5 billion, or less than one-fifth of 1 percent. Admissions to spectator sports comprised a smaller share of total consumer expenditure in 1954, less than one-tenth of 1 percent. Even though professional sports receive revenue from television, radio, and licensed products, and gambling on sports takes in some billions of dollars, you can see that the industry is a minor player in the United States economy. In fact, Americans spent much more on tobacco products in 2006 than they spent on admissions to spectator sports. Professional sports are more visible than many industries and have their own section in most daily newspapers, but we should not lose sight of the industry's relative unimportance in the overall economy.[1]

When Michael Jordan retired (again) from the Chicago Bulls, local television reporters wrung their hands about the economic impact upon the city. What would happen? Some people bandied about figures of half a billion dollars in lost revenue.

The Chicago Bulls continued to sell out for a season or two after Mr. Jordan left. One could argue that the Bulls did not pay the remaining players as much as Mr. Jordan, so there was less spending in Chicago by Bulls' players. But even had the fans deserted the Bulls, all would not have been lost for the city. After all, Chicago has many cultural and entertainment venues. Instead of trekking to the United Center, people could mosey over to Second City and get a few laughs, increase their patronage at local movie theaters, or grab a good dinner. The overall effect on spending in Chicago ought to have been minimal. One could grant that the city gained more utility from having the Bulls win the championship than from having people patronize the other venues mentioned, but in terms of spending, there should be almost dollar-for-dollar replacement.

Some observers argue that having an NBA, NFL, or MLB team makes a city "major league." Such a status is wonderfully vague. Without the Bulls, Cubs, White Sox, Bears, and Blackhawks, would Chicago really be a significantly worse place to live? After all, the lakefront, the Art Institute, Museum of Science and Industry, Field Museum, Shedd Aquarium, two zoos, comedy and dramatic theaters, Chicago Symphony Orchestra, and ballet and opera companies would still exist. Frankly, losing the United Center and the refurbished Soldier Field would enhance the city's architectural heritage. Perhaps the city's bars would suffer, especially those near the stadiums, but other venues and restaurants would gain business.

What about tourists? Some people undoubtedly come into Chicago for the express purpose of taking in a game. Conversely, many people come into the city to visit the cultural and historical sites. Other people might be deterred from visiting the city when there's a game being played, fearing the traffic and occasionally unruly crowds. Indeed, researchers have discovered that such events as the Olympics and World's Fairs may essentially be a rearrangement of tourism flows.

Suppose Kalamazoo, Michigan, is going to host the Olympics in 2012. There would certainly be an influx of tourists in 2012, but many people who were planning to visit Kalamazoo sometime in their lifetime might have re-arranged their visit to coincide with the Olympics. Tourism might well fall off in 2011 and 2013. On the other hand, some people who had planned to visit in 2012 may avoid the city because of the hubbub. Some Kalamazoo residents might stay in town to watch the Olympics instead of traveling to Detroit to see a professional game. Conversely, other Kalamazoo residents might leave town during the games because of the anticipated crowds.

The concept of the multiplier is closely tied with the idea of increased tourism because of sports teams. Jane Roe travels from New York City to visit Kalamazoo and see the Olympics. She spends $500 on motels, meals, gasoline, tickets, and sundries. Suppose she spends $300 at the Bates Motel. According to the multiplier effect, Norman, the motel owner, and his employees now have $300 more in revenue that they spend in the local economy. Suppose Norman spends an additional $100 at the local taxidermy shop. The taxidermy shop owner and employees now have an additional $100 to spend. The process continues ad nauseam. When all is said, each of Jane's original dollars generates more than a one-dollar increase in the local economy. Depending on the enthusiasm of the consultant making the calculations, the multiplier might be as high as three or four.

Disputing the multiplier is akin to shooting fish in a barrel. First of all, we've already seen that Jane's presence in Kalamazoo might have displaced someone else who would have visited the city but was dissuaded by the crowds attending the Olympics. Her visit may not be a clear-cut gain. Second, the Bates Motel might have been owned not by the kindly local, Norman, but by an evil international corporation, and much of the $300 she spent there might go to corporate coffers in Delaware, where incorporation laws are favorable. In other words, there is leakage in the multiplier. The $100 spent at the taxidermy shop might or might not remain in the community. Indeed, the fixation on keeping the spending local is provincialism writ large. A Kalamazoo resident might choose to take some of his earnings to the big city of Detroit and sample the wider cultural amenities in that city. To be fair, Kalamazoo has an impressive amount of cultural activity for a city of its size. The multiplier is quite literally an elastic concept. Depending upon the assumptions made, one could tailor the multiplier to please almost any client.

People also make the argument that having well-paid athletes in town will bolster the local economy, because the athletes will spend their money and pay their taxes locally. To use a motif from a television western, a town could also hire a group of gunfighter mercenaries in the hope that they would spend money in the local saloons and pay some taxes. Such hopes are laughably naïve. As you may know from watching westerns, most gunfighters, if they haven't been shot, mosey on down the road with their pockets bulging after the excitement dies down. The majority of professional athletes do not reside in the city in which they perform. They may spend some money in the city, but they probably spend more in their hometowns, where they will probably pay most of their taxes as well.

We can conclude, then, that sports teams are a relatively unimportant but heavily publicized aspect of any local economy.

Because of the publicity surrounding sports, team owners can leverage the apparent importance of retaining the local team in order to "extort" public funds. Major League Baseball teams developed the technique of getting publicly built stadiums during the 1950s. Not all observers were overjoyed. An editorial in *Barron's* claimed the San Francisco Giants' sweetheart deal with the city:

> Seems to play hob with the precepts of sound municipal finance, as well as those of free enterprise. The blunt fact is that in order to break into the big leagues the Bay City has agreed to underwrite the construction and operation of a ball park and related facilities. Thereby, in effect, it has placed the public credit behind a private venture. The deal may represent a smashing victory on the West Coast for better baseball and civic pride. But it also stands for the triumph, in a great U.S. metropolis, of expediency over principle.[2]

New York Yankees General Manager George Weiss also excoriated public financing of sports stadiums, although there was a self-serving element in his complaint:

> It's damned unfair for a stadium financed by public funds to operate against a private corporation that pays the city $200,000 a year in taxes. Anyone who says the [new Shea Stadium] will pay for itself is crazy. Every municipal stadium in the country is a white elephant.... The city won't lift a finger to help us get the parking space we need desperately at Yankee Stadium, but it's ready to pour money down the drain to accommodate the Continental League.[3]

Today's owners appear to have preferred public financing and ownership of stadiums to privately built stadiums. Relatively few stadiums in the past forty years have been privately built. If you were an owner, you might think that owning the stadium is beneficial, since you dictate what goes on inside. You also collect the parking and concessions revenues. Finally, you don't pay rent. The owner still incurs an opportunity cost, however, even when her team plays in her stadium, as she could have booked another event there instead. Moreover, you tie up a large chunk of capital in the stadium, possibly running into the hundreds of millions of dollars. Even at 3- or 4-percent rates of return, an owner gives up three or four million dollars per year on a capital outlay of one hundred million dollars not to mention the maintenance required to delay depreciation of the stadium. If the team tanks or the demand falls, perhaps because of declining population within the metropolitan area or falling incomes, any move to greener pastures means leaving an empty stadium behind. When you own a stadium, therefore, your capital is at risk. The city may also begin levying punitive property taxes.

With a publicly owned stadium, the city might try to keep most of the concessions and parking revenues, but an owner has leverage, too. If the owner is considering relocating to a city with a vacant stadium, the original city may offer generous terms to prevent the move. As long as there are vacant stadiums in large cities, teams can play musical chairs and threaten cities with the loss of their beloved teams.

The availability of substitutes is a major reason why city financing of sports stadiums usually does not yield a positive return. Don't forget opportunity costs: The dollar spent on a stadium could have been spent on building a school, improving roads, or, most radically of all, returned to taxpayers for them to spend as they see fit.

Economist Rob Baade examined the experiences of forty-eight cities during the 1980s. He analyzed the data to see whether cities with new stadiums enjoyed a higher per capita real income growth rate than those without new stadiums. His findings suggest that building a new stadium has no real effect upon a city's economy. In a few cases, the new stadium negatively affected the economy.[4] In addition, while the athletes' large salaries mesmerize fans, the typical stadium worker makes a low wage. Baade concludes, "The data suggest that stadium subsidies and other sports subsidies benefit not the community as a whole, but rather team owners and professional athletes.... The failure of professional sports to demonstrate a significant impact on economic growth suggests that either team owners and athletes spend little of their revenues in the area, or that professional sports does not generate economic growth as substantial as alternative uses of the funds invested in sports."[5] Other economists have found generally similar results, although a few claim that positive benefits occur in some cases.

If the economic benefits of having the public build sports stadium are so dubious, how do the owners prevail? After all, isn't America a place where the "majority rules?" What sort of evil conspiracy lurks in our political process that allows the few to be enriched by the many?

Consider a hypothetical owner: George Steinmodell, owner of the Palookaville Punks soccer team.[6] While George is wealthier than 99.9 percent of all Americans, he moans piteously that he cannot afford a plush, new stadium for his team that will also pump up the local economy. Your first clue that something is amiss occurs when he makes his claim. If a new stadium is such a good deal, George should be able to convince his friendly neighborhood banker to ante up a loan. The irony of shills touting publicly financed stadiums as money-makers for a city is that the owner typically pleads poverty or inability to undertake such a large project with even a scant hope of turning a profit, yet somehow the selfsame project is assumed to be a good deal for the local government. If there are non-monetary benefits from the stadium, such as a general feeling of joy from having a successful team or increased ability to publicize the city as an attractive place, it might be possible that the overall gains, both private and social, justify public subsidy. However, one should be very wary of such claims concerning large "intangible" benefits.

George goes to the mayor. "I need a stadium. If you help me get public funding, you'll be able to cut a ribbon when the stadium opens and tout the jobs created." The mayor likes such publicized opportunities. The local news reporters always show up and breathlessly announce during the construction phase, "This project is creating 1,000 new jobs and is pumping $100 million into the local economy." The mayor may even lift the first shovelful of dirt on the site.

Aside from kissing babies and saving lives, there's nothing a politician likes to do more than to create jobs. The argument that building the stadium "creates jobs" is just sleight-of-hand. After all, if you gave me dictatorial power (and we know how much short men like me relish power), I could create a job for every person. Some people might end up digging ditches and then filling them up under the scrutiny of armed gendarmes, but at least they'd get a paycheck. Alternatively, in our white-collar society, I could employ many people in such make-work jobs as adding up numbers and then subtracting them out. Creating jobs is not an impressive feat if the creator is given sufficient coercive power. Of course, a privately built stadium presumably creates jobs, too.

There is a real asymmetry at work. As stated, a politician loves to stand in front of a construction site, with workers hovering in the background, and say, "We're creating jobs by building this stadium." Television reporters love the spectacle.

Such largesse is not conjured out of thin air. The losers in the deal, various entertainment venues throughout Palookaville and other businesses, lose dribs and drabs of revenue. These losses require an imagination to recognize. Few television news crews are adept at covering abstract stories, so they don't show up when Joe's Bar has to lay off a couple of employees. "All of the crowd goes to the Palookaville Stadium these days. Nothing more depressing than an empty bar." In any event, the idea of building publicly funded stadiums is tantamount to lifting oneself by one's civic bootstraps. Our highly televised mayor gains from having a visible "benefit," but he avoids taking the blame for the less visible and hard-to-prove costs.

But, you say, why don't the majority of Palookaville citizens protest this enrichment of mogul Steinmodell? Even if his family and employees vote along with George, they have a few hundred votes at most. Businesses that stand to gain from having a new stadium built, such as construction firms, nearby hotels and restaurants, and media outlets (who gain from covering the team) also add some votes. Part of the difference between political democracy as compared with economic democracy is that the political process is ill-suited to directly register passion or intensity of preferences. In the economic democracy, all consumers have votes. Certainly consumers vary in the number of votes they can cast, but most consumers can employ Chicago-style voting habits in the marketplace: They vote early and often. In the political arena, you might be forced to choose between McDonald's and Burger King. If you really, really like McDonald's, you have but one vote. In the economic arena, you can vote many times for McDonald's, thereby registering the intensity of your preference.

Obviously, George Steinmodell has a strong preference for the stadium. Although a majority of Palookaville residents may be against the stadium, their opposition may be lukewarm. Although George can only indirectly buy individual votes from citizens, he can subvert the political process by registering the intensity of his preference with local legislators. In other words, since the benefits of a new stadium are concentrated upon George, his players, and his employees, they will find it worthwhile to lobby and to expend resources to persuade legislators to vote for what they want. George can afford top-flight consultants to make "enthusiastic" financial forecasts and to massage the news flow. Indeed, local newspapers may face financial incentives to support the sports teams, as professional teams sometime help spur demand for newspapers and other news media. While most citizens may not make the connection that they will each have to pay an additional twenty or thirty dollars for the stadium, they may not do anything about this added tax cost even if they recognize it. After all, Americans are currently paying extra money each year for sugar-based products, thanks to the domestic sugar industry's cozy deals with Congress.

Suppose you discovered that you were paying fifty dollars a year for this subsidy. You might be angry to discover such a transfer, but would you be angry enough to undertake organizing millions of Americans to end it? I think not. George can, therefore, leverage his passion for a stadium against a relatively indifferent public.

Even with privately funded stadiums, chicanery lurks. Lately, some owners have created PSLs, Personal (Private or Permanent) Seating Licenses. By earmarking the money to pay for stadium construction costs, the owner can mislead unwary patrons into thinking that the extra charge is not enriching the owner. The mistake here is a matter of fungibility. Suppose you put your leftover money into various jars labeled, "Christmas fund," "gas fund," and "birthday fund." You might put the five dollars you saved today by skipping lunch into the "Christmas fund" jar, but, in reality, it doesn't matter in which jar you place the money. The money is fungible. If you're short of gas money, you just take some out of the "Christmas fund." Although the owner earmarks the money for stadium costs, it is, aside from possible tax issues, the same as putting the money into his general fund.

Of course, owners of professional teams are not the only folks to use this sleight-of-hand. Often college alumni can direct where their donations go. The real question, though, is whether it really matters. A provost could say to the athletic department, "Well, you got $10,000 in donations for new equipment, so we'll cut your budget by $10,000." It's the net change that matters. State-run lotteries that designate profits for education often do similar switching. The million dollars from the lottery does, indeed, go to education, but, as many educators ruefully note, money from the general fund is cut, almost dollar-for-dollar. On net, many state education budgets are unaffected by lottery winnings.

What Brings 'Em to the Ballpark

We now turn to what actually draws folks to ball games. As George Steinbrenner once stated, he was interested in what "put fannies in the seats," whether it be a winning team or a marquee player.

Bill Veeck, Jr. (not to be confused with his father, William Veeck, Sr., who helped pilot the Cubs to success in the late 1920s and early 1930s), once wrote that team owners are in the business of providing fun and entertainment for fans. He wrote with suitable capitalization, "Although you are dependent upon repeat business, you have NO PRODUCT to sell. The customer comes out to the park with nothing except the illusion that he is going to have a good time. He leaves with nothing except a memory. If the memory brings on either yawns or head pains you have lost him until next year." The trick was how to create the "good time" fans are seeking? Veeck suggested that you guarantee that they will have a good time.

> You can give them a MONEY-BACK GUARANTEE. You can tell them that if they don't have fun, you want them to march, singly or *en masse*, upon your box office and demand their money back. No stalling, no box tops, no questions asked. To prove that you are not making this offer frivolously, it would be well to grab the public-address microphone the first time you have been soundly trounced and insist upon everybody coming back whether they want to or not. "No one," you announce, your voice throbbing in agony, "should have to pay good money to see this kind of a monstrosity. I implore you to come back as my guest."[7]

Did it work? Veeck's Cleveland Indians beat the Yankees in attendance in 1948–49 and his White Sox also did so in 1960 (after their 1959 pennant). I quote Veeck at length not only to use his point about promotion but also to encourage readers to consult his books. His books are entertaining, if occasionally self-serving (if I had out-drawn the Yankees and beaten them twice for pennants, I'd be self-serving, too).

In general, holding all else constant, the higher the ticket price, the lower the quantity demanded. In other words, ticket price and quantity demanded are negatively or inversely related. Imagine them poised opposite each other on a teeter-totter. When price rises, quantity demanded falls and vice versa. Economists have documented few, if any, exceptions to this "law of demand."

The usual approach to estimating the demand for a product consists of gathering data, including the price and amount sold of the commodity or service being considered. Quantifying sports ticket prices is difficult, since teams usually offer several different classifications of seats simultaneously. To cope with the multiplicity of ticket prices, researchers might opt for an "average" ticket price, perhaps weighted by the number of seats in each classification: box, reserved, general admission, or bleacher. Such a method implicitly assumes, however, that the proportional mix remains constant regardless of whether the stadium is sold out or is sparsely filled. In addition, owners often offer discounts for season tickets or as special promotions. The difficulty of ascertaining which ticket price to use in estimating demand may be reflected by the perverse result found in some studies: Price is positively related to quantity demanded.

The economist must also be careful in differentiating whether a higher price triggers a change in the quantity demanded or whether a change in the underlying demand drove the price higher. An example of the latter effect might occur if fans faced higher ticket prices for other entertainment options in their city. They might react by switching to the local sports team (assuming the team hadn't already raised ticket prices). When consumers substitute sports for other entertainment, the demand for sports tickets increases and the ticket price should increase eventually.

The problem in ascertaining price's effect upon quantity demand, therefore, is holding other factors constant, so the researcher also needs information on prospective customers' incomes, prices of substitute goods, prices of complementary goods, product quality, weather, preferences, taxes and subsidies, and expectations about future prices.

Such a differentiation between the effects of a higher price or of a shift in the underlying demand is important in thinking about why ticket prices have increased. Many fans blame escalating player salaries. But the real question is, "What came first, the increase in fan demand or the increase in player salaries?" An increase in demand, perhaps because fans have more income to devote to sporting events, would increase a team's ticket prices and revenue. With the increased revenue, an owner might be inspired to improve the team, increasing the demand for star players and thereby driving up salaries. When baseball free agency and its attendant jump in star players' salaries occurred in the mid–1970s, ticket prices jumped, too. However, the decade was one of relatively rapid increases in the Consumer Price Index. (We'll return to this episode in a later chapter.) As television revenue and gate revenue began to increase, the demand for star players increased and players received higher salaries. The situation works in reverse. If the demand for sporting events diminished, we would expect an eventual decrease in demand for star players and reduction in salaries.

If demand for a team's games falls, ticket prices should fall. During the Great Depression, though, baseball owners refused to lower their ticket prices. They did begin offering discounts in the form of Ladies' Days, but they claimed that they had not raised prices during the Roaring Twenties and were thus loath to lower ticket prices during the Great Depression. In addition, the diminished demand occurred concurrently with a major deflationary episode, where the Consumer Price Index fell by over 20 percent. Thus, ticket prices became more expensive in terms of purchasing power. Owners may have counted on people literally voting with their feet by moving their fannies around the stadium, substituting cheaper grandstand or general admission tickets for reserved and box seats.

Demand for games is also affected by the team's perceived quality. In the sports context, economists often measure product quality in terms of a team's win-loss record or finish in the standings. Typically, it is assumed that the higher the quality, the stronger the demand: More people will buy tickets at any given price for a higher-quality team than for a lower-quality one.[8]

There might, of course, be limits on the quality variable. Athletic contests have one aspect not typically found in other commodities or services: uncertainty regarding the outcome. In theater or opera, if you've read the play and the director remains true to the original script, you can know the outcome in advance. The bromide about opera — everybody dies — is serviceable. In sports, while the Yankees may usually win, they don't win all of the time. Fans typically enjoy the uncertainty, to a degree at least.

Quality can be considered in two ways: absolute and relative. Do fans care about attending a contest where the score is likely to be close, or do they simply prefer watching "the best?" During the 1950s, the Brooklyn Dodgers and New York Yankees provided evidence that fans preferred the latter. The Yankees were the best draw for every opposing American League team. In other words, fans preferred to see the best, regardless of the likely competitive imbalance. Fans were not enthused by relatively competitive games between the sad-sack Philadelphia Athletics and St. Louis Browns.[9]

Winning always helps, but such factors as a new, comfortable stadium; convenient access and parking that reduces the time cost of attending games; alternative entertainment opportunities; fan loyalty; population base; income; and even such arcane aspects as corporate tax codes affect how well a team draws or what sort of local broadcasting deal it can cut.

Although New York City has the largest population base in the country and reasonably high incomes, the city has a myriad of entertainment options. There are not just multiple professional sports teams in each league; there are also great museums and many other cultural amenities. During the 1950s, New York's per-capita attendance at Major League Baseball games was one of the lowest in the game. While the low rates of attendance were partially mitigated by the higher ticket prices charged for Giants, Dodgers, and Yankees games, it appeared that the wider variety of entertainment venues siphoned off some of the demand for Major League Baseball.

During Portland's NBA championship finals against the Chicago Bulls, local Chicago television reporters were amazed that not all Portland residents were mesmerized by the finals. The Chicagoans could not understand that many Portland residents were outdoor enthusiasts who preferred being outside to sitting around watching television. To the big city reporters, this was an unheard-of example of "rural" yokels missing out on truly important events.

Generally, higher incomes or greater wealth among the residents of a city make it more likely that fans will attend games. Major League Baseball owners did not consider New Orleans a good candidate for a team because its residents had lower per-capita incomes than residents of other major cities.[10] At extremely high levels of income and wealth, though, fans might begin switching to fancier entertainment venues.

Fan loyalty is an interesting phenomenon. After the Dodgers and Giants left New York City, the Yankees did not experience much of an uptick in attendance. Apparently Dodger and Giant fans did not assuage their loss by transferring their loyalty.[11] In cities such as Chicago, Cubs and White Sox fans view each other with barely concealed loathing. Had the White Sox left the city for Florida, as seemed possible two decades ago, many observers doubted that the Cubs would have received an influx of refugee White Sox fans.

In any event, there are many factors that might increase demand and thus increase ticket prices. Fans wax nostalgic about the good old days when ticket prices were low and games were affordable for family outings. In a sense, "high" ticket prices are a misnomer. If fans still voluntarily pay such prices, they must still feel better off paying and attending the game than they would feel about undertaking an alternate activity. They might wish they could pay $20 instead of $30 to see a game, but as long as no one forces them to attend, I have scant sympathy. Moreover, I suspect few fans thumb through old *Sporting News* to see what ticket prices were in 1954 or 1964. A savvy fan might use the Consumer Price Index to convert yesterday's ticket prices into today's dollars. An even savvier fan might heed the warnings of the President's Blue-Ribbon Panel which studied the Consumer Price Index during the 1990s. The panel suggested that, partly due to technical problems, the index overstated the true rate of increases in prices. An economist might also argue that "affordability" is better measured against a fan's potential earnings. Thus, an economist might examine "average hourly earnings" for non-supervisory manufacturing workers, adhering to Bill Veeck's claim that most baseball fans are blue-collar, beer-drinking folks. Of course, Yankees' fans might well be the white-collar, play-it-safe types, for whom the blue-collar "average hourly earnings" figure would be inappropriate.

You could construct a "market basket" for a family of four attending a game, including four reserved seat tickets, four soft drinks, four hotdogs, and maybe a couple of tubs of popcorn. Many Major League Baseball teams listed concession prices in their scorecards during the 1940s and 1950s, although the New York teams, serviced by the Stevens brothers, did not do so. By adjusting such market baskets for changes in the Consumer Price Index and by comparing them with typical hourly earnings, one could better discuss the affordability of games then and now. There is one considerable difficulty here, however. With any market-basket approach to comparing prices across time, the compiler has to hold quality constant. The scorecards and yearbooks themselves demonstrate changing quality over time, with more pages, better photos and paper, and slicker production. You are probably aware that contemporary Americans are losing their battles of the bulges. In an era of "super-sizing," comparing concession prices from fifty years ago with current prices is literally comparing "regular" with "super-size." A soda pop in the 1950s might have been eight or ten ounces. I'm not even sure whether McDonald's or other fast food franchises have cups that small anymore, except for coffee. My guess is that a 1954 hot dog resembles a shrunken version of its great-great-grandpup. Fans today are also offered a much wider array of food than in years past. "Nachos, we don't need no stinkin' nachos," would have been the refrain at 1950s ballparks.

The difficulty of comparisons does not end with concessions. Major league stadiums in the 1950s were old, cramped, and endowed with "superstructure obstructions," to be flowery about it. Aside from Cleveland's Municipal Stadium, all of the stadiums were at least thirty years old by 1953. Many were built just before World War I. Given the architectural standards and technology of the early 1900s, many stadiums had huge beams interspersed among the seats to hold up the roofing. Fans attending the games at the Polo Grounds were said to have watched games as though "through a picket fence," shifting one way and then the other to follow the ball in play. Apparently the restrooms at some stadiums were so filthy that one owner, Bill Veeck, forbade his wife to use the facilities until they were refurbished.[12] As teams moved to cities possessing newer parks, the "evil" Walter O'Malley and his henchman Charles Stoneham built modern stadiums with public help in the form of land giveaways or subsidies.

O'Malley and Stoneham touted the new, wider, more comfortable seats in Chavez Ravine and Candlestick Park. (Charles discreetly neglected to mention the winds ravaging his ballpark.) Seats at Candlestick Park were twenty-one inches wide instead of the eighteen-inch seats at Ebbets Field in Brooklyn. If you think three inches are trivial, get a yardstick and an average-sized friend. Sit side-by-side on the yardstick and check the measurements. In addition, the seats possessed backrests and were made from more comfortable material. Teams were just beginning to construct fancy box seats, and eventually the closed suite emerged. Naturally, a football fan with access to an enclosed, heated "suite" would have difficulty comparing the affordability of his seat to that of a bleacher seat in the elements among the hoi polloi in the good old days.

Of course, owners faced increased competition from television. Although they quickly sold rights to telecast games, the new medium offered competition that was quite literally spotty at first. If you've ever gone to a science or broadcasting museum and seen the early televisions, you know that today's youth would cringe in shame if the family's only television were like the early sets. The screens were small. Bars in the late 40s had "big screen" sets which were roughly seventeen to twenty-one inches in size. There was no instant replay and camera angles were limited. Owners wanted to insure that the televised images were no better than the vantage points of the worst seats in the stadium. For most of a decade, they probably need not have worried. Eventually, color, instant replay, zoom lens, and other amenities improved the telecasts. Indeed, the technological marvels of television have allegedly contributed to America's growing obesity problem, as men in 1950 could not channel surf as readily as men today. In the past, changing channels required getting out of the chair and manually turning a knob. Depending upon the reception, you might have to fiddle with the antenna and the knob controlling the rolling of the screen. I doubt today's children would even understand that last sentence: "What's rolling of the screen?" "Horizontal control" now seems more appropriate as a sleazy SPAM header. In an extreme case, you might have to go outside, fetch a ladder, climb the roof, and tinker with the outside antenna. Today, of course, a guy can sit his butt in his La-Z-Boy recliner, replete with cup holder and place to hold his nacho chips, and channel-surf with a flick of his finger, thus driving his female friends or wife nuts. I need not add that, in 1954, few cities had more than three or four stations, compared with today's Cecil B. DeMille cast of thousands of channels. Given all these advantages, I prefer televised football to attending in person.[13]

Contemporary fans, then, have much greater degrees of comfort and more amenities than their grandparents did. This observation should not surprise readers. After all, despite the disclaimers of some politicians and media and scholarly pundits, the material well-being of current Americans is far greater than that of their grandparents and parents. The suburban boom of the postwar era often took place in Levittown-style homes, small, squarish houses of less than 1,000 square feet. Today, many Americans have garages larger than their grandparents' homes. Comparing affordability across decades is more difficult than it appears.

Let's set aside the question of whether prices are too high and ask whether the owners set prices at profit-maximizing levels. Walter O'Malley made an interesting claim during the 1950s. He believed that an owner who was building a new stadium would take a loss on building general admission and bleacher seats (take that, Cubs fans), because such seats were unlikely to recover construction costs:

> [T]he public doesn't like those seats either. They're very seldom well filled. The public wants reserved seats even if the view sometimes isn't as good — it's some kind of snobbery. I could sell all the general admission and bleacher seats I don't sell now if I wanted to cheat and raise the price a dollar and make them "reserve." But it's a tradition that you've got to have them. And you figure you're getting some people into the park, kids and others, who otherwise couldn't afford to come to the ball game, and getting their loyalty, and you know they'll climb the ladder to the reserved seats and boxes just as soon as they get the money.[14]

O'Malley's claims, if they are accurate, address some interesting questions. While teams often raise ticket prices for premium events, such as the World Series or Championship Series, the market usually doesn't clear. How do I know this? The presence of long lines of willing buyers provides strong evidence.

The presence of consumers who can't get tickets at the listed price creates an arbitrage opportunity. You often see characters wandering in front of sports venues holding up tickets for re-sale. In unenlightened times, such activity was labeled ticket scalping, but we'll use the less pejorative term, ticket arbitraging. Occasionally, these arbitrageurs are victims of unfortunate circumstances: "Honey, I scored two tickets to the Super Bowl." "Really? But don't you remember it's Aunt Josephine's birthday that Sunday? You'll have to sell the tickets." A less savory character is the professional ticket arbitrageur. This character anticipates the excess demand for tickets, guessing that the sports team failed to place a high enough price to clear the market. In the financial market, such activity is known as speculation, and there's a class of people who specialize in guessing how high or how low the market will go. We call them speculators, usually not politely. Indeed, my students who worked in the futures market at the Chicago Board of Trade referred to themselves as traders and never as speculators.

An economist often views speculators or arbitrageurs with more sympathy. A competent arbitrageur improves the efficiency of the market. Let's consider the following event: a game of HORSE featuring Larry Bird, Michael Jordan, and Charles Barkley, recreating the classic McDonald's burger ad. These three legends are going to shoot off in a 60,000-seat football stadium. You are the promoter and you figure fans would be willing to pay $30 a ticket for this exercise in nostalgia. However, you have underestimated the fans' demand for nostalgia and there are 200,000 people willing to pay $30. Ordinarily such an excess demand would cause the price to rise, but you've already published the price.

With such excess demand, there are long lines of fans surrounding the stadium's ticket booths. In addition to the $30 for the ticket, fans are using up valuable time waiting in line. Now, I don't know about you, but I despise standing in line. I would have fared poorly in the former Soviet Union, where standing in line was the national pastime. Fans attempt to mitigate waiting in line by bringing lounge chairs, boom boxes, ice coolers, etc. Assuming that no fan can "cut" in line and usurp an earlier position, the 60,000 fans that get tickets undoubtedly waited for hours. Suppose the wait was five hours. That would mean that each of the 60,000 people who got tickets wasted five hours standing in line. The lost time represents what economists call a deadweight loss. No one really gains from having people wait in line, unless you argue that the owner gains from the free media publicity attendant upon the long lines. How much would you be willing to pay to avoid waiting in line for five hours? In other words, what is the value of your time (this can be considered in before-tax or after-tax dollars)? For many of you, the cost of the five hours waiting in line would exceed the cash cost of the ticket.

Indeed, we can predict what sorts of people are more likely to stand in line: younger people (predominantly students), retirees, or unemployed people. These people may place a lower value on their time and are more willing to stand in line. Many white-collar workers making $40 per hour would find standing in line prohibitively expensive.[15]

Thus, the 60,000 tickets end up in the hands of the young, the unemployed, and the retired (which would be an intriguing title for a soap opera). However, many of the other 140,000 fans might have been willing to pay more than $30 for a ticket, perhaps much more. Since a fan's reservation price for a ticket represents his or her "top dollar" valuation of a ticket, almost every fan getting a ticket valued the game at more than $30 plus the cost of waiting in line. Fans with only a passing interest in the game might be able to re-sell the tickets to someone who values the game much more.

Why did the erroneously low price happen? Two possibilities exist. First, suppose the owner was able to legitimately claim that the newspaper ads printed the wrong price. The true price was $75. Suppose, too, that $75 per ticket would have cleared the market. Who would have been better off? Obviously the owner would have been better off, receiving more revenue. Collectively, consumers will be better off. While they pay $75 in cash costs for the tickets, the additional $45 is probably much less than the value of the time spent waiting in line. Remember that unless you could saunter up to the front of the line and get your ticket without waiting, you were willing to pay $30 plus the value of five hours of your time. We could show graphically that the value of five hours is greater than the $45 in additional cash cost. The consumers willing to buy tickets valued the tickets at a minimum real cost of $75. The market price eliminates waiting in line and saves resources.

If the owner has placed an unduly low price on the HORSE match, the ticket arbitrageurs can step in and help improve efficiency by matching people with a willingness to pay a high price with those who only a passing interest. Each transaction benefits both the original and new ticket holders. We might be stretching things by suggesting that fans should honor the ticket arbitrageurs, but fans should at least realize that arbitrageurs can be socially useful.[16]

We should also note that ticket arbitrageurs are running a risk. The possibility exists that the listed ticket price is too high and that the HORSE match won't sell out at $30 a ticket. In this case, the arbitrageur will lose money. Years ago, the Chicago Art Institute had a Claude Monet exhibit. At first the exhibition was wildly popular, and ticket arbitrageurs took note. They purchased blocks of tickets for the final days of the show. Unfortunately, the anticipated demand did not materialize, so the arbitrageurs took an impressionistic bath.

The second possibility requires us to return to Walter O'Malley's claim. If owners continue to build unprofitable general admission seats, or if we always see lines for World Series tickets, then we should ask why the owners would not set a market-clearing price. After all, they like revenue as much as the next person; some might even argue that owners enjoy revenue more than is healthy. Perhaps they don't want to be accused of gouging. Some economists studying pricing suggest that owners may not charge market-clearing prices at peak periods. One example would be the refusal to raise winter prices at ski resorts — in order to maintain goodwill.[17] In other words, the ski resort or sports team owners value repeat customers and are hesitant to jeopardize their goodwill. Such behavior does not violate our assumption of rationality or profit-maximization. An owner would consider how much revenue they might forego today by not charging market-clearing prices in return for increased future revenue (or the possible loss of future revenue). Obviously, there is a limit to how much revenue an owner would forego today in return for future benefits, and the owner would use the marginal analysis and present-value calculations described earlier in the book. Owners rely upon their experience in gauging these tradeoffs. Usually the effect of such a tradeoff is not directly observable. Of course, if an owner was planning to pull a Robert Irsay, secretly moving his Baltimore Colts in the dead of night, then maintaining fan goodwill becomes moot. Mr. Irsay would presumably be loath to jettison any revenue today in Baltimore in hopes of future revenue.

O'Malley's refusal to act opportunistically by reclassifying general admission seats as reserved, at least while he was in Brooklyn, suggests a tradeoff between today's revenue and goodwill. In effect, an owner invests in a future fan base by attracting younger people, including children, to games with lower prices. The Brooklyn owner made an effort to attract kids with the Knot-Hole club. Given that he eventually moved the franchise to Los Angeles, one is entitled to question his sincerity. However, he might not have viewed the move as inevitable until 1956 or 1957, or he might have been camouflaging his intention to relocate. In any event, the desire to let a wider audience afford premium sporting events such as the World Series or Super Bowl might also explain consistent under-pricing of tickets.

I would suggest, though, that in the context of a Super Bowl or World Series the affordability issue is extraneous. Back in 1984, Michael Jackson went on his "Victory Tour." People were outraged when the promoters charged $25 or $30 per ticket. Pundits wrung their hands over the specter of poorer fans missing their chance to see the Moonwalk. Suppose that the true market-clearing price was $60 but for publicity purposes, the promoters charged only $20. A low-income fan could wait in line and purchase four tickets for $80. The fan and three friends could attend the concert, or the fan could re-sell three of the tickets and get $180. The opportunity cost of attending the concert is the same for the low-income fan as it would be under the market-clearing price. What the promoters have done is allow the patient fan to reap the arbitrage opportunity. While we might not bemoan the promoters' loss, it is fallacious to think we've lowered the price for the low-income fan. The low price did create an opportunity for the low-income fan to collect some economic rent.

O'Malley's remarks are interesting on another level, though. Despite his disclaimer, he did re-classify seats for Sundays, holidays, and double-headers. Seats that were usually general admission were upgraded to reserved. Since some of the reserved seats had the same price as general admission, it's not entirely clear whether he reaped more revenue per seat. He may have used reserved seating as a convenience for the fans. The Cincinnati Reds explicitly charged more and also reclassified some seats for Sunday, holiday, and night games. Variable pricing for seats is not an entirely new tactic.[18]

Of course, to plagiarize *The Six Million Dollar Man*, we have the technology to get money from putting fannies into La-Z-Boys in homes across America. As early as the 1950s, O'Malley dreamed of pay-per-view television for his team's games. His scheme, aborted by various factors that included an unfavorable state ballot measure, promised to solve some difficult problems. First, since pay-per-view revenue would be tied to a particular game, sharing such revenue with visiting teams would be easier to calculate than it would be under a system where the home team received a lump-sum payment for a season of games. While O'Malley despised "baseball socialism" and often refused to share his local media revenue with visiting teams, many of whom thought television hurt gate revenues, he eventually acquiesced to sharing some with the visiting team. Second, such direct payments might help owners ascertain whether television hurt or hindered gate revenue. Many National League owners had decided not to televise home games by the late 1950s. O'Malley and Stoneham only telecast the games between their two teams and no others, when they relocated to the West Coast. Owners had hesitated to embrace radio, a weaker substitute than television but hurriedly agreed to televise their games; ironically, they might have been better off doing the opposite.[19]

Profits, Profits, Who Has the Profits?

We now discuss profits. Owners have traditionally pled poverty. "If salaries continue to increase, it's the end of sports as we know them." Such doom and gloom is specious. Assuming that the underlying demand for professional sports experiences no persistent downturn in demand, how can owners *not* make profits? Are teams profitable? Few readers will think of baseball labor activist Marvin Miller as a humorist, but in his *A Whole Different Game*, he satirized baseball owners' penchant for moaning about their profit/loss statements despite rising franchise values. He devoted two pages to a "mock advertisement." With such headings as "Own Your Labor Supply," and "Enjoy the Finest Tax Shelter in the Nation," he concluded:

> Your methods of operation, your business practices — such as the use of blacklists, group boycotts, and conspiracies in restraint of trade, including combinations with foreign associates — are free of legal restraint. The United States Supreme Court has determined that the industry is not subject to the antitrust law of the United States or of any state, *unlike your closest competitors, who are subject to such restraints.* You are therefore free to utilize what would otherwise be illegal sanctions to enforce your will in controlling the entire skilled labor complement of the industry, to deprive cities and entire areas of your product when you choose to do so, to maintain with your associates a complete monopoly by barring would-be competitors, to fix prices and to allocate divisions of the market.[20]

Succinct, acidic, and accurate.

I reiterate the sports owners' advantages vis-à-vis owners of non-sports businesses. Owners have price-setting power, enabling them to set a higher price than would occur in a more competitive industry. For a long time, owners had the ability to exploit players by using the reserve clause and the reverse-order draft, thereby keeping salaries low. Certainly, free agency and arbitration have led to higher salaries, but we can presume that owners still pay salaries that are based upon revenue considerations. Modern owners often do not have to tie up their capital in a stadium, and since they usually negotiate sweet deals regarding parking and concessions, they continue to reap these revenues. Finally, highly favorable tax rulings enable owners to report "paper losses" while reaping real benefits. Given these advantages, it would take an inept businessperson to earn true losses.

Entire books could be written on the various accounting tactics used to camouflage or enhance profits. Many of the tactics are perfectly legal, but can mislead the general reader. Professional team owners don't like to brag and are modest in public forums. They prefer to present a sad, dismal portrait of their profitability. Their allies in city councils or in the state-house may agree that such modesty is best for gaining support for publicly financed stadiums. A swaggering owner bragging about his obscene profits is an unlikely candidate for public largesse. Most owners opt for pleading poverty. "Me and my orphan Yankees need a fancier stadium in the Bronx. We're just hanging on by our jockstraps in decrepit Yankee Stadium. Did I mention it was built in 1923?"

Some legal accounting tactics are quite lucrative. Owners gained a huge benefit when Congress countenanced depreciating the value of player contracts. If you purchased a sufficiently large share of a team after World War II, you could use this depreciation allowance for five years. With the high corporate tax rates of the period, this depreciation allowance could have saved you at least half of the value of your players. Exercising your annual depreciation allowance could artificially reduce your reported profit or inflate any loss, yet you would not be out a single dollar. This is what people meant by "paper losses." The allowance was so valuable that owners worried when Congress considered lengthening the period of depreciation to ten years instead of five. If that had happened, owners could only have depreciated half as rapidly, which would have diluted the value of the allowance.

The right to depreciate players also adds to a franchise's value. Bill Veeck explained the benefits of being able to depreciate the value of one's players: "As a seller [of a franchise], you are selling more than just the franchise and the players. You are selling the right to depreciate."[21] Economists James Quirk and Rodney Fort point out that Veeck, since he was only moderately wealthy and not able to afford a large enough share of any team, was unable to cash in on this depreciation allowance until he bought the Chicago White Sox the second time during the 1970s.[22]

If you hire your friends and family and pay them salaries, those salaries reduce your profits. Of course, if you were already planning to give your wastrel nephew, Willie, a million dollars, you might as well make him vice-president of navel contemplation. At least you get a tax write-off.

Some teams are owned by media conglomerates. The Atlanta Braves and TBS or the Chicago Cubs and WGN are examples. TBS and WGN telecast Braves and Cubs games respectively. Normally, the Braves and Cubs would sell their broadcast rights in an open market. The sales price would be recorded as revenue. TBS and WGN presumably "pay" the Braves and Cubs for broadcast rights. In essence, the amount paid is simply a transfer between divisions. Indeed, the amount may be selected with no regard to a market price but may, instead, be chosen for tax purposes. If TBS is already making a lot of money, while the Braves are floundering in red ink, TBS may "pay" a large amount for broadcast rights. By doing so, TBS incurs a larger expense and thereby reduces its profits and tax liability. Conversely, if the Braves were hoping to induce the public to ante up for a new stadium but were doing well and in danger of publicly having to admit a profit, then the team could sell its broadcast rights to TBS for a smaller amount, thereby reducing the team's revenues and profits. Such shifting, then, can produce a desired effect on profits and public perception.

The early NBA provides some good examples of the difficulty in comparing profits. The basketball owners, as with their football, hockey, and baseball brethren, supplied financial information to Congress during the 1957 hearings inquiring into professional team sports. The league presented dismal profit/loss figures for 1951 to 1954. Hardly any owner reported profits, except for the New York Knickerbockers. The dismal figures were not the result of chicanery among the owners. Most of the owners simply did not attract enough patrons to turn a profit. The Knicks's accountant suggested that the team's profits were a mirage by appending the remark, "No rent or any part of Madison Square Garden general overhead or administrative salaries included in above expenses. Had this overhead or rent been charged for each game, operations for 1952, 1953, and 1954 would have resulted in a loss and 1955 and 1956 would have about broken even."[23] Even this caveat is ambiguous. Madison Square Garden owned the Knicks. The opportunity cost to the arena owners was the amount they could have earned by renting the stadium to their hockey team, a visiting rodeo, a Harlem Globetrotters game, an ice show, a boxing match, or evangelist Billy Graham. If there was no alternative booking, the opportunity cost of hosting a Knicks' game would have been the minor expenses involved in turning on the lights; paying for heating; and hiring ushers, cleanup, and other labor.

A strong piece of evidence regarding the desirability and profitability of owning a professional sports team is the market value of the franchise. Although franchise prices don't always escalate (just ask the Columbia Broadcasting System, CBS, which fared badly with its ownership of the New York Yankees), most franchises have appreciated, sometimes much faster than the Consumer Price Index. The franchise's market value incorporates all of the relevant factors, direct and indirect. Although, as with many auction-type sales, the most optimistic bidder buys the team and may overpay, the general upward trend suggests that teams are inherently profitable.

Yes, some owners have reaped almost fantastic capital gains from selling their franchises. Eddie Gottlieb seemed to have made out like a bandit. He bought the Philadelphia Warriors for a pittance ($25,000) in April 1952 and sold the franchise for $875,000 a decade later.[24] This amounts to an annual nominal rate of return of 42.7 percent. An economist would argue that Eddie should adjust his rate of return for changes in the general price level (inflation) and also for risk. Inflation was moderate during this period and reduced the real per-annum gain to about 41 percent. During his initial years of owning the team, two other teams (out of ten) ceased operations. Gottlieb, too, came perilously close to going bankrupt, as the team lost money during his first years as owner. If one adds these losses (perhaps $50,000 to $100,000) to his initial purchase price, his rate of return would be whittled down considerably. In addition, Gottlieb was able to boost his team's value by convincing his fellow owners to grant him rights to Wilt Chamberlain.

In addition to earning profits, when owners purchase a franchise, they are buying a bundle of property rights. Some of these rights are anticipated, such as territorial monopoly (although this was, on occasion, abrogated), but some may not be. A lucrative national television contract, favorable tax treatment of player depreciation and other tax avoidance rules, the advent of free agency, surprising population growth or shrinkage, and other factors may affect the franchise values. During the late 1970s, baseball's new rules pertaining to players' property rights for their labor meant that owners would have to pay closer to market salaries instead of the artificially depressed salaries under the strict reserve clause. This change, if unanticipated, should have suppressed franchise values. However, unanticipated jumps in television revenue may have offset the deleterious change in player property rights during the introduction of free agency in the 1970s. Some cities went into decline. Detroit, like several Northeastern and Midwestern cities, lost population between 1940 and 2000, although much of the out-migration was to surrounding suburbs.

Although outside observers often must guess at whether professional sports teams earned profits, presumably prospective buyers of existing franchises demand access to the "true" figures. A business that persistently loses money shouldn't command a very high selling price. Thus, information pertaining to profitability can be found in actual franchise sales figures.

Of course, franchises are not sold every year, so the information is spotty. Don't forget that assets that appreciate, even at a low rate of 4 percent per year, double in value roughly every eighteen years. This means one shouldn't be impressed just because a franchise doubles in value over a period of time.

In addition to a team's direct profitability, there are other factors which affect its value.

Early owners of baseball teams hoped to reap synergy with their other businesses. For instance, an owner of a cable-car company might think it advantageous to buy a team and build a stadium adjacent to a stop on his line. A brewer, seeking a way to advertise his beer, might buy a team on the assumption that baseball patrons are thirsty beer-guzzlers.

The brewer-owner's "free advertising," though, is largely a mirage. Suppose you own a team and sell advertising on the outfield walls. You also own Butz Beer — "Butz fer Yer Gutz." You could get free advertising by placing Butz ads on the leftfield wall. However, you are foregoing the opportunity to sell the ad space on the leftfield wall to another company. Your advertising costs remain unchanged from an economic viewpoint, though your accountant might love the situation because there's no explicit cost.

A more modern quest for synergy was the Columbia Broadcasting System's purchase of the New York Yankees in 1964. The purchase caused rival National Broadcasting Company news commentator, Chet Huntley, to grumble, "Just one more reason to hate the Yankees," on the air.[25] So much for journalistic objectivity.

CBS purchased 80 percent of the team for over eleven million dollars. Earlier, NBC had attempted to purchase the New York Giants football team, so Huntley's gripe was truly sour grapes. The purchase price stunned observers, as the wildly successful Milwaukee Braves had been sold for only half that amount a year or two earlier. CBS was such a large entity that the purchase price was less than 2 percent of its annual revenue. The company could have purchased the Yankees out of the profits from its successful Broadway hit, *My Fair Lady*.[26] In a weird cosmic irony, according to legend (and legend it is, indeed) the Yankees had purchased Babe Ruth from the Boston Red Sox because Sox owner Harry Frazee needed cash to finance *No, No, Nanette*. To misquote Chico Escuela, for the Yankees, "Broadway been bera, bera good to me."

CBS President Dr. Frank Stanton hoped that the "affinity of management skills" used in running both a television network and a baseball team would create the necessary harmony of interests. After all, both endeavors involved attracting large audiences. Some legislators bemoaned the sale, with Congressman Emanuel Celler smelling the stink of profits: "I don't think CBS would be interested in the Yankees purely from an entertainment standpoint. CBS must feel there is a huge potential profit from the transaction. This deal confirms my belief that baseball is big business. I think the Department of Justice should examine this sale."[27] Somewhere, Sherlock Holmes is not trembling over Celler's powers of deduction.

Some commentators thought CBS was hoping to launch a pay-per-view scheme with the Yankees. Certainly, the team might have been a gem for such a scheme. The network was already paying the Yankees $400,000 or more per season for appearances on the "Game of the Week," much more than any other team.[28] The Yankees were the best draw for a national audience. Indeed, some wags suggested that the telecast be called, "The Yankee Game of the Week." You might think, "Well, if CBS owns the Yankees, they no longer have to fork out that money." True enough, but CBS still incurs an opportunity cost, as they could have sold the rights to telecast Yankees games to NBC or ABC.

The idea of synergy, then, is less straightforward than most people think. For synergy to exist, the merger of the two companies must bring about some increase in productivity. A tanner that purchases a slaughterhouse might capture synergy by eliminating the need to transport hides from the slaughterhouse to a separate tannery.

In popular culture, perhaps the best example of synergy occurred on *The A-Team*. You may recall that four disparate characters formed the team: Hannibal, Face, Murdock, and B.A. Baracus. Hannibal concocted the plans that "always came together." Since he always had a stogie in his mouth, he wasn't much for fisticuffs. Thus, he needed an enforcer. Mr. T played B.A., strongman of the team. Face was the ladies' man, while Murdock was the pilot with alleged psychological issues. The team helped underdogs and occasional damsels in distress, while working in an opportunity for Mr. T. to voice his signature line, "I pity da fool." Together, the A-Team was invincible, able to defeat large numbers of foes by blowing them up with nary a fatality, thereby avoiding those pesky wrongful death suits; individually, they were useless misfits. By melding their talents they epitomized synergy, the idea that the whole is indeed greater than the sum of the parts.

In professional sports, Bill Russell and Bob Cousy enhanced each other's skills. Russell's defensive and rebounding prowess gave Cousy extra opportunities to run the Celtics' lethal fast break. Teaming each player separately with other talented but less complementary teammates might not have resulted in NBA titles.

In the event, CBS's purchase of the Yankees, despite the valiant efforts of the suave, gallant Mike Burke, became that era's Snapple debacle. If you'll recall, Quaker Oats bought Snapple hoping for synergy. After all, Quaker Oats dealt in food and beverages, so it seemed to make sense to acquire the hot new Snapple label. The acquisition was a major flop, as was CBS's purchase of the Yankees. By 1973, George Steinbrenner was able to purchase the Yankees from CBS for around $10 million. Steinbrenner, like Dan Topping, Del Webb, and Larry MacPhail in 1945, got a bargain, although, to be fair, it took even that forceful shipbuilder time to right the Yankees' ship.[29]

If you subscribe to the theory that owners are greedy, rapacious scoundrels, who do not care about fans, then these owners are fortunate that sports fans love the game so much. Fans continue to flock to games, even after the disillusionment of player strikes and owner lockouts, boorish player behavior, and other shenanigans. If, instead, you believe owners are sober, hardheaded business men and women, you may applaud their efforts not only to put a good team on the field but also to provide fans with greater creature comforts and amenities at the old ball games. In either case, the owner of your local pro team needs you (and a healthy dose of television revenue). The next time an owner of a sports team pleads poverty in the face of stable, if not growing, demand, he is probably either prevaricating or is inept. In either case, he is not a good candidate for your sympathy.

CHAPTER 5

Competitive Balance, Player Movement, and the Reserve Clause

Sports pundits and fans love to discuss the ills of the game. The perceived imbalance between teams' abilities to compete for championships ranks high among the ills of professional basketball, football, and baseball. Fans hearken back to some supposedly halcyon days, when teams with deeper pockets did not "buy" their way to championships. I'm afraid to report that there wasn't much halcyon in professional sports. From the time of Harry Wright and his Cincinnati Red Stockings who won eighty or eighty-one games in a row against a motley of foes to the dynasties of the New York Yankees and Boston Celtics, professional sports has been characterized by the good, the bad, and the ugly. Come to think of it, Clint Eastwood's "Man with No Name" wasn't a paragon of competitive balance either, witness his long win streak in gunfights.

What Is Optimal Competitive Balance?

When I was in graduate school, a bunch of us gathered in the dormitory television room to watch the NBA playoffs. At halftime, NBA Commissioner David Stern held the lottery to determine the draft order. The New York Knicks were one of seven teams involved in the lottery. The contemporary rules gave each of the seven teams an equal opportunity to get the first pick, unlike today's lottery. When the New York Knicks won the lottery, the group burst into shouts of, "Fix! Fix!" Although the lottery was conducted by a prestigious accounting firm, rumors later swirled that the Knicks' envelope had a small crease.

Why would sports fans assume that the lottery was rigged? The obvious answer was that the NBA wanted New York to have a strong team.

The Knicks finished 24–58 in 1984–85; with Ewing, the team's 1985–86 record was 23–59. They didn't register a winning record until 1988–89. Indeed, the franchise has only two championships for its sixty-plus seasons in the NBA. Still, the hope that such a strong player would bolster the franchise in America's largest city, excuse me, media market, remained a plausible reason for suspicious fans to cry, "Fix!"

Similar things have happened in baseball. Upon the formation of the American League and the transfer of the Baltimore team to New York, the league president and the other owners recognized the importance of having a strong team in New York. Allegedly, they helped stock the team with some good players, though the Highlanders (as the Yankees were known then) were still mediocre for the better part of two decades. There was a good reason for the other owners to lessen their own team's chances of winning in order to help create a strong team in New York: The potential fan base was huge.

While it seems plausible for sports leagues to desire strong teams in New York, there is no general agreement about the optimal competitive balance. Competitive imbalance, like art, is something you know when you see it. One definition of competitive balance would be for every team in the league to have, on average, the same win-loss record. Even the NFL, with its lauded competitive balance, does not have this form of parity. I suspect few fans would prefer such a situation.

Moreover, there is little reason to think that the owners forming a league would truly desire complete parity, unless, of course, their team won the pennant on the last day of the season, with every other team tied for second.

The best way to start thinking about optimal competitive balance is to pretend to be the benevolent planner for the league. If we make the simple, but not always accurate, assumption that a winning team draws more in New York than in St. Louis, then the league is collectively better off if the Yankees win more frequently than the Browns. How much better the Yankees should be than the Browns is a difficult question. If the Yankees win every year, fans may get bored.

Of course, the idea of a benevolent planner itself raises suspicions. Fans may believe that the pennants are rigged, making the sport similar to (fans of the World Wrestling Federation may want to skip the next phrase) professional wrestling and its reliance upon theatrics and not upon true competition. The National League, circa 1900, faced a challenge from some of its owners who wanted to re-organize the league, with all of the teams forming a single entity. The league would allocate players, with the New York and other teams in large cities getting an advantage. The idea was not radical. Team owners had previously owned more than one team in a league or across leagues. These owners often transferred the best players to the team with the biggest potential draw. Fans disliked such shenanigans, and eventually both leagues were forced to prohibit such interlocking ownership. While I said at the outset I wouldn't discuss hockey, the National Hockey League was notorious for having one family, the Norris clan, controlling, at times, half of the teams in the league. As late as the 1950s and 1960s in baseball, the New York Yankees and Kansas City Athletics sparked fears of interlocking ownership, as the Athletics owner also owned Yankee Stadium. You wouldn't have had to been Oliver Stone or Michael Moore to smell a conspiracy.

If the New York Yankees had not been so successful, I doubt the issue of competitive balance would elicit as much attention from fans and sports economists. While basketball has had the Minneapolis Lakers, Boston Celtics, Chicago Bulls, and Los Angeles Lakers, and football has had the Cleveland Browns, Green Bay Packers, and now the New England Patriots, the New York teams have not dominated. There seems to be room for the smaller cities at the championship banquet. In any event, sports leagues probably want to have strong teams in the larger cities.

Certainly competitive imbalance has been a problem for professional sports leagues since their inception. The Boston Red Stockings dominated the National Association between 1872 and 1875, compiling a 205–50 record. The National Association was a loose formation of professional teams. Often at least three or four teams would fail to play an entire season. The ill-fated Union Association featured one very strong team in St. Louis and several rotten clubs in such small cities as Altoona, Wilmington (Delaware), and St. Paul. St. Louis went 94–19 and cruised to the league's only title. The lopsided competition did not help the fledgling league in its desperate bid for survival.

Of course, the National League and American League did not achieve competitive balance, but at least there was some churning. After being the class act of the American League's first eighteen seasons, the Boston Red Sox fielded losing teams between 1919 and 1933, including last-place finishes nine times during an eleven-year stretch. Note that the team's misfortunes started before the sale of Babe Ruth. After another dormant period between 1959 and 1966, the team's "Impossible Dream" pennant in 1967 started a lengthy streak of winning seasons, yet also triggered talk of the

"Curse." Other teams were not even fortunate enough to have a Sox-like cycle of winning seasons. The woebegone St. Louis Browns had twelve winning seasons during their fifty-three years. The Chicago Cubs, a wealthy team by most standards, had just one winning season between 1946 and 1966, when Leo Durocher rekindled the team's fortunes between 1967 and 1972. Thereafter, the Cubs never had back-to-back winning seasons again until the 2003 and 2004 campaigns. Although Pittsburgh Pirates fans can trace the decline of their franchise's success to the defections of Barry Bonds and Bobby Bonilla, among others, the team's woes existed long before. After starting the twentieth century as the National League's best team with four pennants in nine years, the Pirates nose-dived during the 1950s, including five last place finishes in six years and a truly ghastly three-year period where they won less than 32 percent of their games. Ever wonder why Philadelphia Phillies fans are so cranky? Their great-grand-parents watched some spectacularly inept baseball, especially between 1918 and 1948, when the team had just one winning season and twelve seasons with one hundred or more defeats. For fans in these cities, the concept of competitive balance was ludicrous. There's no need to recount the glories of the New York Yankees, whose dominance between the acquisition of Babe Ruth and when CBS took over in late 1964 is unparalleled in pro-fessional sports: just one losing season in 1925.[1] The National League never had as dominant a franchise, and the Giants, Cardinals, and Dodgers took turns being temporarily dominant over the same period.

The National Football League took its time in promoting competitive balance. During the mid–1950s, the Chicago Cardinals were typically inept while the Cleveland Browns usually won. The league did have a reverse-order draft during the decade but with one important wrinkle. The first pick overall was awarded by lottery. Every team was guaranteed a number-one pick once during twelve years. After the first pick, teams drafted in reverse order of the previous year's finish. More recently, until their Super Bowl win, the New Orleans Saints were poster children for competitive imbalance, despite the NFL's more generous revenue sharing, a reverse-order draft of college players, and free agency.

As mentioned, the National Basketball Association had dynasties in Minneapolis, Boston, Chicago, and Los Angeles. Until the 1980s, the Detroit Pistons were typically also-rans, despite Dave DeBusschere and Dave Bing. The New York Knicks did not dominate the league, barely playing over .500 ball for the first sixty years. Despite having several high draft picks, the Los Angeles Clippers have epitomized ineptitude. Conversely, the Portland Trailblazers, without many early draft picks and with a small stadium, consistently posted winning records for the better part of two decades. The Utah Jazz relied upon keeping Karl Malone and John Stockton together and compiled a lengthy record of successes.

So, it is entirely possible for teams in large cities to mismanage their advantages and not dominate their leagues, while teams in smaller cities, with adroit selection of talent, can prosper for years. Still, a team such as the Yankees can probably afford to make more mistakes and still come out on top. The Yankees allegedly passed on Ernie Banks and Larry Doby while looking for the "perfect" black player. Because of the team's surplus of talented white players, it took years before their hesitance to sign blacks would haunt them. The Boston Red Sox nixed Jackie Robinson and Willie Mays. Amazingly, the Portland Trailblazers survived after choosing Sam Bowie over Michael Jordan in the draft. At the time, Bowie's history of injuries was known, but he was considered a more polished center than Hakeem Olajuwon. Of course, had the Trailblazers taken Hakeem and Houston selected Michael Jordan, the Bulls probably would have ended up with Sam Bowie, and I would have been able to catch NBA games on the cheap in Chicago.

There are two interesting questions. First, what would be an optimal level of competitive balance? No one seems to have an answer, except Mets fans and baseball fans outside New York City, whose perennial answer is, "The Yankees win too often." Second, why, despite reverse-order drafts, revenue sharing, and free agency, do some teams wallow in ineptitude for years while other teams without any obvious advantages keep on winning?

In considering competitive balance, a researcher may use different measures. The standard deviation of the win-loss percentages is an excellent start. Of course, to compare standard deviations across leagues, you have to make adjustments for the different lengths of seasons. Since baseball plays the most games, one would expect a smaller standard deviation for baseball (if all teams were truly equal) than for football. Researchers have found that the standard deviation of win-loss records has narrowed over time in baseball, although they differ on why this is so. The issue of stability is important, too. A situation where the Excelsiors always win the pennant with a 59 percent win-loss record and the Bums always finish last with a 41 percent record would be different from one with a bigger spread in the win-loss records, but churning of pennant winners. Some of the studies have failed to examine whether the teams generally maintain their status over time. For many fans, having their home team face a chronic 41 percent win-loss record is less desirable than having the team face winning 30 percent or 52 percent in alternate years. At least there is the hope of participating in a pennant race on occasion. Finally, one might note that the National Football League deliberately rigs its schedule to give weak teams an easier schedule in the subsequent season. In theory, this might compress the standard deviation.

One might want to also consider the number of championships won. The wonder is that few fans bemoaned the Atlanta Braves' lengthy domination of their National League division. The Yankees re-emerged as divisional champions in 1994, but they still lagged the Braves in regular season win-loss records until the 2006 and 2007 seasons.

One approach to ascertaining optimal competitive balance would be to observe the owners' actions. Although there are random elements to any team's finish in a given season, presumably teams would reveal their long-term equilibrium win-loss record over a number of seasons. In the postwar American League, the Yankees usually finished around .600, while the Browns, Athletics, and Senators muddled along at around .400. The remaining teams hovered around .500. However, the equilibrium changed during the mid–1950s, when the Browns and Athletics moved to more lucrative markets that could better support higher quality teams. After a decade in their new homes, a new equilibrium might have been established, but the Senators moved to Minnesota and two new expansion teams popped up in Washington, D.C., and Los Angeles upsetting any developing equilibrium.[2]

Shifting demographic and economic factors make ascertaining the optimal competitive balance more difficult. Many of the original cities with Major League Baseball franchises stagnated or decreased in population, although their metropolitan areas might have continued to grow. The cities of the west and south grew and began to surpass the older cities in population.

Despite these considerations, the past offers clues as to what the owners may consider the profit-maximizing win-loss record, given the other teams' situations.

How Owners Built Winning Teams During the Reserve Clause Era

Let me first shatter a comforting myth. Star players rarely stayed put, even before free agency. Tracking the movement of Hall-of-Fame baseball players provides evidence that even before free agency, star players moved frequently. By 1999, there were 137 players in the Hall of Fame who had started their careers in 1903 or later. Only thirty-eight of those players spent their entire careers with their original major league team, while another eighteen spent all but the last year or two years with their original team. Thus, a majority of Hall-of-Fame players moved during their careers, and, of course, most of these players completed their careers before free agency.

The New York Yankees and Brooklyn/Los Angeles Dodgers tended to keep their Hall-of-Fame players for most of their careers, while the Philadelphia/Kansas City/Oakland Athletics did not retain any of their big stars. The Philadelphia Phillies and both St. Louis teams also tended to relinquish their star players. While the Yankees acquired fourteen future Hall-of-Fame players during those players' prime years, the Dodgers, Braves, Cubs, and Reds acquired similar numbers. The Phillies, Pirates, Athletics, Indians, and Tigers did not acquire many Hall-of-Fame players during their prime years.[3]

Fans today might bemoan the fate of such small-market teams as the Seattle Mariners and Kansas City Royals. The Seattle Mariners are an amazing team. They lost Ken Griffey, Jr., Randy Johnson, and Alex Rodriguez, arguably the best players of their generation at their positions, yet the team continued to win until recently. On the other hand, the Kansas City Royals, the very model of a successful expansion team, fell upon hard times in the 1990s. This movement of superstars from Seattle and Kansas City is not a new phenomenon. Consider Connie Mack's dismantling of the 1929 to 1931 Philadelphia Athletics, a team that was arguably superior to the 1927 Yankees. Mack sold or traded Lefty Grove, Jimmie Foxx, Mickey Cochrane, and Al Simmons, as well as other regulars. He had already busted up one championship team after 1914. Later Athletics owner Charlie O. Finley also dismantled his A's, although commissioner Bowie Kuhn did him no favor by rescinding a couple of the sales. Vida Blue, Catfish Hunter, Reggie Jackson, Sal Bando, Joe Rudi, and Bert Campaneris left via trades or free agency. Unfortunately for Athletics fans, the team went into prolonged funks in all three instances.

While the Athletics were the poster child for teams in weak markets having to get rid of stars, they were not the only such team. Although the St. Louis Browns didn't have many stars, they did unload their best players to the Boston Red Sox in the late 1940s. While many fans bemoaned the Kansas City Athletics' proclivity for trading players to the New York Yankees (including Roger Maris, Clete Boyer, and Ralph Terry), the Browns' transfer of Vern Stephens, Ellis Kinder, and Jack Kramer was probably a bigger transfer of productivity. If you think I'm joking, just take a gander at Stephens' run production as a shortstop, including 300 runs batted in between 1949 and 1950. Things were so bad that the Yankees cried "Foul!" They wanted the commissioner of baseball to investigate, ostensibly because they worried about St. Louis becoming an even worse draw. Later, of course, when people complained that the Yankees had stripped the Athletics of their best players, the owners of the two teams recognized the ill-will emanating from the trades. Immediately after he purchased the team, Charlie Finley announced a ban on trades with the Yankees. Characteristically, Finley immediately did a volte-face and traded pitcher Bud Daley to New York.[4]

The other St. Louis baseball team, the Cardinals, often sold players to other teams, including the sale of seven players to the Boston Braves right after World War II. The Cardinals won the pennant in 1946 and still had a strong farm system, so they were selling excess players. The Brooklyn Dodgers did the same thing during this period.

During the 1950s, after languishing for two decades, the Chicago White Sox became the second-best team in the American League for fifteen years. The Sox improved by twenty-one games between 1950 and 1951, gaining their first winning record since 1943. The team continued winning through the 1967 season. The White Sox are instructive because they built a winning team without a productive farm system. The team used a series of clever trades and purchases, plus a few judicious acquisitions from the waiver list. Although fans like to think that the New York Yankees swiped good players from the downtrodden teams in St. Louis, Washington, D.C., and Philadelphia/Kansas City, Chicago actually did far more such swiping than New York. The majority of the players in Chicago's starting lineup and pitching staff during the mid–1950s had been acquired from the bottom-dwelling teams.

There are some puzzles, too. Consider the New York Yankees in 1964. CBS purchases the team in August. The team wins the pennant by a single game and loses the World Series. The team then fires rookie manager Yogi Berra and hires Johnny Keane from the world-champion St. Louis Cardinals. The team still includes Mickey Mantle, Roger Maris, Whitey Ford, Mel Stottlemyre, Elston Howard, and a host of others. The Yankees falter in 1965, which can be attributed to injuries, and Minnesota wins the pennant. At the outset of the 1966 season, manager Keane brags that the Yankees outclass the Twins at every position except shortstop. The Yankees lose early and often to begin the 1966 season, and Keane is fired within thirty games. Ralph Houk cannot offset another wave of injuries, and the team finishes last. The team trades an injury-plagued Roger Maris after the season. One can understand the Yankees' reluctance to make a big deal after the 1965 season and their refusal to panic as they hoped for their stars to heal. During the 1965–66 meltdown, the team only acquired journey-men players, while other clubs acquired Frank Robinson and Orlando Cepeda (MVPs in 1966 and 1967), among other stars. The Yankees would not return to the top until 1976, after they signed Jim "Catfish" Hunter. Steinbrenner later signed Reggie Jackson, who helped the team win two World Series. It remains difficult to explain why the Yankees, with CBS's deep pockets at their disposal, continued to flounder for so many years.

Even without free agency, the general flow of talent was from teams in smaller cities to teams in medium-sized and large cities. Free agency might have increased the amount of movement as players exercised location preferences, but in terms of net redistribution of talent, the general flow from smaller to larger cities existed before and during free agency in baseball.[5]

Football's restrictive rules effectively precluded the movement of play-ers via free agency until relatively recently. For many years, the Commis-sioner of the NFL could determine the compensation due to a team that lost a free agent. The threat of such compensation was enough to dampen enthusiasm for signing free agents.

Did Free Agency Increase Big-City Teams' Dominance?

What might alter competitive balance? Does free agency matter? Many observers think the advent of free agency enabled the Yankees to sign the big stars and become paramount. Indeed, the team signed such early free-agent luminaries as Catfish Hunter and Reggie Jackson and started winning pennants again.

Now I am going to say something that will shock you. Most econo-mists believe that it is quite possible that competitive balance will not be much different under free agency than it was under a strict reserve clause. They base their belief upon a theory developed by Nobel Prize winner Ronald Coase, although economist Simon Rottenberg earlier applied the principle to player movement in Major League Baseball. According to Coase, if property rights are well defined and transaction costs are low, then it doesn't matter who has the legal right to determine how property will be allocated. The legal rights matter only as they affect who gets the economic rent from the scarce property.[6]

The theorem is commonly applied to externalities. The reader may recall that an externality exists when two parties conclude a transaction that has costs or benefits upon a third, uninvolved party.

Here are two examples. Suppose you own a waterfront resort down-stream from a fertilizer factory. The factory finds it cheaper to dump its waste into the river than paying to ship it away, creating a negative exter-nality for your business. In fact, if the factory had to pay to ship the waste away, it might not be able to produce fertilizer at a competitive price. While the waste washing upon your beachfront makes staying at your resort less desirable, it will only force you out of business if the levels of waste are high enough to drive people away. In other words, certain levels of waste can coexist with the continuing ability to run your resort. In the traditional interpretation of this situation, too much pollution occurs.

Suppose you have the right to a clean beachfront. You could go to court and force the factory to cease dumping. However, from society's point of view, such an all-or-nothing result is not optimal, as people value both the fertilizer and the beachfront amenities. You could negotiate with the factory to pay you for the right to pollute. Presumably you would get the factory to pay enough to cover the cost of cleaning your beach, which might still be cheaper than shipping the effluence away. Now the factory has to consider the cost of polluting and will likely reduce but not stop its production. If, instead, the factory has the right to pollute (perhaps it existed before your resort), it could pollute at will, which puts you out of business. However, people like staying at your resort, so, again, the all-or-nothing solution is not optimal. You could pay the factory not to pollute so much. Now the factory has to take in the opportunity cost of polluting in terms of the foregone payment from you. In either case, the factory owner and you are both facing the true costs of your activities. The amount of fertilizer produced and the cleanliness of the beach will be the same no matter who has the legal rights. If you have the property rights, you gain the economic payments; if the factory has the property rights, it gets the economic payments. Thus, fighting to get the property rights is important in terms of the payments (economic rent) but not in terms of the amounts of fertilizer produced and the number of guests served.

A second example consists of a group of small retailers on a city block. Currently, young people with bad attitudes loiter on the sidewalks and deter elderly shoppers from patronizing the businesses. One day, a social activist opens a for-profit youth club in a vacant storefront. The club fosters good behavior and gives the young people constructive recreational opportunities. The loitering ends, and businesses attract more shoppers. The social activist provides an external benefit for the businesses. In planning for her youth club, the activist may not have considered the benefits that would accrue to businesses along the street.

In the case of external benefits, too little of the good or service is produced. Lighthouses were long considered the classic example of a positive externality, as their services lowered the costs to ship owners. Traditionally, people thought that not enough lighthouses were operating, but owners of lighthouses charged a fee for their services to ships in the harbor. If our social activist could charge businesses for the benefits she provides, she would be more likely to open the youth club and to make it financially successful.

What do these examples have to do with professional sports? The issue here is: Who owns the property rights to a player's labor? Under the reserve clause, once a player signs with a team, the team owns the rights to the player's labor. Conversely, under complete free agency, players own the right to their labor and are freely able to contract with any team they desire. Does this affect the overall distribution of talent, as reflected in teams' win-loss records?

Economist Simon Rottenberg wrote his seminal paper on the distribution of playing talent in Major League Baseball in 1956, presaging the Coase Theorem. His thesis suggested that the distribution of players under a free market probably wouldn't be too different than that under the reserve clause.[7] Congress grappled with the reserve clause during its almost-annual hearings in the 1950s, but Rottenberg was not asked to present his ideas before Congress. Baseball owners claimed that the reserve clause was important in maintaining professional baseball, primarily for competitive balance.

Some of the members of the Congressional committee were skeptical. A Senate counsel, Paul Dixon, grilled Washington Senators owner Calvin Griffith. "Does not the reserve clause, and the unlimited number of ballplayers that the other major league teams can get, make it harder for you to get good ballplayers?" Griffith answered, "Well, we are not in financial position to go out and bid $100,000 to get ballplayers."[8]

Dixon then queried commissioner Ford Frick: "But isn't it also true that even with this reserve clause that you have had so long in baseball, the wealthier clubs are presently outbidding the poorer clubs by the use of the bonus rule that we have talked about?"

"The reserve clause only keeps clubs from raiding each other."

"But you say you do not want anybody to legislate mediocrity. God save us from mediocrity. But hasn't baseball, by the handling of its own house, in effect legislated mediocrity? A good example is the comparison of the New York Yankees and the Washington Senators."[9]

A senator (U.S., not baseball) made the conundrum explicit: "The fact is you have the reserve clause in the American League, but you do not have the equalization of competitive strength?" Frick could only answer, "Senator, that is true as of the year of our Lord 1958."[10] Although legislators were skeptical regarding the reserve clause, they did not withdraw baseball's antitrust exemption.

The reserve clause and its attendant strengthening of owners' bargaining power against that of their players, as well as other collusive agreements, increased the value of their franchises. Some senators understood this, with Senator Karl Mundt stating:

> [granting antitrust exemptions] we should do it with our eyes open that we are thereby expanding tremendously the financial value of a baseball franchise. We are giving to the fortunate owner an exclusive right which increases vastly his economic investment, and his economic opportunity, and increases vastly the resale value of the investment that he already has. Now I ask you, sir, whether in good conscience we can, by legislative fiat, make dollar bills out of 50-cent pieces for the people who own these baseball clubs without assuming some responsibility to be sure that public service is considered by the owners of the club.[11]

I would like readers to remember the apt phrase, "make dollars out of 50-cent pieces." We'll allude to it later.

To see how Rottenberg's and Coase's ideas work, suppose there is a brilliant football quarterback prospect, Norm van Unitas. Every professional team is drooling at the thought of having this "Mozart of Quarterbacks," and there ain't no better prodigy than Mozart. Suppose a scout for the Chicago Cardinals had signed the youngster, before his ability became well known. Now the Cardinals draw small audiences; their attendance numbers are well below those of the more glamorous Chicago Bears. Although Unitas improves the team's record somewhat and helps attract an additional 50,000 paying fans to the Cardinals' rundown stadium, the New York Giants owner is thinking, "Norm van Unitas could bump our attendance by 150,000, especially since our current quarterback is mediocre." In other words, Unitas can put a larger incremental increase of fans into the New York stands than he can in Chicago. Economists would say that his marginal revenue product is greater in New York than Chicago. There is an arbitrage opportunity here: 100,000 additional fans, representing, say $300,000 per season (at $3 per seat, back in the good old days of 1950s America). The football league, as well as the two teams, would be better off with Unitas in New York. All the Cardinals and Giants owners have to do is figure out how to split the $300,000 gain. Since both will be better off making the deal, they will probably do so.

If Unitas has the property rights to his labor, the story is similar. Teams would bid for his services. Since he is more valuable to New York, the Giants would likely bid more for him. Assuming Unitas has no strong preference regarding location, he will sign with New York.

In our simple story, Unitas is likely to wind up in New York regardless of whether there is free agency or a reserve clause. What is different is that under the reserve clause, the owners get most of the economic rent from Unitas' unique talent. The economic rent is the payment for the unique factor of production (Unitas' labor) above his reservation price (the minimum required to get Unitas to forego his best alternative). Under free agency, Unitas gets most of the economic rent in the form of a higher salary.

Now this is a very simple story. It would be erroneous to say a player has a specific marginal revenue product. Much depends on the existing situation. A New York Giants team that already possessed a top-notch quarterback might get less marginal revenue product from acquiring Unitas. If the Giants were already champions, the potential gain might be lower than it would be if they were also-rans.

There is another factor to consider in our story. It is the existence of friction, in the form of transaction costs, in transferring players. Implicit in our story is the assumption that the transaction costs are low. By transaction costs, I mean the cost of finding someone who is interested in making a transaction; the cost of negotiating an agreement; and the cost of monitoring and enforcing the agreement. Early in baseball's history, owners grappled with setting up the prototypical set of property rights to players' labor that would facilitate transferring players. Theoretically, in order to transfer a player from, say, Troy to New York, the two owners had to release the involved players and then re-sign them. Such a tactic was risky since once the players were released, any other team could attempt to sign them. At first, owners relied upon "gentlemen's agreements" not to tamper with the players being transferred, but baseball owners during that era were rarely "gentlemen." In one case, an owner took the safer but more expensive route of buying an entire rival team just to get a desired player. These ill-defined property rights to players' labor clearly needed revision before transaction costs would be low enough to ensure an efficient re-allocation of players. The reserve clause evolved slowly. Until they had fully established a team's property right to players' labor, owners found making trades and selling players fraught with difficulty.

As I've mentioned, one transaction cost is finding a willing trading partner. Unless cash is used, two teams must have the "double coincidence of wants" that underlies barter transactions. The Lakers need a power forward. Utah has Karl Malone but needs a center. The Lakers don't have a desirable center they are willing to trade. The two teams cannot find a double coincidence of wants. Utah needs to find a team wanting a power forward. That team must want a power forward and have a center to offer in return. If there's no prohibition on cash transactions, Utah could simply sell Malone to the Lakers and use the cash to buy a center from someone else. As with the general economy, dollars, being universally accepted, facilitate transactions.

Selling players leads us to another possible cost. Aside from the usual change in attendance due to a worse win-loss record after trading or selling a star, there could be a punitive aspect as fans boycott their home team in the wake of such a trade. Many Hall-of-Fame caliber players have been sold, although teams often camouflaged the true nature of the transaction by including young players. Apparently, a straight sale may raise the ire of fans, so an owner might use the "rebuilding" excuse to justify the trade. Quick now, can you recall which three Los Angeles Lakers players went to the Philadelphia 76ers in exchange for Wilt Chamberlain, or the three players that San Francisco received from the 76ers for Chamberlain, or the four players that went to Milwaukee in exchange for Lew Alcindor/Kareem Abdul-Jabbar? Going further back in history, who did the Red Sox get along with cash for Tris Speaker after the 1915 season? Indeed, the sale of Speaker to Cleveland should have sent shock waves through the league, but Boston bounced back to win two more World Series in 1916 and 1918. If they had not, we might be talking about the curse of the "Speaker." In fact, the $55,000 Cleveland paid for the centerfielder, in addition to young hurler Sam Jones, was not far different in purchasing power than the $100,000 the Yankees spent on Babe Ruth after the 1919 season. Since Speaker ranks among the top ten in Thorn and Palmer's Total Player Ratings, the transaction could compete with the Ruth sale as having precipitated the eventual collapse of the Red Sox.

With free agency, the fear was that rich teams would sign every star. Will George Steinbrenner sign every all-star free agent available? He faces several limitations. First, the Yankees, although a wealthy team, do not have unlimited resources. The team might afford even a $300 million payroll, but a $400 million payroll ($16 million per player on a twenty-five-man roster) probably taxes its financial wherewithal. Second, the benefits of adding more all-stars begin to dwindle, both on the field and in the stands. Suppose the Yankees' current roster is capable of winning ninety games. Adding the clone of Mickey Mantle might ensure ninety-nine wins. Getting the clone of Ted Williams might boost the wins to 106. The ghost of Lefty Grove in his prime might mean a near-record 112 wins. Walter Johnson, Christy Mathewson, and Napoleon Lajoie might mean a total of 121 wins. Each additional all-star is likely to boost the number of wins, but at some point, the number of additional wins begin to fall. Economists designate this as diminishing marginal productivity.

Aside from diminishing benefits on the field, what about the effects on attendance and revenue? Although the gate is usually boosted by winning games, too much winning can eventually squelch demand.

First, a team which wins over one hundred games typically runs away with the division/pennant. After the pennant race is decided, attendance tends to fall, even for the pennant winner. Winning too many games within a season, therefore, can adversely affect the gate.

Second, when the Yankees dominated the American League, with pennant runs from 1936 to 1939, 1941 to 1943, 1949 to 1953, 1955 to 1958, and 1960 to 1964, league attendance tended to fall off during each pennant run. In addition, the Yankees themselves saw a diminution in home attendance as they continued their dynasty. Consecutive pennants can, therefore, be deleterious to a team's attendance. Of course, part of the attendance decline at Yankee Stadium might have been the result of increasing ticket prices. However, in the past, teams did not automatically raise ticket prices after winning a pennant.

We conclude that George Steinbrenner is unlikely to pursue a team comprised of twenty-five all-stars.

Scheduling Unfairness

During the off season, sports fans and pundits need something to talk about. College and NFL football observers debate "strength of schedule" during the off season. Strength of schedule affects competitive balance.

The NFL explicitly rigs the upcoming schedule by pitting fourth-place teams against other fourth-place teams and first-place versus first-place teams for at least two of the sixteen games each season. This would be equivalent to Major League Baseball pitting the traditionally last-place Kansas City Royals against the Pittsburgh Pirates for twenty games each season. The NFL's schedule tinkering has a long history. The league's immediate predecessor, the American Professional Football Association, was a ramshackle collection of teams. Owners scheduled games on a haphazard basis. Some teams played almost all of their games at home, while other teams played most of their games on the road. Hardly anyone played every other team in the league. The league standings were so meaningless that the owners voted on which team would be anointed the champion. The owners did not create rational, balanced schedules until several seasons later. Even after World War II, some biases remained. The Chicago Bears got to play the Chicago Cardinals twice per season, even after the Cardinals were placed in the other division. Since the Cardinals were the perennial "sick man of the NFL," the Bears received an easier schedule than its Western Conference rivals. The league countenanced the skewed schedule, because the Bears provided the Cardinals' best gate attraction.

The early National Basketball Association, though, may have provided even more skewed scheduling than the NFL. The home court advantage was especially pronounced in the NBA during the 1950s, with home teams winning 64 percent or more of the games. The league also promoted doubleheaders, where four teams would play two games at a single arena. The owners hoped that by scheduling doubleheaders in the larger arenas owned by New York and Boston, the overall gate receipts would be greater than staging two separate games. The net result exacerbated any competitive imbalance. The impoverished Milwaukee Hawks played only eighty-three of their 281 regular-season games at home during the team's four seasons in Milwaukee. The team played 101 road games and 97 games at neutral sites (part of doubleheaders). The Hawks finished last in the Western Division all four seasons, and twice had the league's worst overall record. Over the same four seasons, Syracuse Nationals played 131 games at home, 114 road games, and just thirty-six games on neutral courts. The team boasted winning records each of the four seasons. While St. Louis was obviously an inferior team, the teams' skewed schedules exacerbated any latent difference between Syracuse and them. Whether because of Syracuse's exuberant and sometimes rabid fans (attacking players was de rigueur at Syracuse) or because Nats players were more rested due to their lessened travel, the team's home win-loss record was 110–19 during these four seasons compared with their 42–72 road record (20–16 at neutral sites).[12]

Major League Baseball's inter-league games also add an element of inequity between teams' "strength-of-schedules." The New York Mets play six games with the New York Yankees each season, surely a detriment to the Mets' win-loss record. The other National League teams rotate playing the Yankees. Given the drawing power of the Yankees, I suspect many owners secretly envy the Mets.

Importance of Competitive Balance in Launching a New League

Competitive imbalance may have contributed to the demise of some upstart leagues. The Union Association was a classic example of "Snow White and the Seven Dwarves." (There were actually thirteen teams in the league during its sole season, but five played fewer than twenty-five games of the one hundred-plus game season.) The champion St. Louis team won 83.2 percent of its games, while four teams won fewer than 25 percent of theirs. Not surprisingly, none of these four teams finished the season, with one team lasting only eight games. In the American Association, the St. Louis franchise won four consecutive pennants (1885 to 1888), three by wide margins. The imbalance did not improve the league's chances for survival. Even the National League was not immune to chronic competitive imbalance. During the League's monopoly era (1892 to 1900), Baltimore, Boston, and Brooklyn dominated the circuit. Several teams were perpetually inept. However, tight pennant races did not insure a league's survival, as both the Players' League and Federal League featured competitive races during their short lives.

The American League succeeded in promoting tight pennant races for most of its first decade, which helped it outdraw the National League. For the first two decades, the American League's New York franchise was a contender, but it was never a champion until 1921. Although Babe Ruth is renowned for triggering the Yankees' "dynasty," the team won just seven pennants during his fifteen seasons with them. Joe DiMaggio and Yogi Berra would experience more pennant success, as the Yankees' monotonous pennant routine hurt the American League during the late 1930s and through the early 1960s.[13]

These examples reveal that scheduling can affect competitive balance.

Only the NFL consciously rigs the schedule to create compression in the league standings, but one wonders whether the other leagues will emulate pro football in the future.

Possible Remedies for Competitive Imbalance

We now examine some proposed remedies for competitive imbalance. Revenue sharing will receive a separate chapter.

What about creating parity by having a reverse-order draft? The reverse-order draft may simply shift economic rent from wealthy teams to poorer teams with little, if any, effect on the overall distribution of talent. If the woebegone Cardinals had drafted Norm van Unitas, the impetus to trade or sell him to the New York Giants would still exist. With a reverse-order draft in baseball, the woebegone teams would become intermediaries, developing talented young players before trading or selling them to the Yankees. There might be a short-run spike in a team in a smaller city's record, if a rookie was surprisingly good. Therefore, the amateur draft may have affected the movement of players but not the overall competitive balance. In the past, the Yankees dominated because they were adept at developing or acquiring top minor league talent. They signed Joe DiMaggio at a fire sale price, because he had sustained a leg injury. Mickey Mantle cost them very little to sign.

In addition, by having a productive farm system or by astute purchases of top minor league players, the team could plug whatever holes it had by shipping surplus minor leaguers off in exchange for an established player. As Yankees' general manager during the 1950s, George Weiss, summed up: "Because the Yankees were substantially built on developed players, we seldom did any trading for front-line men. Pitchers were the exception ... we had trouble developing good pitchers.... We were fortunate that we had good men we could spare to get these men we wanted, which is another tribute to our system."[14] Indeed, the team had trouble developing durable starting pitchers, with Lefty Gomez, Whitey Ford, and Mel Stottlemyre being the best.

Even before the initiation of a reverse-order draft of amateur players in 1965, the distribution of rookie talent had narrowed during the postwar era as more teams invested money into their farm systems. After relocating to Baltimore, the Orioles used much of their new-found gains in revenue to sign amateur players. Thus, the Yankees' advantage in developing players was eroding, as other teams increased their financial strengths. The amateur draft may well have further reduced the team's ability to dominate minor league talent, although the team had already begun to dismantle its farm system in the early 1960s. If the Yankees had had difficulty developing talent, they could have shifted to purchasing top talent from teams in smaller cities. While the movement of players might have quickened, the overall distribution of playing talent, as reflect by teams' win-loss records, should not have changed greatly before and after free agency.[15]

Ironically, given the Yankees' deterioration after the 1964 season, the team benefited from high draft choices in the June 1966 to 1968 drafts. One of their selections was Thurman Munson. On the other hand, teams that consistently did well in the standings during the late 1960s, such as the Cincinnati Reds and Boston Red Sox, did quite well in the early amateur drafts.

Baseball's current "tax" on excessive payrolls makes economic sense and may promote parity. We've seen that owners should hire top talent up to the point that the marginal revenue equals the marginal cost. By placing a tax on excessive team salaries, a team like the Yankees faces a steeper marginal cost for signing additional stars. Signing an additional star becomes less likely to satisfy the team's optimizing rule: Marginal cost is now more likely to exceed the marginal benefit.

Competitive imbalances within and across seasons are crucial concerns for professional sports leagues. When the Yankees won their fourth consecutive pennant in 1939 in another runaway, rival American League teams, fearing further erosion in attendance and revenue, enacted a rule that a pennant winner could not make trades with other teams in the league for one year. The Yankees finished second in 1940, and the rule was rescinded. After the team's 1958 pennant, there was talk of renewing the trade prohibition.

The best way to prevent dynasties would be to implement a reverse-order draft with strict prohibitions against player movement. Once a player signed with a team, he would be there for his professional life. Teams and players would lose their freedom to choose. Aside from the civil rights violations, this would have another undesirable effect. Is it really desirable that every professional sports team have a nearly equal probability of winning a title? This question returns us to the issue of optimal competitive balance. Wealthier teams would, of course, continue to seek some sort of an edge. They could hire the best scouts, coaches, managers, and even the best sports physicians. Conversely, a player might be able to leverage his way onto a stronger team in a big city by making it clear that he won't

sign if drafted by the Podunk Gophers instead of the New York Yankees
à la Eli Manning. Or owners of teams in large cities might try to "persuade"
an owner of a team in a small city who held the first pick to forego selecting
a particular player.

Another way to redress the New York Yankees' advantage is to place
more teams in New York City. Remember, there used to be three teams
in the city; the Yankees, the Giants, and the Dodgers. Remember also that
these three teams often dominated the sport. Long-time Brooklyn residents
might recall that the borough used to be the third-largest city in America
and was only brought into the larger city kicking and screaming. In any
event, another American League team in New York City might not be as
disastrous to the incumbent Yankees as one might think. A strong rivalry,
like the classic struggles between the Giants and Dodgers, might actually
swell the gate. Of course, having too many more teams in the city would
lessen any such rivalry. A clever marketing ploy for the newcomers would
be to almost, but not quite, co-opt the Yankees' nickname. There's the
George Foreman route, bestowing a number on each team. The current
Yankees would be the New York Yankees 1.0 and each subsequent team
would become the New York Yankees 2.0, 3.0, and so on. Of course, this
might violate some sort of trademark protection. A multicultural approach
would be to designate the next team as the New York Yanquis. Although
having multiple teams in New York City might erode the probability that
the Yankees would make it to the World Series, television networks might
still be pleased with the relatively high probability of having at least one
metropolitan team in the series, whether that team was the Yankees 1.0 or
the Yankees 3.0. Between 1949 and 1964, with the sole exception of 1959,
at least one New York team appeared in every World Series. In 1959, one
of the participants, the Los Angeles Dodgers, was only two years removed
from being a New York team.

Putting more teams in New York City would require compensating
the Yankees and Mets. George Steinbrenner purchased the Yankees in 1973
with the understanding that there would only be one American League
team in the city, as well as only one National League team. In other words,
Steinbrenner purchased the exclusive right to play American League baseball in New York City, and the purchase price reflected this right. Abro-
gating this right would injure him, although the severity of that injury is
an interesting question in its own right. Just as the reserve clause helped
owners "make dollar bills out of 50-cent pieces," so did territorial protection. "Hey, I paid for the right to make dollar bills out of 50-cent pieces,

and I demand compensation for losing this right!" This is one moment that I might pity George, or at least grant him the justice of his claim.

These issues of territorial rights are longstanding. When the National League first organized in 1876, it was informal. Eight existing teams anted up $10 each for membership. Although the New York franchise was thrown out after the 1876 season for violating the league's rules pertaining to playing all of its scheduled games, the exclusive property rights to the New York City territory were a steal at $10.[16] Assuming the team played in all subsequent seasons, any purchase price paid by later owners would reflect the value of the monopoly rights. The exclusive territory rights would be capitalized, and all subsequent owners should theoretically earn just normal profits from possessing the rights. The original owner undoubtedly received a windfall, but barring miscalculations, later owners would pay full value for the monopoly rights.

The National Football League and the National Basketball Association have salary caps. Ostensibly, a cap is supposed to rein in spending and also promote competitive balance. While it is possible to design a salary cap that promotes competitive balance, owners are probably more enamored of such legislation for its ability to curb salaries. In practice, salary caps are akin to the Federal government's EPA mileage ratings for automobiles: highly publicized numbers signifying little. NBA teams quickly sought "exemptions" in order to sign star players, making the cap all but meaningless. Salary caps can be evaded by structuring contracts with future payments.

Some observers talk about "soft" and "hard" caps, but the reality is that probably no one really wants a hard cap. Why? Because a salary cap, as with most price controls in the economic world, is likely to force owners to do things they don't want to do. While they'd like to limit salaries in general, there are always those pesky particulars. A strictly defined and enforced cap might force small-market franchises to field stronger teams than they intended (or even find profitable). At the other end of the scale, teams in large cities might resent being unable to pay high salaries to generate a profit-maximizing winning team. Players, too, may dislike the cap for its deleterious effects on salaries, especially for top players.

Typically, teams in large cities that acquiesce to salary caps want teams in small cities to face a minimum team payroll (a salary floor). As with speed limits on freeways, it's the variance that causes accidents. This is why many freeways also have minimum speeds. Whether there is a binding minimum team payroll or there are minimum individual salaries, such rules may encourage (coerce) teams in small cities to field stronger teams than they would freely choose. Binding minimum salaries also imply that players at the bottom of the roster might be paid more than their marginal revenue products, especially if a team has to have a set number of players.

In any event, the evidence suggests that existing salary caps have ambiguous effects on competitive balance.

Some people may think of salary caps in terms of individual player limits. At times, owners have suggested a predetermined pay scale. Suppose you could only pay Barry Bonds, Manny Ramirez, and their ilk $5 million per season. Their free market salary might be three times that amount. You might assume, then, that owners of teams in small markets would have a better chance of signing top talent, especially if such players have preferences for smaller towns. Whenever there is any arbitrary artificial impediment to the market, owners will try to circumvent the rules. There could be "under-the-table" bonuses or deferred payments. Conversely, the players might benefit from a predetermined salary scale because they would not have to pay agents, but such a gain probably weighs little in the balance. Owners, players, and commentators all wondered whether baseball players (as well as other professional players) could ever effectively coalesce as a bargaining group. Most people assumed that the biggest stars would disdain collective bargaining, and certainly the traditional union contract of "one salary fits all" held little appeal for most athletes. The genius of Marvin Miller and other players' organizers was getting solidarity between stars and benchwarmers.

People lament competitive imbalance, but only rarely do professional sports leagues do anything about it. Ultimately, most professional sports leagues desire successful teams in the largest cities. The owners collectively may not feel sufficient impulse to radically tilt the playing court or field towards teams in small markets. We will devote the next chapter to another presumed palliative for competitive balance: revenue sharing.

CHAPTER 6

Will Revenue Sharing Enhance Parity?

Most fans and commentators believe that revenue sharing is the big hope for redressing competitive imbalance. Some economists believe that revenue sharing tends to transfer money from franchises in larger cities to those in smaller cities. However, many economists believe that revenue sharing may not have much effect upon competitive balance, especially when local television revenue is not shared. According to these economists, revenue sharing might, at most, increase the survivability of weaker teams. This is not a trivial consideration.

John Vrooman differentiated between revenue sharing that was sensitive to a team's win-loss record and that which was not sensitive to a team's record.[1] National broadcasting revenue that was shared equally would, of course, represent revenue that was not sensitive to a team's record. Home gate revenue in professional football, with its shorter season and large proportion of season-ticket holders, might not be as win-sensitive as it is in professional baseball.

There is a perverse consequence associated with revenue sharing. Revenue sharing may act to reduce the marginal benefit of winning more games across the board. Teams may end up at the same equilibrium win-loss records, but because the marginal benefit in terms of additional revenue from larger crowds is reduced as the revenue sharing becomes more generous, owners are less willing to offer as much in salaries. Thus, revenue sharing may fool the public into thinking competitive balance will improve, while artificially eroding the players' ability to generate additional revenue (marginal revenue product) and thus their pay.

History of Revenue Sharing

Revenue sharing has been around since the dawn of professional team sports. Early on, two competing baseball teams agreed on a method to divide the gate. Harry Wright, manager of the first overtly professional baseball team, the Cincinnati Red Stockings, negotiated the gate-sharing arrangements with captains of other teams. His team won almost eighty games in a row against a variety of opponents. As the team's acclaim grew, presumably Wright's leverage increased, too. When the National Association of Base Ball Players formed in 1871, it assumed a very loose structure. For ten dollars, your team could be a member. Unfortunately, clubs also felt free to drop out, whenever they liked.

Baseball historian Harold Seymour claimed that revenue sharing arose because teams, "Appreciat[ed] the results of inequality of markets, the owners tried to compensate by sharing gate receipts, giving 50 per cent of the base admission price to visiting teams. Anything above that, taken in through the sale of seats that cost more than the base price, was kept by the home team as an incentive to improve its stands by adding more box and reserve seats."[2]

When William Hulburt of the Chicago White Stockings and other owners formed the National League, they set both a minimum ticket price of fifty cents and a simple gate-sharing rule: Fifteen cents of each paid admission went to the visiting team. However, teams in larger cities often preferred a fixed guarantee instead of a percentage version of revenue sharing. The teams in the smaller cities disliked the fixed guarantee. This tension belies the popular belief that revenue sharing exists to help teams in smaller cities and to maintain competitive balance. The reality is more likely to be that teams playing in large cities want revenue sharing to reward them for bringing a strong team to (smaller) towns.

There was another way to deal with the "inequality of markets," of course: allowing multiple teams in the larger markets. Notice that while the National League owners implemented a minimum population rule, which was immediately ignored with the inclusion of Hartford, they did not remedy the "inequality of markets" by placing more teams in New York City and Chicago. Perhaps they recalled past experiences. The National Association had allowed multiple teams in the same city, although with decidedly mixed results.

In any event, baseball's gate-sharing plan through most of the twentieth century was a flat amount per paid admission. In the American League after the mid–1920s, the rules stipulated twenty cents for bleacher and general admission seats and thirty cents for reserved and box seats. The National League opted for a simple 22.5 or 27.5 cents per paid admission. The home team paid nothing to the visiting team for patrons who bought discounted tickets, such as for Ladies' Days, or for season ticket holders who did not show up for a particular game. The flat rates amounted to between one-seventh and one-quarter of the home revenue during the postwar era.[3]

The National Football League's revenue-sharing plan, sometimes touted as effectively promoting greater competitive balance during the postwar era, was more and less generous than its baseball contemporaries. Naturally, fans of the Chicago Cardinals might wonder about competitive balance in relation to the Cleveland Browns. Football had a reverse-order draft of college players, which baseball did not. On both metrics, according to popular opinion, football should have featured more parity during the 1950s.

Football's 60 percent to 40 percent split of gate revenues seemed to be more generous than baseball's during the 1950s, but there were two tiny details we should notice. First, the 40 percent applied only after the home team skimmed off 15 percent to cover the "expense" of hosting the game and another 2 percent to cover the league's expenses. The home team then paid 40 percent of the remaining receipts to the visiting teams. In practice, home teams paid one-third of the gross home receipts to visiting teams. While this proportion was larger than that in baseball, football's proportion was not as large as it initially appeared to be. The second point was that the home team guaranteed a payout of $20,000 to the visiting team during the 1950s. The guaranteed payout had increased over the years, indicating that the owners wanted a binding guarantee.

The National Basketball Association and the National Hockey League do not have gate revenue sharing. The NBA's antecedent, the Basketball Association of America, was comprised of hockey arena owners looking for another event to book for their arenas. Since the NHL, circa 1946, did not have gate-sharing rules, it is no surprise that the BAA did not either.

Effects of Revenue Sharing

Baseball's revenue-sharing plans suffered from some defects. First, the flat rate per admission meant that teams which charged more for tickets paid a lower proportion of their home revenue to the visitors. The postwar

New York Yankees, for instance, usually had higher ticket prices than did their rivals and thus paid a smaller proportion to the visitors. Second, most economists investigating revenue sharing assumed that the stronger a team is, the better it draws at home and the worse it draws on the road. The reality, for the mid–twentieth century at least, was that the Yankees and the Dodgers were by far the most attractive teams on the road. The "Boys of Summer" Dodgers didn't get much of an attendance boost at Ebbets Field, when Jackie Robinson broke the twentieth-century color line in 1947. The team, however, quickly became the best road draw in the National League. Although the Dodgers had good but not great attendance at Ebbets Field, their ability to draw on the road made the team a beneficiary of revenue sharing.

The New York Yankees experienced an almost one-third drop in attendance at Yankee Stadium between the late 1940s and the middle 1950s. Although it was fashionable to root against the Yankees (rooting for the Yankees was likened to rooting for U.S. Steel), fans flocked to see them when they went on the road. Between 1949 and 1966, the Yankees were usually the best road draw in the American League. By the mid–1950s, the team drew more on the road than at home and thereby also became beneficiaries of revenue sharing. The middle-class teams in the American League, such as Detroit and Chicago, frequently funded the revenue-sharing plan. From the Yankees' perspective, this form of gate sharing, which weakened the strongest rivals even as it may have boosted the inept Browns, Athletics, and Senators to mediocrity, was perhaps the best of all possible worlds.[4]

In the National League, when the Braves moved to Milwaukee, they became the largest donors by far. Indeed, after the Braves' success in 1953, the National League increased the rate from 22.5 to 27.5 cents. It may be telling that the rate increase did little to improve the dire circumstances of the Pirates, Reds, and Cubs. When the league had an opportunity to help weaker members, it chose not to; instead the owners revised the plan in a way that mostly benefited the Brooklyn Dodgers and the New York Giants. The Dodgers and New York Giants gained the most revenue, while the downtrodden Pirates and Reds got a few crumbs.[5]

Some sportswriters praise professional football's "generous" revenue-sharing plan, but it is important to note that making baseball's revenue-sharing plan more generous would not necessarily have kept Brooklyn and New York from being net recipients. Doubling the visitor's share to fifty or sixty cents per paid attendee would simply have doubled the Dodgers' and Yankees' gains.

Had the revenue-sharing plans been made on a proportional basis, the Yankees' high ticket prices would have eroded their benefits from revenue sharing. However, the team's ability to draw on the road would still have muted the plan's effectiveness in transferring revenue from New York to Washington. The Brooklyn Dodgers would have been net recipients under even a 100 percent revenue-sharing rule, assuming that owners would not have changed ticket prices or promotions in the face of such a plan. Walter O'Malley, owner of the Dodgers, excoriated "socialism" in baseball, even though he was the chief beneficiary of revenue sharing. Rarely has taking such a strong, principled stand against socialism paid so well. Because the Milwaukee Braves did not televise games for many seasons and earned most of their revenue at the gate while Brooklyn earned the most television revenue, O'Malley's refusal to share television revenue was nakedly self-interested, which is fine as far as it goes, but also hypocritical.

As described earlier, the NFL's revenue sharing plan was not as generous as is reputed. The guaranteed $20,000 minimum payout meant that such weak-drawing teams as the Chicago Cardinals had to pay more than one-third of their home receipts to the visiting teams. Indeed, on a proportional basis, the Cardinals and the Green Bay Packers usually paid out the most of any NFL teams. While the Cardinals and Packers did gain revenue from the plan, the guaranteed minimum reduced the amounts transferred.[6]

Why did football mandate a minimum payout? While I haven't been privy to the minutes of league meetings, I suspect that owners of strong teams wanted to insure that their ne'er-do-well brethren wouldn't be tempted to strip their own teams of talent. Baseball's St. Louis Browns had sold or traded their best players after World War II. They still might get respectable crowds when the Yankees and Dodgers visited, but they killed the gate at Yankee Stadium and Ebbets Field. Other owners harshly characterized the Browns' owners, the DeWitt brothers, as, "parasites, who feed on the drawing power of the better teams while on the road and keeping themselves weak and without support at home."[7]

There was a major difference between pro football and baseball during the 1950s. Unlike baseball, strong teams in pro football proved only slightly better draws on the road than their weaker peers. The NFL's plan, therefore, was more likely to transfer revenue from strong teams to weak ones.

Baseball might have redressed the problem of strong teams becoming the recipients of revenue sharing by rearranging the redistribution. Regardless of whether home teams paid a flat amount per paid admission or a proportion of gate receipts, redistribution towards the poorer teams would have been increased by taking the visitors' shares collected from all of the teams and *dividing them equally* between all the teams. This method would have severed the link between a team's ability to draw on the road from the amount it received from the pool.

Any revenue-sharing plan has to be careful not to erect perverse incentives. Like state and federal programs to help indigent families, revenue-sharing plans can actually make it more difficult to escape from poverty. A team in a small city that tries to improve will likely put more fannies in the seats. As it does so, though, the revenue-sharing payments may begin to dwindle. In other words, some revenue-sharing plans may lower the marginal revenue of additional wins, just as earning income may result in lower welfare payments. A parent thinking of taking a $8.00 per hour job may lose, on average, $3.00 per hour in welfare payments. The incentive of working for $3.00 net is less than working for $6.00, and we haven't even brought in income and social security tax considerations and the time spent away from the children. The indigent parent is not necessarily "lazy" in refusing to work for $6.00 per hour: It's simply not a good deal. Similarly, a team receiving revenue-sharing aid may find improving the team, with its attendant higher payroll, a losing proposition. Economists debate the "welfare trap" aspect of many programs, but a similar trap may exist for professional sports teams if the revenue-sharing plan is ineptly designed.

We could create the ultimate abuse of revenue sharing. Let's say that owning an American League baseball team gives you a set of property rights, including the expectation that teams like the New York Yankees will play your team a set number of times each season. Imagine how valuable it is to have the property right to have the Yankees visit Podunk Stadium six times per season. Just as many colleges would love to play Notre Dame's football team, many baseball teams would love to play the Yankees, even if they would get routed and have to invoke the softball "slaughter rule." Of course, the Yankees don't want to cast their figurative pearls before the baseball swine of the world.

However, suppose you buy the Kansas City Royals. You could stock the team with major league journeymen and lose a lot of games while paying only twenty million in payroll. Or, you could get players who would *pay you* to perform for the Royals. In what could be considered the ultimate Fantasy League, you could offer Hollywood celebrities, dot.com survivors, aging politicians, and any other folks willing to pay big bucks to step in and bat against Mariano Rivera or pitch to Alex Rodriguez. I could imagine that Billy Crystal, Mark Cuban, and even Fidel Castro might think it fun to play ball and enjoy the camaraderie of riding on the team bus across the country (if you're going to save money on payroll, you might as well cut corners on transportation, too). Each celebrity might ante up $1,000,000 to play an entire season. You might even get the Fox network to stage the antics as a reality show, with celebrity manager Donald Trump screaming, "You're cut!"

You might draw fairly large crowds to begin with, as fans revel in the novelty. Chances are, though, that fans would quickly tire of the constant massacres of the Kansas City Royals "Hollywood Stars." Rival teams could object to this "mockery" of the game — just recall the outrage when Bill Veeck sent the vertically challenged Eddie Gaedel to the plate for one lousy appearance — and might invoke the clause that allows them to boot out owners who injure the game. Still, if an owner does try such a stunt, I hope he'll remember to pay me consulting fees.[8]

Your owner peers would undoubtedly censure such activities, as well they should. We've seen how the St. Louis Browns were accused of stripping their team by selling players to the Boston Red Sox. Under Major League Baseball's current revenue-sharing rules, wealthier teams want to ensure that weak teams re-invest some of the revenue-sharing loot in acquiring good players. Thus, Major League Baseball owners of stronger teams have lobbied for a minimum payroll. In addition, the players' union negotiated for minimum salaries, which also helps insure that owners field a modicum of talent.

Even in the NFL, owners are quick to find ways around the revenue-sharing rules. Luxury boxes, aside from being lucrative, are also largely exempt from revenue sharing. If owners were truly worried about helping the poor and maintaining competitive balance, you'd think they'd vote for the league to plug such loopholes.

Baseball owners had been wary of radio broadcasts of games at first, but they embraced television more enthusiastically during the late 1940s. Although Bill Veeck and some other owners warned that televising home games would hurt the gate (and the visiting team's revenue share), most owners opted to televise home games. Since, as mentioned, television revenue was not subject to revenue sharing, it was as though "tax-free" income fell into their laps. A potential "Prisoner's Dilemma" arose. If televising hurt home gate receipts by, say, $12,000 per game and revenue sharing took one-quarter of the gate receipts, television revenue in excess of $9,000 would be a net gain to the home team's owner. The league, however, would be collectively worse off if the television revenue was less than $12,000, and if all owners pursued such policies everyone could be worse off. This is a Prisoner's Dilemma story, if there ever was one.

By the mid–1950s, many National League owners decided that televising home games was not beneficial and opted to televise only their road games. Even Walter O'Malley telecast just eleven home games per season after moving to Los Angeles, and those were only the games with the San Francisco Giants. Ironically, O'Malley got at least as much television revenue, if not more, in Los Angeles as he did in Brooklyn televising all of the home games.[9]

The New York and Los Angeles teams received much larger sums from televising games than did teams in St. Louis or Pittsburgh. The disparity continues today, as the New York Yankees reap several times the media revenue that Kansas City does. Such media revenue helps the Yankees afford their lavish payrolls.

During the 1950s, NFL teams had fairly even distribution of media revenue, while Major League Baseball teams had relatively larger disparities in such revenue. The NFL's more even distribution might have made it easier for that league to settle on a national television package in which all the teams received equal shares of the media revenue.

The National Football League eventually received an exemption allowing the organization to negotiate national television contracts on behalf of all teams. From an economic perspective, national television revenue that was shared equally would be win-inelastic and would be a lump-sum windfall that might keep some weak teams viable but might not affect marginal revenue product and competitive balance.

A more effective method of improving revenue distribution was to get teams to move from smaller cities to more viable venues. When the Athletics and Browns moved in 1954 and 1955, the American League achieved a reduction in the disparity in revenues far greater than the league's revenue-sharing plan ever achieved. In an ironic twist, the Yankees gained road revenue from having the Athletics and Browns drawing more. Eventually, the Browns/Orioles, Athletics, and Senators/Twins improved on the field, and these three teams displaced the Yankees as the strongest teams in the league between 1965 and 1975.

Revenue sharing may not be much of a cure for competitive balance ills. It may, instead, work against the players' interest while giving the appearance that something is being done.

CHAPTER 7

Why Professional Athletes Make Big Bucks

Sports fans and reporters are amazed, frustrated, and envious of the salaries that top professional athletes earn. "They're getting paid all that money to *play a game*?" Maybe athletes are playing games, but they are simultaneously amazing, frustrating, and entertaining us.

Never Have So Many Paid So Few So Much

Ballplayers make more money than most Americans. One should never forget, though, that they represent the apex of a large pyramid of participants in high school and college sports. Major League Baseball, the NBA, and the NFL employ a total of fewer than 3,000 players. As such, they represent perhaps less than one-tenth of 1 percent of all participants in sports. Hollywood stars and bestselling novelists are comparable talents, but few people complain about Tom Hanks', John Grisham's, or Stephen King's mega-bucks.

Because many Americans have played and coached sports, most fans feel that they can comment and criticize upon coaches' decisions and players' performances, while believing that they, too, are just a cut below being able to play professionally. Indeed, a poll commissioned by a brewery back in the 1990s (this may have been a skewed and soused sample of males), echoes the Terry Malloy lament in the movie *On the Waterfront* that he "coulda been a contender." The poll found that a majority of American males thought they could have been professional athletes, "if only the [junior high and high school] coaches had spent more time with them." Such thinking is frightfully delusional. Not many people think, "I could have been a nuclear physicist if only the math teacher had spent more time

139

with me in algebra class." Since scientific endeavors are generally not televised, most of us would have little ability to ascertain the relative merits of the top physicists in the world. Given the widespread fear of numbers, much less abstract mathematics, even someone with an undergraduate degree in physics may be able to befuddle friends with its arcane nature. From personal experience, I know the exalted cachet associated with having majored in mathematics as an undergraduate: "Wow, you must be smart!" We do not witness physicists in action very frequently, and any Hollywood depiction is likely to be long on physical appearance, madness, and action and short on mental gymnastics.

Part of the difficulty in perceptions arises from fans watching professional athletes interact only with other professional athletes. A 6' 8" player going up against the gang at the YMCA looks positively gigantic, but if he plays center in the NBA, Yao Ming and Shaq are almost ten inches taller. The players that Michael Jordan and teammates beat every night look like a bunch of bums, yet any one of those bums could beat almost every other male on the planet. There's a long continuum of talent that stretches from the guy who got cut from the junior high team to the high school starter who never quit talking about his exploits to the high school star cut from a small college team to the Division-1 bench-warmer to the All-American to the guy playing in Europe to the NBA journeyman to the NBA star to the select few such as Michael Jordan, Tim Duncan, Larry Bird, and Magic Johnson (just to name the more modern ones). You could get a better idea how good these players really are if they played a wider spectrum of ordinary joes.

While NBA players are so obviously different than most of us because of their great height, professional football linemen are different because of their girth and strength. While most of us know 300-pound men, men with the requisite girth, most of our heavyweight acquaintances cannot run a 40-yard dash in less than five seconds as many of the NFL behemoths can. These men are big, strong, and QUICK. It's the same thing with the seven-footers playing in the NBA, many of whom could beat most American males in a full-court sprint. These athletes are marvelously talented.

In addition to being gifted, professional athletes are not anonymous cogs in a machine. Professional team sports market individuals. Reporters and experts help identify the truly great from the merely gifted. Otherwise, many fans would have difficulty recognizing differences between AAA baseball players competing amongst themselves and a major league game. A good AAA pitcher can throw almost as fast as his major league counterpart; a good AAA hitter can hit almost as well as a major leaguer. If all the major leaguers disappeared into the Bermuda Triangle, promoting all AAA players to the major leagues would not cause a ripple, if the fans didn't know of the shift.[1]

This process of the very best crowding out other highly talented performers is not unique to professional sports. Frankly, most of us couldn't tell the difference between a Monet and a "second-line" Impressionist. The critics and art historians have inculcated the idea that Monet is among the best, so we view his paintings with this reputation. There may be some objective way to demonstrate that Monet is the best, but the judging process is similar to that of figure skating in being imbued with much subjective content. Who is the best tenor or soprano in the world? Even the most knowledgeable critics might rank the top dozen differently. Can anyone explain why one contestant is Miss America and another contestant achieves instant obscurity by being first runner-up? Does Miss America really look that much better in a bikini, excuse me, swimsuit; answer the innocuous questions posed to her more charmingly; or sing light opera much better than the runner-up?

Whatever the vagaries of judgment, the cachet of being the very best is highly rewarding. Number one often makes much more money than a runner-up. Huge disparities in prize money, like those found in golf tournaments, spur athletes to play extra hard.

While early promoters of sports events wanted to have the best teams, there was some resistance to focusing attention on the best individuals on those teams. Once individual players became widely identifiable, their bargaining power increased. Baseball owners took their sweet time in putting numbers on their players' uniforms. In the movie industry, producers hesitated to list the actors who were appearing in their films. Anonymous actors have difficulty demanding more money. Not until the days of "that girl with the curl," Mary Pickford, and of Charlie Chaplin, did individual movie actors gain public recognition. Pickford became the highest-paid female actor of her time and used her clout to become a producer, eventually forming United Artists with husband Douglas Fairbanks and friends Chaplin and director D.W. Griffith.

As an aside, why do movie stars often make more for one film than top athletes make in any given season, even though going to a movie costs less than attending a game? Few movie theaters charge even ten dollars for a show, while there are precious few bleacher seats or seats in the nosebleed section at ballparks that go for fewer than ten dollars. You are getting a couple of hours of entertainment at either venue. There is a difference in the nature of the performance, though. Today's showing of *Titanic* will be the same as tomorrow's showing. Leo DiCaprio doesn't survive in any showing. In a sense, tomorrow's showing is close to a perfect substitute for today's showing of *Titanic*. His performance is not ephemeral. In contrast, today's baseball game is not the same as tomorrow's showing. "No two games are exactly alike" is a hoary shibboleth. For example, today's game may determine the pennant winner, while tomorrow's game might not affect the pennant outcome. Today's game might see Barry Bonds hit homerun number 756, while tomorrow's game might be anticlimactic. Sure, you can watch the replays, but the drama is essentially ephemeral. Drama aside, though, motion pictures often draw many more patrons. Few professional teams draw even four million fans in a season, whereas *Titanic* sold tens of millions of tickets.

In any event, being perceived as "the best" enhances one's bargaining power. The great economist Adam Smith recognized this back in 1776.[2] "The exorbitant rewards of players, opera-singers, opera-dancers, etc. are founded upon those two principles: the rarity and beauty of the talents, and the discredit of employing them in this manner."[3] If Smith had been writing a century later, he might have included ballplayers in the discredited category. Today, the "discredit" of being a player, opera-singer, opera-dancer, or other performer has been transformed into credit, leading to ever-greater numbers of aspirants.

Productivity and marketability are crucial ingredients for high salaries. To be imbued with unique talent and to hone it through long, hard, and often lonely hours of practice is to be singularly blessed. However, you have to be additionally blessed to reap really big money: There has to be a large demand for your services. Orvil Finkleblatt, the "best there ever was" bird-caller, may be the Michael Jordan, the Pavarotti, the Tom Hanks of bird-calling, popular at every bird-calling exposition, but unfortunately there isn't a big demand for bird-calling. The Olympic-champion synchronized swimmer, that event which causes so much sniggering every four years, doesn't even rate a spot on a box of Wheaties, much less a chance at big bucks. There's no need to denigrate the synchronized swimmer's ability. True, most of us can hold our breath under water and can even swim, but can we do the intricate movements? I think not. I shudder to think how many times I would have drowned practicing the requisite movements. Still, synchronized swimming has a limited fan base, so don't look for a AWUSS (Association of World Underwater Synchronized Swimmers) league coming to a town near you anytime soon. Perhaps if they allowed trash-talking and full-contact styles, then the sport would gain adherents.

The drive to be the best has costs, of course. If all youngsters spent equal time practicing, the overall ranking might not differ much from the original distribution of natural ability. Although the absolute quality of play might suffer if the youngsters devoted their time to something else, the youngsters collectively would have been better off doing something else with their time.

With the huge prizes for being the best, there's also an incentive for participants to gain an edge, whether by fair means or foul. Such endeavors are not endemic only to athletics. Parents pay lavish sums for tutors to prepare their children to college entrance examinations, for instance. Young people (and their parents) are interested in memory-enhancing products. Heck, even United States Senators seek to gain a competitive edge by dyeing their hair, injecting Botox, undergoing tummy tucks and chin lifts, and other endeavors.[4] I suspect some use "elevator heels" to appear taller, since height appears to sway voters, at least on a subconscious level. Meanwhile, they criticize athletes who would ingest or inject dubious products, such as steroids. I'm not sure what level of hypocrisy is involved here, but I think it's pretty high.

Of course, the potential danger of steroid use is that pretty soon, "everyone has to do it" to compete: A slippery slope argument applied to sports instead of Communism. I can understand not wanting children to use steroids, and I can countenance professional leagues proscribing such substances, but I do not understand why the Congress should be involved. In the case of football players, I think the hand-wringing over steroids is misplaced concern. During an NFL players' strike in 1987, former player Ron Mix bemoaned the dangers involved with professional football. He claimed that a majority of players ended up disabled and that players' life expectancy was only fifty-five years, some fifteen years below the national average and approaching Third-World standards.[5] Unfortunately, Mix did not provide a citation for his figures. A recent research letter to the *Journal of American Medical Association* detailed that, no surprise, NFL players had body mass indexes well above average. The authors concluded that, "The high number of large players was not unexpected given the pressures of professional athletes to increase their mass.... The high prevalence of obesity in this group warrants further investigation to determine the short- and long-term health consequences of excessive weight in professional as well as amateur athletes."[6] Another study suggested that football players, being heavy, are more likely to suffer from sleep apnea: "The estimated prevalence is higher than that found in a cross-sectional study of men of similar age, and emphasizes the importance of physiognomy over physical conditioning as a risk factor for sleep-disordered breathing.... The presence of sleep-disordered breathing, even in persons without symptoms, is a known risk factor for the development of hypertension."[7] There are clear and present risks to playing football at any level, and certainly players voluntarily accept the risk. I suppose I could paraphrase the Dan Aykroyd character in *Point-Counterpart*, by saying, "They knew the risks, let 'em croak," but worrying about steroids at this juncture seems a little silly.

Baseball players were the first team sports participants to gain national recognition. Their salaries tended to be higher than those of players in the fledgling professional football leagues and, later, those of professional basketball players. Almost from the beginning, players on the top baseball teams made more than the typical working man. By the 1950s, they made several times more. Aside from reading newspaper accounts of their heroics, most fans never saw a major league player. Before 1955, there were no major league teams very far west of the Mississippi River or south of the mouth of the Ohio River. While people residing in the west and south might have been willing to pay some small amount to watch, say, Ted Williams, the opportunity rarely arose.

In addition, the reserve clause undoubtedly suppressed player salaries during the 1950s. After winning the World Series in 1959, the Dodgers' highest salary for 1960 was Gil Hodges' $39,000. If you convert $39,000 in 1960 dollars to today's dollars, Hodges was making less than the current major league minimum. Mickey Mantle had to fight to get a $13,000 raise after his 1961 season (fifty-four homeruns and a .317 batting average). He did not attain a $100,000 salary until the 1962 season, despite two Most Valuable Player awards. On other occasions, the team threatened Mantle and two-time MVP Yogi Berra with pay cuts.

Under the reserve clause, owners had to pay you more than your reservation salary. Your reservation salary would be the amount of money you could make in your best alternative employment. In the early days of professional baseball, few players had college degrees. Many players were blue-collar workers, so a salary greater than, or possibly even slightly lower than, that paid to blue-collar workers (given the more pleasant aspect of ball-playing), could entice you onto the ball field. Of course, such a decision would need to be adjusted for the seasonal nature of playing baseball.

In professional football and basketball, with their highly developed collegiate training grounds, most players are close to, or actually possess, an undergraduate degree.[8]

If you're drafted to play professional sports, one of your considerations, therefore, is how much money you can make using your college degree. As more players gain college degrees, the reservation price needed to induce them to opt for playing games goes up. In most cases, though, the alternative employment doesn't offer nearly as much money as the minimum professional sports salaries. The argument is probably more germane to baseball players presented with an opportunity to play minor league baseball. Bill Laimbeer, former center for the Detroit Pistons, was a rarity in that he was born with the proverbial "silver spoon" in his mouth. His father was a high-ranking executive for one of the Big Three automakers. At one point in his career, Bill was said to be the only NBA player who made less money than his Dad did. Bill's non-basketball alternatives might have been rosier than the typical NBA player had, but I suspect his lowest NBA salary still greatly exceeded his reservation price.

Players should have been disgruntled. Yet, several star players, including Mickey Mantle, testified before Congress during the 1950s that the reserve clause was necessary for the good of the game. Only one professional athlete testified against any form of the reserve clause, and this football player requested anonymity. Players needed to have their consciousness raised, but Karl Marx had been long dead. The public, mesmerized by the players' higher salaries, would have had difficulty accepting the fact that the players were among the most exploited workers in America in terms of the proportional difference between their hypothetical free-market and actual salaries.

Owners bemoaned player salaries under the reserve clause throughout the history of all the sports. Meanwhile, baseball player payrolls as a proportion of club expenses fell from roughly half around 1900 to below one-fifth by the mid–1950s.

In baseball, Marvin Miller and the Players' Association first won the right to arbitrate disputes. They used this right to get favorable rulings pertaining to the reserve clause. Once the arbitrators conjured the specter of free agency, Miller, the players, and the owners struggled to implement a mutually agreeable plan. Miller recalled: "The owners wanted as few players as possible to become free agents. I wasn't entirely opposed to this; I didn't want so many free-agent players as to flood the market. I had no doubt that my position was sound, but I agonized over the eligibility requirement. What would be likely to produce the optimal mix of supply and demand?"[9] The players and owners also created a system for salary arbitration for players ineligible for free agency. While this system received and continues to receive less attention than free agency, the arbitration system has greatly contributed to rising player salaries.

Early NBA owners were between a proverbial rock (low gate revenues) and a hard place (high player reservation wages). Professional basketball occasionally attracted large crowds, but most teams averaged fewer than 5,000 attendees per game. George Mikan and Bob Cousy struggled to reach $30,000 salaries at a time when baseball star Ted Williams could get $100,000. Like most owners, NBA owners wanted to reduce player salaries. While NBA owners boasted that their teams were comprised of collegiate stars, this fact was a mixed blessing; in general, college graduates earned more than the average working stiff. NBA owners could not reduce salaries much below $5,000 before many potential players would opt for jobs with companies sponsoring "amateur" teams, such as the Phillips 66ers. Such talented players as Bob Kurland, George Yardley, and Jim Pollard spent some or all of their post-college careers with top amateur teams. Yardley, an engineer, and Ernie Vandeweghe, father of Kiki Vandeweghe and an aspiring physician, had lucrative outside offers. Vandeweghe's leverage was such that the Knicks allowed him to skip road games with western opponents. George Mikan earned his law degree while playing professional basketball.

The punitive marginal income tax rates of the 1950s exacerbated the players' suppressed salaries. With marginal tax rates of up to 90 percent — at high enough income levels, for every additional dollar you earned, you lost ninety cents — players often had to work during the off-season. Winter was not a time of endless rounds of golf and recording rap albums. Even in the early 1970s, baseball players, including established regulars, frequently had off-season jobs. If I recall correctly, Richie Hebner, the Pirates' third baseman, was a gravedigger during the winter.

Some players, recognizing the tax bites, resorted to clever tax shelters. Ted Williams had a $100,000 contract late in his career, but $25,000 was placed in an "expense account" and was therefore tax-exempt. Players considered cooperating with Hollywood actors to get tax relief, including income averaging and a form of self-depreciation. Owners already had tax relief; they were able to depreciate the value of their players over a period of years. Surprisingly, it was a Democrat, President John F. Kennedy, who provided tax relief for players with his push for sharply reduced marginal tax rates, an action that presaged the Reagan revolution twenty years later.

Role of Technology in Affecting Player Salaries

Modern professional athletes are fortunate to be living in these times. Advances in technology have allowed owners to reach ever-wider markets, which, in turn, spur greater demand for top athletes.

Due to a fortunate concatenation of events, professional team sports became viable after the American Civil War. Harry Wright and the Red Stockings proved the feasibility of an explicitly professional baseball team. Wright's Cincinnati Red Stockings featured the best-known and possibly the most-talented baseball players. The team won eighty or eighty-one games in a row, albeit against competition that varied wildly in quality. Part of the primitive nature of the Red Stockings' endeavor is the dispute over exactly how many games in a row the team won. Since the team won most of these games on the road, Wright's team was spared the overhead of maintaining a ballpark. Because his team became renowned, he was able to get favorable shares of the gate.[10] The drawback to being a road team was, of course, increased travel expenses. In any event, the Red Stockings' model proved successful, and other entrepreneurs entered the market.

Wright was successful, because post-bellum America had a dense network of railroads, canals, lakes, and rivers in the northeast. Steam-powered transportation was more reliable and cheaper than animal-borne transportation. Players working in Boston could board a train and play a game in New York and return that day. There's no way Wright's Red Stockings would have been viable in an era with only stage coaches, wagons, canoes, and flatboats. What steam power was to transportation, the telegraph was to communication. Wright could speedily arrange games with teams in towns down the railroad lines. Results of his team's games were rapidly reported. His team's prowess would have meant nothing had there been no speedy communication and cheap newspapers, combined with, of course, widespread literacy. The penny press needed material to attract readers and sporting events proved ideal. Newspapers heralded the Red Stockings' exemplary record, and the sporting public could keep track of its exploits. Just as Davy Crockett became more than a local colorful character through the power of cheap printing presses, the Reds Stockings became famous due to communication technologies. They were not merely a Cincinnati phenomenon; the whole Northeast was alerted to the team's feat. Fans and other teams eagerly sought their date with the Red Stockings. The publicity generated large crowds of people willing to spend thirty-five cents to see their local favorites battle the Red Stockings.

The next step was to field professional teams that were tethered to a locale. Whether Wright's team could consistently draw fans to the same venue for many games during a season was an intriguing question. Wright next built the Boston Red Stockings into a power in the National Association.[11] The National Association teams needed places to play. While the earliest baseball teams used open fields, baseball owners eventually sought enclosed fields to prevent "free watchers." (This is a perennial problem for owners; the modern Chicago Cubs' management has frequently battled denizens in Wrigleyville who can watch games from apartment rooftops.) Building enclosed ballparks entailed investing significant sums of capital. Technology again affected the development of professional sports. Wooden ballparks had the unfortunate tendency to burn down. Steel girders and concrete made larger and more durable ballparks feasible, but these stadiums required larger sums of capital. The need for capital helped transform baseball from a player-run enterprise into a capitalistic venture.

With franchise relocation and expansion and air transportation, professional sports eventually spanned the USA and Canada as well, extending the market. Almost concurrently, television spread across the nation in almost the same way, beginning in the Northeast and upper Midwest and spreading westward and southward after a number of years. By 1960, 90 percent of American households had a black and white set. Tens of millions could see Ted Williams play each season rather than the two or three million at the ballparks. Later, cable television would exponentially increase the medium's appetite for sporting events. Sports are attractive for television: Sporting events come with free advertisement thanks to newspaper sports sections; they happen on predictable schedules; they are cheap to produce; and they are endlessly variable, as no two games are alike.

As the old television ads for Ronco boasted, "You'd be willing to pay $29.99 for the Veggie-matic, but wait, you also get...," more than just Milton "Uncle Miltie" Berle and a host of locally produced shows. Now almost everyone could watch Ted and his chums play. Perhaps you were just a lukewarm fan, unwilling to pay even the $2.50 to get a good seat in 1960 but willing to sit in your living room and deposit a quarter into a hypothetical pay-television meter or to pay indirectly through watching advertisements on "free" television. The demand for Ted became wider, albeit shallower — but a wide and shallow demand can be quite lucrative. Ted probably made less than $125,000 in 1960, with the team still largely dependent upon revenue from live attendees. You might scoff at the potential of people willing to pay up to twenty-five cents to watch you perform. But if forty million Americans, less than a quarter of the 1960 population, had been willing to pay even twenty-five cents to watch Ted in an All-Star game (since the Red Sox were hopelessly out of contention during the latter part of his career, a World Series appearance was highly unlikely), his potential earnings would have run into the millions. Years ago, columnist Bob Greene did an article on a grocery store box boy. The boy made the request that people send him a dime. Many people did, despite the fact that the postage was greater than the donation. This was just an anonymous box boy. Remember this: If you can figure out a way to get a majority of Americans to send you even a dime, you'll get rich. If one hundred million Americans send you a dime, you would have ten million dollars. The potential to tap into a wide, shallow market interested in professional sports would take years to fully exploit, but it was foreseeable even in 1960.

Changing technology, therefore, boosted players' earnings. One often hears the complaint that teachers should be paid more money, since they are doing something really important by educating young minds. Yet taxpayers apparently don't subscribe to this plaint, opting not to vote for tax revenue to finance higher teacher salaries. Even if we grant that a teacher does more valuable work for society than does an entertainer ballplayer, the argument that teachers should be paid as much still does not hold. A ballplayer can entertain millions, even billions, of fans. The ballplayer's performance can be almost endlessly replicated through television and, now, computers and the Internet. The best teacher, even if videotaped, is not likely to reach many students. And, what often makes a teacher great — individual attention and a sense of caring for an individual student — is not easily replicated on videotape. While an individual might be willing to pay much more to have a particular teacher, only so many students can sign up for that teacher, limiting the teacher's potential earnings. The teacher faces a deep but narrow demand.

The factors of technology and free agency helped to increase player salaries. Although local television revenue has been increasing for most teams, its uneven distribution and free agency have helped the Yankees resume and maintain their dominance. At least they have had to pay more for their pennants under free agency. During the 1950s, the team often had the highest payroll, but as with all teams, the payroll comprised roughly one-fifth of the total costs. For any given win-loss record, the Yankees incurred an added $120,000 per season in player salaries compared with other teams, but the team's payroll was rarely twice that of the team with the lowest payroll, the Washington Senators. The team did not greatly outspend the Cleveland Indians or Detroit Tigers, perhaps spending 20 percent more than its rivals on payroll. On occasion, Cleveland outspent the Yankees.[12]

Today, the Yankees maintain a larger proportional payroll edge over the Boston Red Sox and any of the National League big spenders, such as the New York Mets. Moreover, the Yankees' current payroll comprises a much larger proportion of its total expenses, and the team often spends four or five times as much on player pay as do the teams with the smallest payrolls.[13] There is a much larger proportional disparity in payrolls today than in the past, even though the Yankees' win-loss records don't exceed those of the reserve clause era.

Effects of Rising Salaries

Did salary increases trigger rising ticket prices? Although Jim Hunter was the first modern baseball free agent, signing with the New York Yankees for the 1975 season, 1977 was the first season with significant numbers of free agent signings. According to popular wisdom, ticket prices should have gone up because free agency, along with arbitration, drove up salaries. Therefore, we should have seen increases in ticket prices between 1976 and, for instance, 1979. Ticket prices did rise between these seasons, typically by one-quarter to two-fifths. Fans easily persuaded themselves that the greedy players were responsible for the higher ticket prices. However, the consumer price level increased by over one-quarter during the same period, so most of the increase could be attributed to owners attempting to keep the ticket prices constant in purchasing power. Some teams, such as Oakland, Atlanta, and Philadelphia, did not even raise prices during the period. The teams that raised their prices in excess of the general change in prices were not necessarily gouging fans. In previous years, owners might have raised prices every third or fourth year, with a 15- to20-percent increase. In the year of the increase, their ticket prices rose faster than prices in general, but after a number of years, they might only keep up. In addition, some owners reclassified some seats, upgrading them to higher-priced categories. A few owners reclassified seats downward. Still, there is little evidence of dramatic ticket price increases, net of inflation.

Even the Yankees, whose stadium was refurbished in 1976, did not raise prices dramatically between 1975 and 1979. Most of the changes, aside from some box and general admission seats, barely kept up with inflation. Free agency was a convenient scapegoat for ticket price increases, but the relationship was dubious at best.

Some of the owners undoubtedly raised their ticket prices after signing a top free agent, as they anticipated increased demand for the perceived higher-quality product. If the owner had gotten the star player gratis, he still would have been likely to raise ticket prices because of the anticipated increase in demand emanating from the stronger team. In these cases, it was not the greater salaries being paid that triggered the price hike, but the anticipated increase in demand.

Baseball owners could complain that the change from the reserve clause to limited free agency during the second half of the 1970s eroded their franchise's value. Poor George Steinbrenner, buying the Yankees at a fire sale price in 1973, undoubtedly considered the nifty reserve clause property rights to forty players on the major league roster in considering how much to pay for the team. As we've seen, the reserve clause served to suppress salaries, so the property right was valuable. Rescinding the property right later undoubtedly hurt the owners, although I doubt many readers will shed tears over Georgie's plight.[14]

If free agency and higher salaries damaged Major League Baseball teams, then franchise values should have fallen or remained stagnant. Franchise values did not appear to fall in the late 1970s, although such values might have been even higher had free agency not existed. The burgeoning cable and national television revenues may have more than offset the monopoly rent from players' labor.

Top professional athletes earn much more than the typical American. They do so because millions of people are willing to pay relatively small sums to watch them perform. Their high salaries are a reflection of strong consumer demand, as witness by the number of tickets sold, the price paid per ticket, and by television's willingness to pay for telecasting rights. With the relaxation of the reserve clause, modern-day athletes are free to earn close to market salaries; they are no longer exploited. Along with top movie stars, musical artists, and novelists, top athletes bring entertainment, diversion, and even joy to millions of people. When you and I can do so, then we, too, will earn millions.

CHAPTER 8

Discrimination in the World of Sports

Economists studying discrimination find professional sports a fruitful arena for study. The availability of productivity measures, player attributes, and salaries allow us to measure whether there is discrimination.

The Economics of Discrimination

How would discrimination work? Recall that owners are interested in a player's marginal revenue product, which is a mix of the player's productivity during the season and the effect such productivity has on getting fans to buy tickets. If players from Group A are less productive than players in other groups, then their marginal revenue product and their salaries would be lower. Whether this is "discrimination," I leave to the reader's opinion.

If fans have a preference for players from Group B over Group A, then for any given level of production players from Group B would attract more fans and their marginal revenue product would be higher. Players from Group A would be employed less frequently and paid less for any given level of talent. Owners and teammates, too, may have preferences. Suppose Owner A prefers players with freckles to players without freckles. Owner A would hire a freckled player over a non-freckled player, even if the latter was a somewhat better player (Owner A might suspend his preference if the difference in talent was marked), or Owner A might pay a freckled player more than an equally talented non-freckled player. If teammates have preferences, then, the outcome may depend in part on the size of Group A versus other groups. We'll see that the market provides some protection from discrimination arising from owner preferences but not much protection if there is widespread fan preference.

152

One form of discrimination arises from statistical considerations. As a thought experiment, suppose you are in a room with thirty strangers of various backgrounds. A moderator comes in and announces that all of you will take a math exam. You will not just take the test; you will also guess which person will get the highest score. The winner of the guessing game gets $500. You could choose the person most likely to get the highest score randomly, but I suspect that for $500 you would suspend your hesitance to indulge in stereotyping. You might fall back on generally held beliefs, or perhaps you've read which groups get the highest math scores on the SAT or ACT exams. Of course, such generally held beliefs are crude measures, at best. Let's say that people of Group A get the highest scores, on average, on the math section of the SAT. Membership in a group is no guarantee of performance, however, since a group average covers a wide range of performances, and there is usually considerable overlap in scores between groups.

The preceding is pretty straightforward and may occur frequently. On basketball courts across America, if a group of relative strangers collect for a game, the "team captains" will certainly express a marked preference for taller players. While there are certainly going to be some more-talented shorter players, a team captain is playing the odds by going for the taller players first.

In the controversial field of IQ scores, apparently the mean male and female scores are identical out to several decimal places, but the distributions are different.[1] There are higher percentages of men in the very high and very low categories; in other words, the men's distribution has fatter tails.

Most of us would think NBA owners reasonable in not hiring a lot of Asian players. First, until recently, Asian males were shorter, on average, than white and black males. Second, relatively few Asians played basketball. Of course, Yao Ming has changed perceptions, and given the billion or so Chinese, one can imagine that the pendulum may swing too far the other way: Owners may become overly optimistic about the talent pool in Asia. Before Yao Ming, owners probably didn't even bother to scout Asian countries, relying on statistical discrimination, as, on average, scouting one thousand Asian players was likely to be less productive than scouting one thousand American, European, or African players.

Sometimes "statistical discrimination" is based upon flimsy statistics. Sixty years ago, Major League Baseball owners undoubtedly comforted themselves with the fiction that black players weren't good enough to play in the major leagues. Some owners may have admitted that a handful of black players could "cut the mustard," but these owners might have rationalized their exclusion on the basis that black players were "happier playing against themselves than competing with whites." A few may have even claimed, sanctimoniously, that signing top black players would hurt the black leagues.

When black players won interracial exhibition games against white players, owners dismissed the victories with the assumption that the white players were goofing off. However, some astute managers, such as John McGraw, realized that some black players were very good indeed. McGraw apparently hoped to sign a black pitcher and create the fiction that he was Cuban, as Cubans played in Major League Baseball during the 1920s. The Washington Senators were pioneers in signing Cuban players, and while such players were usually lighter-skinned, a historical possibility remains that some were part black. Other owners got wind of McGraw's scheme and got commissioner Kenesaw Mountain Landis, an avowed racist, to stymie McGraw. McGraw probably had no special affection for blacks, but he wanted to win. Certainly, he would have subscribed to the Vince Lombardi "Winning is the only thing," and Al Davis "Just win, baby," philosophies.

During Babe Ruth's career, opposing players sometimes taunted him by claiming that he was black, based on facial characteristics. There is no hard evidence to support their taunts, but let us conduct a thought experiment. Suppose someone produced evidence that the Babe was partly black. Given the goofy mores of the time, a player with a single grandparent who was black would have been considered black (just as Tiger Woods is considered today, even though he is actually one-half Asian). What would Major League Baseball have done? Landis might have wanted to ban him, but Ruth was the biggest draw in the game. Some observers and historians believe that Ruth was as responsible as Landis for saving the game after the Black Sox scandal. No one could claim that Ruth, black or white, was not capable of playing the game at the highest level. Would fans stop attending Yankees games if they knew he was black? Would Jacob Ruppert, owner of the Yankees, acquiesce in banishing his best player and crowd pleaser? Great as Lou Gehrig was, he never attracted the fans as did Ruth. No other player drew fans the way Ruth did.

In Ruth's case, statistical discrimination would not be a tenable argument. He had re-written the slugging record book. Ruppert would have been an all-time bigot if he had thrown Ruth off the team. The other owners, seeing Ruth's ability to pack their stadiums, might have remained silent, whatever their racial preferences. I suspect even Landis would have backed down. Much would have depended upon the fans' reaction. The owners may well have set aside their racial beliefs and protected their profits by retaining the Babe.

Let's consider the economics of discrimination based on preferences in general.[2]

Suppose I own a business in a small town and employ unskilled workers. The workers are currently all paid the same market-clearing wage determined by supply and demand. I sponsor a city league co-ed basketball team drawn from the ranks of my employees. Other employers in town do the same, also using unskilled workers. Players wear jerseys bearing the company's logo and results are printed in the local newspaper. Aside from illegal betting, there's no cash remuneration for players or employers, just the fun and thrill of competition. An owner who really wants to win may find herself opting to hire taller people, based on the observation that "you can't coach height." Since all workers are unskilled, there's no inherent productivity gain or loss from hiring mostly taller workers.

If I'm the only employer with a keen desire to win the city league, then there probably won't be too much effect on the local labor market. If all of the employers want to win, though, things change. There will be increased competition for tall employees that will likely be manifested in higher wages for such people. Since being tall has nothing to do with the principal work, we could label this "discrimination."

As the heightened demand for tall workers boosts their wages, the diminished demand for short workers lowers their wages. So far the predictions are straightforward: The favored workers gain, while the other workers lose. Less noted is that the employers have to pay to indulge their preference, as economist Gary Becker pointed out. Prejudice costs. (Of course, the basketball-loving owners believe that the benefits of having a winning team outweigh the higher cost.) A possible exception to this result would occur if there were severe unemployment in town, perhaps due to a minimum wage set above the hypothetical market-wage. Then employers would face reduced or no costs for discriminating.

While our example seems whimsical, studies show that, in reality, taller men earn more than shorter men. In a world where physical labor was paramount, the wage differential might have been a result of higher productivity on the part of larger and presumably stronger men. In our story, though, all workers are equally productive or unproductive, given that they are unskilled.

If you are an employer who doesn't care about fielding a winning city league basketball team, then you face an arbitrage opportunity. You can hire "cheap" short workers, cutting costs. If the other employers are making the same product as you, then you are likely to usurp their market share and possibly drive them out of business. In a real sense, then, a competitive, free market affords an element of protection against spurious discrimination.

Employers in town who still wish to discriminate might choose to get a minimum wage enacted, creating "excess labor." They might get the mayor and city council to pass an ordinance that either prohibits short people from producing the product or mandates that all employers must pay a premium for tall people. The discriminating employers need an outside force to curb the costs of discrimination.

What does our story have to do with professional sports? Although baseball owners appeared to have been able to maintain a "gentlemen's agreement" against introducing black players into Major League Baseball for most of the first half of the twentieth century, such discrimination should have gotten some of the owners of downtrodden teams to thinking: Why not hire cheap black players? Several potential obstacles become apparent. Black players might not be good enough. Games between white and black players could always be explained away as mere exhibitions that white players didn't take seriously. Teammates and fans might not accept black players. In the twenty-first century, though, few owners would be foolish enough to pass over top black players. The loss of productivity would be too obvious. The New York Yankees lagged in promoting black players to the major league, perhaps because they continued to win with their all-white squads. The Boston Red Sox waited until after Jackie Robinson retired before playing Pumpsie Green.

You'd expect discrimination where it's least costly, as in the cases of benchwarmers, coaches, or managers. Owners apparently don't think managers are very important, since their salaries are low in relation to players' salaries. Measuring a manager's ability is difficult. Give Casey Stengel the Yankees, and he wins with monotony; give him the Bums, Braves, or the Mets, and he loses with monotony. Also, the owner may have more face-to-face interaction with a coach or manager. If the owner is not comfortable dealing with people of different hues, then he is likely to discriminate in choosing a manager but not in choosing players.

So far we've dealt only with owners and their preferences. Owners may have been hesitant to employ black players, if they feared a negative response by white players and fans. Players have preferences, too. Some of Jackie Robinson's teammates were hesitant to play alongside him. Rival players taunted him mercilessly, and some refused to play against him. Fortunately, Happy Chandler, the successor to Commissioner Landis, backed Branch Rickey and Robinson. If enough players refused to play with black players, then owners might end up paying more for white players. The resulting team might not be as competitive as the "color-blind" teams. Players who enjoy playing only with similar teammates may pay for their preferences on the playing field.

Fans have preferences too, and it is not difficult to imagine that most fans in the 1940s may have preferred to watch white players.[3] They might have simply thought white players were better than blacks, as music lovers prefer the Chicago Symphony to the Podunk Symphony. Robinson's and other early black players' prowess, however, clearly debunked this argument. Even during the 1970s and 1980s, though, people whispered that the NBA suffered from having too many black players, although it was clear that black players were, if anything, superior.

Owners wondered whether white fans would be willing to sit next to black fans. When Jackie Robinson debuted for the Brooklyn Dodgers in 1947, black leaders encouraged blacks to be restrained in cheering for Robinson to reduce the chance of inter-racial altercations. Before the Milwaukee Braves moved to Atlanta, pollsters queried southern fans as to whether they would mind sitting next to "Negroes." The blacks, apparently, weren't asked whether they would mind sitting next to white folks. Anyway, the vast majority of those polled said such mixing would not bother them.

From an owner's perspective, fan response to black players would affect the marginal revenue. Had Brooklyn fans reacted adversely to Robinson's presence, then the team would have suffered at the gate. In reality, Robinson did not appear to have, on net, affected Brooklyn's home attendance, although the team may have increased ticket prices and thereby received more home gate revenue. Whether or not fans in Brooklyn or in other National League cities liked having black players, Robinson's debut, coinciding with the Dodgers' ascendance to the top of the National League, hiked the team's road attendance. Brooklyn became perennial leaders in road attendance, frequently outpacing even the mighty New York Yankees.

Still, if fans refused to welcome black players, even talented ones, owners might begin to pay premium prices for top white talent. Black players might end up in cities with more tolerant fans. Fans who did not like black players might pay for their preference by having a home team with less talent.

Equal Pay for Equal Talent?

Researchers have studied whether black players get paid the same as white players for given levels of performance. There is evidence that, up to the 1980s, blacks were paid less than equally talented white players. In hockey, there was evidence suggesting that French-Canadian players received less pay. More recently, though, it appears that equally productive black and white players make similar amounts.[4]

While such studies are useful, they may leave out part of the discrimination process. While stars may get the same pay regardless of color, journeyman players may not. An owner may recognize that it is costly to discriminate against star players, but may indulge in replacing black reserves with white reserves. Presumably the cost of discrimination to an owner is lower with regard to second-line players. Or an owner may appease fan preferences and make sure not to have "too many black players" by discriminating against the less-talented black players.

But even if there does not appear to be discrimination at the major league level, there could be other factors at work. First, various ethnic groups have, throughout history, selected certain occupations. Once they have established themselves in some craft, they trained their children in the craft and perpetuated the group's presence in the craft. Thus, it is unlikely that all occupations would perfectly represent the overall population. In the professional sports arena, such a situation is called "stacking." Unlike non-sports groups that self-selected into occupations, stacking was often dictated by employers and not by players. Blacks are found at the speed positions: running back and outfield. There are relatively few black quarterbacks or pitchers. However, such stacking is not done solely on the basis of race. French-Canadians are over-represented in certain positions in hockey. Certainly, observers can measure speed, so putting speedy players who happen to be black at running back or in the outfield makes sense. However, the outdated belief that blacks did not possess the mental capabilities to play quarterback persisted. Here, one can argue that there is discrimination based on inaccurate perceptions.

Second, members of some groups might have decreased access to the initial training for a particular sport or occupation. The lack of tennis courts in poor neighborhoods might keep talented but poor children from taking up tennis. Individual sports such as tennis, ice skating, and gymnastics may require a sizable financial investment by parents. Although those few members of a disadvantaged group who attain major league status may not be directly discriminated against by owners and fans anymore, they may, therefore, represent success against inordinate odds.

Demonstrating that discrimination exists is more difficult than most people realize. Aside from a tell-tale sign, such as an explicit law prohibiting hiring a particular group, discrimination frequently manifests itself in more subtle ways. Even if overt prejudice has been suppressed in our time, other factors may still lead to less-than-desirable outcomes. Sports reflect the larger society, so it should be no surprise to find discrimination in our stadiums and ballparks at times.

The Slow, Painful Process of Integration

Today's sports fans would find it unthinkable that professional sports could be devoid of African-American players. While Jackie Robinson is renowned for integrating Major League Baseball during the twentieth century, his fellow pioneers of integration in the NFL and NBA are less heralded.

Black players had played college football early in the twentieth century. Paul Robeson, a renaissance man if there ever was one, played football for Rutgers before playing professional football. Fritz Pollard was another talented African-American football player. George Preston Marshall, owner of the Washington team, among others, pressed his fellow owners to stop using black players. What can you expect from an owner whose team is nicknamed the "Redskins?" The NFL remained segregated until the end of World War II, when the upstart All-American Football Conference introduced Bill Willis and Marion Motley. These players' success forced NFL owners to seek top black talent of their own. Of course, black benchwarmers were not particularly welcome. Owners and coaches also proved hesitant to use African-American players as quarterbacks. Washington was the last to integrate.

The National Basketball League integrated during World War II. The league even had an entirely black team in the Dayton (New York) Rens. The team's player-coach William "Pop" Gates has never been accorded the recognition he deserved as being the first African-American coach in a white-run professional sports league. After Gates and a white player engaged in a brawl that spread to angry fans, though, the league owners quietly and temporarily released all of its black players.

Basketball owners certainly understood that some black players were outstanding players. The National Basketball League's champion Minneapolis Lakers lost two games against the Harlem Globetrotters. While these were exhibition games, most accounts describe hard-fought games. The Lakers had dominant center George Mikan, but the Globetrotters had smaller but quicker players. The games appear to have generated respect between the players.

The National Basketball Association (formerly the Basketball Association of America with several former National Basketball League teams joining the new NBA) integrated for the 1950-51 season. The owners may have hesitated in signing black talent, since Abe Saperstein, owner of the Harlem Globetrotters, monopolized such talent. Saperstein's team was a godsend to many of the struggling NBA owners, as an appearance by the Globetrotters guaranteed a large crowd, often an NBA team's biggest crowd of the season. NBA owners feared antagonizing Saperstein.

Chuck Cooper was the first African-American drafted; Earl Lloyd was the first black player to appear in an NBA game; and Nat "Sweetwater" Clifton was the first black player signed away from the Harlem Globetrotters. The NBA integrated relatively rapidly thereafter, with every team having a black player by 1955-56, well before baseball and football could make that claim. George Steinbrenner of the Cleveland Pipers in the short-lived American Basketball League had African-American John McLendon as coach. Steinbrenner and McLendon, in a presage of the owner's stormy relationship with his New York Yankees' managers, clashed over the way George treated the players (threatening to withhold their paychecks because of poor play). Most fans are familiar with Bill Russell's role as player-coach of the Boston Celtics. Wayne Embry became the NBA's first African-American general manager (of the Milwaukee Bucks).[5]

Saperstein's Harlem Globetrotters not only provided employment for top black players in the 1940s and 1950s, but it gave top black collegiate stars leverage in bargaining with NBA teams. Bill Russell, Wilt Chamberlain, and Oscar Robertson quickly vaulted to the top tier of NBA salaries because of Saperstein's lucrative offers. Chamberlain opted to forego his senior year with Kansas to play for the Globetrotters. He was able to force Philadelphia Warriors owner Eddie Gottlieb to pay him much more than any NBA player had ever received, when Saperstein tried to keep him on the Globetrotters with a handsome raise.

The black players in the early days of the NBA faced some overt racism on the court but more on the road. NBA owners contracted for many exhibition games in small towns across the country. In some towns, black players could not stay in the same motel with their teammates or eat in a decent restaurant. The earliest black players reminisced that they always ended up guarding each other and doing the "dirty" work on the court. They believed owners and coaches purposely kept them from being the leading scorer on the team, although Don Barksdale and Ray Felix led their teams in scoring as rookies. With the debuts of Maurice Stokes, Wilt Chamberlain, and Oscar Robertson, though, African-Americans quickly began dominating scoring, rebounding, and assist categories. Bill Russell presumably would have led the league in blocked shots, had the league bothered to keep such statistics. Russell and Chamberlain certainly attracted large crowds for their debuts and throughout their careers. Even if fans didn't like black players, they were willing to spend money watching such players compete with and against the white players.

Some black players expressed preferences over where they would play. Bill Russell apparently made it clear that he did not want to play in such small towns as Rochester; fortunately for him, Red Auerbach obtained him for Boston. Although Boston was not free of racism, Russell's ability to elevate the team to championship level helped gloss over unpleasant incidents.

While George Mikan had disagreements with Maurice White, owner of the Chicago American Gears, and Bob Cousy struggled to create an NBA players' association, such African-American players as Oscar Robertson proved more aggressive and persistent in asserting their rights and forming an effective players' association. Curt Flood and other black players were also in the forefront of the baseball players' movement.

Although blacks and whites have played games with and against each other for over a century, sports continue to engender discussion about race. While owners, players, and fans have rarely been at the forefront of progress, neither have they always lagged changes. Sports are probably better thought of as a reflection of social mores. Economics can help explain the ramifications of preferences but perhaps less about the formation of preferences.

CHAPTER 9

Keeping Out the Riff-Raff

Suppose you are the owner of a successful professional sports team. You've tamped down salaries, thanks to the reserve clause and player draft. You've received favorable rental terms from the municipally owned stadium. You've gotten wonderful tax-avoidance rulings from the IRS to shield your profits. Life is good. Life is so good that other people with money want their own team.

Established teams abhorred potential new teams. As we've seen, if owners were making an economic profit, it incited envy, as economic profits are hard to find. Envy inspired other potential firms to want to enter the market. New teams and leagues split the existing demand and eroded profits. In addition, more teams and leagues meant more competition for players, sending salaries upward. These twin squeezes on profitability spurred existing leagues to fight hard against interlopers.

For fans, new teams meant more choices because of the increased competition, and there were other benefits as well. In some cases, the upstart leagues introduced innovations.

If owner wannabes can't buy an existing team, they may band together to form their own league. Major League Baseball, the National Basketball Association, and the National Football League have had mixed success in their attempts to defeat such efforts. The National League defeated the American Association, Union Association, and Players' League. It reached an agreement with the American League. The two leagues successfully either broke or kept out the Federal League, the Mexican League, the Pacific Coast League, and the Continental League. The National Basketball Association was a merger of sorts with the older National Basketball League. The NBA fought off the American Basketball League, absorbing four teams from that league. The NFL knocked out the All-American Football Conference and eventually reached a détente with the American Football League which resembles that achieved by the two baseball leagues.

In order to keep interlopers out of a profitable industry, incumbent firms often erect barriers to entry. Economists have long studied barriers to entry. According to economists F.M. Scherer and David Ross, the rate of entry is higher when, "pre-entry profits are ample, when demand is growing rapidly, and when barriers associated with scale economies and product differentiation are low."[1] In addition, an entrant with an innovation may also be encouraged to enter. Baseball's American Association had such innovations as twenty-five cents admission, beer at the ballpark, and Sunday ballgames. These innovations thrilled many of baseball's German-American fans, who were used to frivolity after Sunday church services. The older, staid National League was aghast at such antics. The American Basketball Association featured the three-point, long-range shot and colorful red, white, and blue basketballs. The National Basketball Association eventually instituted the three-point shot, but drew the line at the colorful and very popular tri-colored ball.

Since a cartel, such as a professional team sports league, has better opportunities to earn economic profits than a purely competitive industry, the cartel will probably face envious potential entrants at frequent intervals.

Tactics to Combat Entry

What tactics can a cartel use to deter entry? Economist Robert Smiley investigated tactics used by incumbent firms to prevent entry. He surveyed managers and executives in manufacturing and service-industry firms and found that most of the managers and executives used at least one of the following methods occasionally:

(1) Set prices and market products to exploit learning and scale economy effects aggressively.
(2) Expand capacity.
(3) Advertise to cement customer loyalty.
(4) Seek patents on likely substitute products and technologies.
(5) Talk tough about responding to entry.
(6) Set limit prices to block entry.
(7) Set limit prices to slow the rate of entry.
(8) Introduce new product varieties to fill all product niches.
(9) Avoid disclosing profit data on individual product lines.[2]

Many of these activities are not directly applicable to professional team sports, but owners of sports teams employ the general tactics of using price as a weapon, practicing spatial pre-emption (filling enough desirable cities to keep a rival league out), talking tough, and hiding profitability.

Smiley did not ask respondents whether they had enlisted government intervention to raise barriers to entry. Incumbent firms might enlist political support for legislation directly benefiting the incumbents or stymieing potential entrants. His survey also did not include predatory pricing. Although the public likes to think that firms frequently engage in predatory pricing, the evidence suggests that such tactics as setting prices below short-run marginal or average variable cost are not pervasive. Predatory pricing differs from limit pricing, in that a firm practices limit pricing by setting a price lower than a full exploitation of its monopoly power so that it is unprofitable for a new firm to enter the market but not so low as to fall below marginal or average variable cost.

Playing Hardball with Interlopers

The established sports teams have always erected barriers to entry.

American sports leagues currently use a closed-circuit model: entry and exit happen only at the behest of incumbent teams. While American professional sports leagues guard against the entry of new teams, European soccer leagues sometimes use "relegation and promotion" processes. The bottom teams of the top league are relegated to the next-highest league, while that league's best teams are promoted. I've seen some city league basketball programs do the same. The winner in, say, the B Division is automatically moved into the A Division, while the last-place team in the A Division is demoted to the B Division. The relegation and promotion method spurs teams in the top division to remain competitive so that they can avoid relegation. The method also inspires players to play hard even in late-season games which might otherwise be meaningless. To use an American example, such a method would have forced the old St. Louis Browns and Philadelphia Athletics baseball teams to fight desperately to avoid last place during September.

At one level, though, American owners would dislike the relegation and promotion method, because they've long struggled to establish that their leagues possess, without a doubt, the top teams in their sports. The idea of replacing the bottom teams with teams from a lower-tier league blurs that distinction. Some observers felt that Jack Dunn's International

League Baltimore Orioles and the New York Yankees' top farm club in Newark during the late 1930s could have given the worst American League teams stiff competition. Whether these minor league teams were, indeed, good enough to beat the Athletics and Browns was a question that I suspect American League owners did not want to have answered.

The National League discouraged barnstorming by its teams. The older, looser form of professional baseball, such as the National Association, featured games with a variety of opponents. By avoiding such contests, the National League hoped to create and to maintain an aura of being the true elites of the game. The National League and other major leagues prohibited their members from playing "outlaw" teams; since potential rival franchises could not get games with major league teams, such teams had difficulty establishing credibility. The National League struggled to end the "exhibition" games with other professional teams, though, as individual team owners could collect additional revenue from such games while the league stood to have its reputation diminished by losses. When the major league players barnstormed and played top players from the Negro League, owners quickly emphasized the exhibition nature of the games if the white big-leaguers lost.

In professional basketball, well into the 1950s, top amateur and semi-pro teams, as well as the Harlem Globetrotters, provided reasonable competition for NBA teams. Occasionally, the Globetrotters signed the best collegiate talent, including, as mentioned, Wilt Chamberlain. The team tried to entice Oscar Robertson, but he did not sign. Obviously, a team with Wilt Chamberlain might have fulfilled Moses Malone's later prophecy of "me and four guys from Petersburg" being able to compete with top NBA teams. Conversely, the idea of Chamberlain playing against local amateurs in Globetrotter games seizes the imagination.

Most American leagues play hardball with potential entrants. Although established leagues are loath to countenance interlopers, they rarely relied upon price wars. Your local gas station back in the 1960s might have launched periodic price wars with neighboring stations, but big league moguls usually disdained such tactics. Why? Because making such threats is usually not believable.

Why is a price war usually not credible? Take a familiar example: Mom and Dad take the two kids on a long car ride to Florida's Disney World. After hours of driving with bickering in the back seat, they arrive at the theme park. Once within the gates, Muffy and Billy renew their argument. Dad yells in an irritated voice, "If you kids don't stop arguing, we're going to get back in the car and drive back to Chillicothe." (I've never been to Chillicothe, but it sounds more dramatic than, say, Cleveland.) Any child over three will simply roll its eyes at dad's threat and continue bickering.

Dad has made a non-credible threat. The kids know that Dad, who has anticipated this vacation for months, is not likely to quash his own pleasure, not to mention Mom's, over a common tiff. As a middle-aged bachelor, I'm puzzled why parents make such ridiculous threats, although one of my students claimed that his folks actually made his siblings and him get into the car for the premature return home. I guess it scarred him psychologically, so it was an "Oprah" moment for our class.

Here's another example. Suppose your ne'er-do-well cousin moves into your apartment. Besides being a slob, he monopolizes your couch and munches on your chips. You want him out of the house, so you threaten him: "I'm going to punch myself in the face until you leave." Naturally, your cousin continues to watch his favorite show; he might even have the temerity to ask for more chips the next time you go to the corner grocery store. He may well appreciate the live entertainment that you are providing. Your threat is laughably pathetic. Yet, a price war is, in many cases, analogous to punching oneself in the face. If incumbent owners threaten a price war, a potential entrant will view it as a non-credible threat in most cases.

The conundrum is this: How can one make the threat credible? An incumbent league might decide to launch a price war, hoping to establish a reputation for being crazy. Apparently Richard Nixon understood this point, as he strove to make sure that the Russians and Chinese would never be completely sure about "that crazy Nixon." A nutty price war might deter the current entrants and even future entrants. However, most owners don't appear to put much credence in such a strategy.

Historically, such price-cutting tactics occasionally backfired badly. During the Gilded Age, two rail barons were in a take-no-prisoners struggle to dominate New York shipping.

> The main competitor of the New York Central (controlled by Cornelius Vanderbilt) was the Erie, a railroad controlled by Daniel Drew, James Fisk, and Jay Gould. Vanderbilt fought a rate war against the Erie. He once cut the rate for cattle between Buffalo and New York on the New York Central to $1 a head as part of the battle. However, his rival, Jim Fisk, did not retaliate in kind. He took advantage of Vanderbilt's cheap fares by buying beef in Buffalo that he then shipped

on the New York Central. He thus made a profit on the price of beef in New York City while at the same time weakening the Vanderbilt system, which had to accommodate the extra freight below cost.[3]

Vanderbilt was no fool, but he apparently lost his head (which made it easier for him to lose his shirt) this time. Professional sports owners do make mistakes, but price-cutting doesn't appear to be one of them.

Baseball owners' experiences using price as a weapon has a mixed record. While the American Association charged twenty-five cents admission, the established National League did not match the lower price and continued to charge fifty cents. Only when a National League team was in extremis, such as the Philadelphia club, did the other NL owners countenance a temporary drop in admission prices. The Union Association entered the baseball fray in 1884 against the established National League and American Association. The new league decided to charge twenty-five cents per admission instead of the usual fifty cents. While the lower price helped the league draw fans, it was too low to be sustainable. The league promptly folded, although lack of a pennant race also contributed to its demise. The American Association also found that maintaining a twenty-five cent price was not feasible and increased the price to fifty cents by 1888. On occasion, the National League used the fifty-cent base admission to destroy a franchise. This was the fate of Henry Lucas' St. Louis franchise. Lucas had organized the Union Association and owned that league's St. Louis franchise. In return for turning against his former associates, the National League granted him a franchise in St. Louis. The American Association's incumbent St. Louis club was aghast, but the National League prohibited Lucas from playing Sunday ball, selling beer, or charging twenty-five cents. As these were key selling points for St. Louis baseball fans, Lucas' inability to use them doomed his franchise.[4]

Sports team owners also try to forestall envy, the necessary precursor to entry, by painting a dismal picture of their experiences. When it suits their needs, owners of professional sports teams cry, "Losses!" The owners attempt to camouflage profitability in order not to attract envious potential owners. During the flush times after the National and American Leagues' agreement, the leagues stopped publishing attendance figures. Up until the 1930s, baseball box scores in the *Sporting News* or *New York Times* did not include attendance. Reporters might estimate attendance, and, given that the stadium capacities were known, come close to the actual figures, but owners were hesitant to reveal the true figures. If, instead, they were fighting a new league, owners would baldly inflate attendance figures.

Heaven help an interested reporter or researcher delving into teams' profitability. That was not allowed. Occasionally the Yankees might let a New York sportswriter see some of the books, but more generally any discussion of baseball economics was couched in general terms. One researcher in the late 1940s came across some Yankees' ledgers in a used bookstore. When he returned to purchase them, the bookstore owner informed him that a Yankees' official had come in and retrieved the ledgers. The Yankees firmly rebuffed the researcher's requests to examine them for his undergraduate thesis.[5]

Fortunately for sports researchers, the leagues could not disguise the popularity of such exhibitions as the World Series. In addition, the construction boom and increasing sales prices of existing franchises described earlier demonstrated the profitability of owning a Major League Baseball team. These attempts to hide profitability did not succeed in deterring investors from starting the Federal League.

The early National Basketball Association owners were not crying "Wolf," when they pled poverty. The winnowing of teams from seventeen to eight within four or five seasons indicated the lack of profits. When the basketball owners, along with their peers in football, baseball, and hockey, had to divulge profit/loss figures to a Congressional committee in 1957, I suspect they were embarrassed. The eight NBA teams' combined gate receipts barely topped that of the New York Yankees. Anecdotal evidence also confirmed the NBA owners' extreme poverty. Not until the late 1950s did teams begin earning profits consistently and franchise values begin to rise.

Physical Barriers to Entry

Owners of incumbent teams erected other barriers to entry. The development of steel and concrete stadiums during the first two decades of the twentieth century signaled the burgeoning wealth and stability of major league teams. Early ballparks consisted of wooden grandstands seating fewer than ten thousand patrons and typically costing less than $20,000. For instance, a park in Baltimore cost $5,000 to build in 1883, while another park in Buffalo cost $6,000. However, such inexpensive ballparks were soon replaced by grander wooden structures. Even by the late 1890s refurbishing or remodeling ballparks cost in the tens of thousands of dollars.[6] During baseball's prosperity in the early years of the twentieth century, concrete and steel ballparks replaced the wooden structures. The new stadiums were larger and more permanent than the older wooden stands; in a sense, the new stadiums were a form of expanding capacity to capture more of the demand. Major League Baseball had a frenzy of stadium building between 1906 and 1915, when most of the teams constructed new stadiums. Yankee Stadium arose in the early 1920s. Between the construction of Yankee Stadium and the municipally built stadiums of the 1950s, only Cleveland constructed a new (municipally built) stadium.

These expensive stadiums also served as physical barriers to entry. It's not enough to get eight investors to start a league. Your investors have to own or have access to playing venues. Stadiums are a large capital investment. Getting land for stadiums could be foiled by political chicanery. Despite these potential difficulties, the Federal League hurriedly built several new ballparks early in 1914. According to historian Marc Okkonen, these ballparks were combinations of wood, concrete, and steel. All cost over $100,000 and some of them cost as much as $500,000.[7] The National League Chicago Cubs eventually acquired the Chicago Federal League's ballpark, now known as Wrigley Field. While the Federal League was able to construct adequate ballparks, these parks were not as good as those possessed by major league teams. The Federal League's parks had a maximum seating capacity of 21,000 (Newark), while most of the parks seated 15,000 to 20,000 people. Aside from the Chicago Cubs, Brooklyn Dodgers, and Philadelphia Phillies, all the major league teams played in parks seating over 20,000 and, in some cases, up to 40,000. Shibe Park (home of the Philadelphia Athletics) and Ebbets Field each cost around $500,000.[8] Steven Riess believes the ten major league parks cost an average of $500,000 to construct.[9] Owning superior stadiums helped incumbent major league owners to fight new leagues. By the 1950s, although there were some cities outside of Major League Baseball that possessed adequate stadiums, a new league hoping to plant franchises in New York or Chicago needed to use existing stadiums or get city officials and voters to build a new stadium. The incumbent owners naturally refused to rent their stadiums to interlopers. During the war with the Federal League, the major league owners threatened to operate "continuous baseball" whereby one of their minor league teams would occupy the big league stadium when the parent team was on the road.[10] The minor leagues, of course, disliked the threatened disruption of their leagues, so the proposal was not implemented. The "permanent" stadiums also increased the credibility of the major league owners; any upstart league would confront businessmen who had large sunk costs and were committed to remaining in the market, so the incumbents' threats took on credibility.

Controlling a Key Input: Players

Fledgling baseball leagues in the nineteenth and twentieth-centuries had difficulty getting the crucial input: players. The National League initially co-existed peacefully with the American Association in the 1880s. The American Association initially consisted of previously existing teams. The league did not make widespread raids upon National League rosters prior to its initial season. After the 1882 season, though, the American Association offered contracts to some National League players but had mixed success in signing any. The bidding led to higher salaries for players in both leagues. Any potential hostilities between the two leagues were mitigated by the rise of the Union Association with its heretical ban of the reserve clause. The National League and American Association decided to forestall the Union Association by denying the upstart league's teams' access to ballplayers. The Union Association's St. Louis franchise was successful in signing players from the two older leagues, but the remainder of the infant league signed only a few major leaguers. The Union Association was unable to retain all of its meager collection of major leaguers, as the two older leagues were able to entice contract and reserve jumpers to come back to their original leagues before the end of 1884.

The two incumbent leagues' most prominent method of denying access to players was to threaten to blacklist any of their players who jumped contract or reservation. To make it clear to the reader, a blacklist in, say, accountancy would operate thusly: If a talented accountant, Philbert Figure, sought to leave the Uriah Heep Accountancy firm for the start-up Babbitt firm, Heep might yell, "Figure, you'll never work in organized accountancy again if you leave!" If you think such threats are imaginary, NBA player Ed Macauley recalled a similar threat uttered by league president Maurice Podoloff: "If you so much as think of going to the other league you'll be sued, you'll be out of basketball, and your career will come to an end."[11] Such draconian measures generated unfavorable publicity, and the National League and American Association were forced to rescind the blacklist against some players (although these players were fined); the owners waited to rescind the blacklist only after the Union Association folded. By rescinding the blacklist in 1884, though, baseball owners were reducing the credibility of future blacklists.

Rules controlling players served to deter entry. During the fracas with the Union Association, the National League and the American Association formed "reserve teams," made up of semi-pro and amateur players. These reserve teams not only forestalled Union Association teams from obtaining some of these players but they also served as a threat to current major league players. As major league owners created farm systems, they controlled hundreds of players. During the twentieth-century, owners again threatened to blacklist any player who jumped to a new league. The blacklists may have helped major league owners maintain player discipline, although the Mexican League made a few prominent signings after World War II. The player pension also served to keep players in line. A player tempted to join another league might forfeit his pension funds if he jumped. When some players reacted by threatening to seek legal interpretation of the reserve clause in the aftermath of Mexican League raids in the late 1940s, major league owners quickly retracted the blacklists.

While college football and basketball produced highly publicized players for professional leagues, even the best college baseball players were non-entities until very recently. A nascent baseball league could not hope, therefore, to gain credibility by signing the top collegiate players, while the American Basketball Association strove mightily to sign Lew Alcindor (later Kareem Abdul-Jabbar) and other worthies. The American Football League teams also scrambled to sign top collegiate talent, and their television backers advanced them money in order to do so.

Major league owners' control of minor league teams also helped deter minor league teams in larger cities from aspiring to major league status. The Pacific Coast League owners attempted to stop major league teams from "drafting" their players during the 1940s. The PCL hoped to stockpile adequate talent to attain major league status. Some independent minor league teams were able to protect impressive amounts of talent, such as Jack Dunn's Baltimore Orioles of the 1920s with Lefty Grove and George Earnshaw. In general, though, major league owners stripped the minor league teams of their best talent. The major-minor agreements, though, were not completely one-sided, as the minor league teams received protection of their territorial rights.

League owners and officials denied that the intent of the strict controls over players was to monopolize players. They peddled the party line that the player control rules were necessary to protect the major and minor leagues and to prevent anarchy.

Proclaiming Your Superiority

The National League struggled to establish the reputation for playing the best baseball. Albert Spalding, an early National League pioneer, recognized the league's need for favorable publicity in establishing its elite status. One of his fellow investors in the Chicago White Stockings was the owner of the *Chicago Herald*. Spalding also cultivated the favor of city officials by giving them season passes, the best free seats going to the mayor and other higher-ranking officials.[12]

Other early team owners resorted to bombastic advertising. Chris von der Ahe, owner of the Union Association's St. Louis Browns, boasted in an ad, "THE BROWNS ARE HERE! [caps his] The Hardest Hitters, the Finest Fielders, the Best Base-Runners, and Coming Champions."[13] His team backed his boasts, as they captured four consecutive American Association titles. Other owners employed more discreet advising, placing ads on streetcars, street corners, and handbills. Once leagues prepared schedules in advance, teams were better able to inform their customers of upcoming games.

A recognized and accepted "world's championship" helps sports leagues establish themselves as elite. Having a true championship series was an advantage of having two leagues. The American Association and National League stumbled upon a successful endeavor when the champions played an informal series in 1884. The series generated good crowds and favorable publicity for a number of years until the antipathy between the leagues ended cooperative ventures. Fans appeared to have accepted the series as determining the best team in baseball. After achieving its monopoly in the 1890s, the National League attempted to replicate the success of the post-season series by pitting its first and second-place teams in a set of games, but these series did not appeal to the public as they were anticlimactic. The first-place teams sometimes did not take the championship matches seriously. In this case, splitting the twelve-team league into two divisions might have boosted the League Championship. The American League and National League champions informally held a set of games after the 1903 season; while this series was successful, the New York Giants' enmity towards the American League precluded a repeat in 1904. Thereafter, the World Series became a popular annual event. Even the title, "World Series," helped reinforce the idea that Major League Baseball represented the acme of baseball. Readers will note that in baseball, the "World" was confined to the northeast quadrant of the United States.

If a league did not truly boast the finest players on the planet, its owners could still boast that their teams were superior, at least in front of the home crowd. The threat of new leagues created subtle changes in umpiring in both the new and incumbent leagues in attempts to attract fans. Baseball statistician Craig Wright reports that teams in new leagues, such as the American League in 1902, where the home teams won 63 percent of the games instead of the normal 52–53 percent, and the Federal League in 1914–15, won a higher proportion of home games than normal. The National League, too, often responded with higher home winning percentages during these league wars. In addition, during times of economic downturns, the home teams fared better. As Wright explains:

> The magnitude of the [American League record of 1902] seems unbelievable without conscious intent by either the umpires or the teams themselves to favor the home team. Given the maverick nature of most expansion leagues, I would suspect the umpires, who were direct employees of the league. After the NL accepted the AL in the treaty of 1903, the home-field advantage in the AL dropped below .600, and by 1904 it was all the way down to .535 ... it seemed that whenever the game had reason to worry about attendance or popularity, home-field advantage would escalate. I don't mean to imply there were overt instructions in these latter cases, as I suspect happened in 1902. But there may have been subtle encouragement in one form or another, perhaps in an occasional philosophical hint about the need to entertain the troubled masses.[14]

While the National League appears to have reacted to the new leagues' penchant for tilting the playing field, the possibility of an established league using such subtle tactics to help forestall entry should not be ignored.

The NBA's early years were also marked by home teams winning 64 percent or more of the games. Some observers thought the small fieldhouses and lack of a permanent referee staff contributed to the skewed home/road records.

Enlisting Friends from City Hall to Fight Interlopers

Baseball owners welcomed politicians as fellow owners, as historians Ted Vincent and Steven Riess document. As Riess wrote, "Politically connected owners used clout to benefit their baseball business just as they did for any other investment. Political influence assured lower tax assessments and minimal license fees, cheap or free police protection, and security against interlopers. Friends at city hall also supplied inside information about property values, anticipated land uses, and mass-transit plans, invaluable knowledge for teams selecting a playing field. On the other hand, owners without protection were vulnerable to political pressure for passes or payoffs. Such owners might encounter repeated inspections by fire marshals or even the construction of city streets through the field."[15]

To maintain amity with local politicians or to cultivate future political favors, owners supplied generous numbers of free passes to games. In their war with the nascent American League, National League owners hoped that political connections in New York would prevent the upstart league from placing a franchise in the city. The New York Giants' owner, Andrew Freedman, was an ally of the Tammany Hall political machine and was also a director of the Interborough Rapid Transit Construction Company building the underground. In the words of Dana Carvey's "Church Lady," "How convenient." Freedman and the Tammany Hall machine impeded potential owners from getting property on which to build a stadium that had access to mass transit. Eventually American League President Ban Johnson struck a deal with a Tammany politician by granting part ownership.[16] The rumored threat of the City of Cincinnati building a street through John Brush's Cincinnati Reds ballpark induced him to sell his club; ironically, he purchased the New York Giants in 1902 and stood to gain from Tammany Hall threats against any American League interlopers. Ben Shibe, owner of the Philadelphia Athletics, gained from insider knowledge concerning land that was being used for a hospital for contagious diseases. Shibe found out that the hospital was going to be closed, and he was able to purchase the land cheaply.[17]

The owners also recognized that trolley and rail services were complementary to baseball. Several trolley companies and railroads held stock in various baseball teams. The trolley-owned baseball teams might divert their rails and services away from potential rivals in the city, leaving those rivals without convenient mass transit.

Pre-Empting Entry of Rival Teams

Incumbent leagues could use spatial pre-emption, placing teams in most of the cities capable of supporting teams, to stymie a new league. The National League probably goofed after the 1876 season. Because the New York and Philadelphia teams refused to make their final western road trip, the league booted them. There were other teams in New York and

Philadelphia, but the National League did not select any of them as replacements. The American Association eventually exploited this oversight and established teams in these cities. The two leagues would exist under an uneasy truce for most of a decade. The National League decided to combat the Union Association's attempt to place a team in Chicago by considering a second franchise in Chicago. "Sooner or later there will doubtless be a second club in Chicago, and in the way proposed you might not only secure the advantage of having both clubs, but at the same time freeze out the Union Association, and, possibly, also provide against the contingency of losing your Lake Front grounds (the Union Association did not play in Chicago during 1884)."[18]

Why did the National League succeed in driving out the American Association (after several years), Union Association, and Players' League but not the American League? The National League shrank from twelve to eight teams as the so-called "Gay Nineties" ended. By the time the National League realized that the American League was a threat, the League's actions were inadequate to prevent the new league from attaining major league status. The National League attempted to award minor league franchises in towns recently vacated by Ban Johnson's league, as well as granting the American Association (a minor league that arose after the demise of the major league American Association) franchises in some eastern cities. All these actions were taken to stymie the American League. The National League appeared to have fumbled its opportunity to thwart the American League's survival and acceptance as a major league by not more adroitly pre-empting some choice cities. While the National League tried to prevent the American League from getting a New York franchise, they left some attractive cities open for American League franchises: Detroit, in particular. Some of the American League franchises were teams purged in 1899 from the National League. Collectively these cities were viable options for Major League Baseball, and, indeed, the American League outdrew the National League for most of the first decade of the twentieth century.

With peace declared, the National and American Leagues enjoyed a joint-monopoly for over a decade. Their success inspired the creation of the Federal League. To defuse the Federal League threat (presumably before the 1914 season), the major leagues considered launching a third "major league" by combining the strongest minor league franchises from the International and American Association.[19] They never implemented this measure. The Federal League lasted a few seasons before expiring. One team sued the incumbent leagues, leading to the bizarre Supreme Court ruling that baseball was not interstate commerce and was thus exempt from antitrust legislation. The league left Wrigley Field in Chicago as its main legacy.

With the demise of the Federal League, the major leagues survived the Great Depression and World War II. With prosperity returning in the late 1940s, two threats to the leagues' hegemony arose. Some wealthy Mexican brothers decided to bankroll their own league. There seemed to be a surfeit of players available, given the wartime backlog of players returning from military service. A few prominent major leaguers signed with the Mexican businessmen, but most quickly became disenchanted with playing conditions south of the border and as the Mexican owners' money began to run out. A few years later, Los Angeles and San Francisco, of the Pacific Coast League, agitated for major league status. The other teams in the PCL were in cities not quite large enough, though, to support big league baseball in the 1950s, and the idea was stillborn.

The Major Leagues Fight the Continental League

After remaining with a stable roster of teams for fifty seasons, the National and American League saw the migration of six teams to new venues during the 1950s. The relocation wave culminated with the Brooklyn Dodgers and New York Giants vacating New York City after 1957 for Los Angeles and San Francisco. The National League again failed to replace the Dodgers and Giants immediately. With the growth of cities such as Houston, Minneapolis, Atlanta, and with an obvious vacancy in New York, the sixteen-team major leagues were vulnerable to a potential entrant, such as the Continental League. In the Continental League case, the existing leagues did not practice spatial pre-emption, until it was almost too late.

When the fledgling Continental League attempted to become the third major league, observers felt that getting major league caliber players would be its biggest obstacle. The big league teams whined that there weren't enough such players, and they certainly didn't want to share any of theirs with the interlopers. After the Continental League scheme collapsed, the major league owners suddenly "solved" the player scarcity problem and stocked four expansion teams with "major league" players via expansion drafts. Expansion teams could select the dregs of existing clubs' forty-player rosters, although a large proportion of the players offered had to be on the twenty-five man major league roster. In addition to this pool of talent, expansion teams had another significant advantage over potential teams in upstart leagues: Major league teams would condescend to play them. Thus, the Washington Senators 2.0 and the Los Angeles Angels got to host the mighty New York Yankees, which was something a potential Continental League team could only dream of. The Yankees provided as much as a third of the expansion teams' home gates for the first few years. Apparently, watching half a major league game was enough for Senator and Angel fans.

The established major league teams might have resorted to using political pressure to keep out new entrants, but Congress' tenor changed during the 1950s as growing cites in the west and the south clamored for big league baseball. Congress began pressuring baseball owners to relocate or expand. Branch Rickey recognized an opportunity: seize New York City for a new league and hope for favorable Congressional intervention.

Since the baseball owners could not be perceived as stonewalling efforts to place major league teams in the growing cities, they prevaricated. The major league owners issued unctuous greetings to the prospective Continental League. The incumbent owners claimed to welcome the Continental League owners if these owners would meet certain standards, as set by the incumbent owners. These standards included placing teams in cities with sufficiently large stadiums and matching the existing player pension rules. The incumbent owners tried to appear reasonable, but, upon reflection, an astute fan would see how ludicrous the proclamation was. The incumbent owners' proclamation would be similar to two grocery store chains in a city dictating the terms for new grocery chains to enter the market.[20]

Ultimately, major league owners always possessed a trump card in forestalling a new league: They could expand into viable cities and forestall a new league, such as the Continental League.[21] By expanding by four teams in 1961 and 1962 and four more teams in 1969, Major League Baseball filled enough of the viable cities to preclude further talk of new leagues.

Of course, expansion, while pre-empting potential entrants, had its disadvantages. More teams meant greater pressure to obtain good players; divided the national television pie into smaller pieces; and reduced exclusivity. In addition, having more teams often means that established teams played each other less frequently, diminishing crucial rivalries. We can assume that existing owners considered these factors when establishing fees for new franchises. Note that expansion fees have generally risen faster than changes in the Consumer Price Index, strongly suggesting robust economic health.

The owners in other sports used many of the same tactics as did the National League, but these football and basketball owners were not completely successful with the tactics either. The American Football League was relatively successful in challenging the National Football League, but the new league received crucial infusions of cash and credibility by landing a national television contract. The American Basketball Association was not as fortunate, although four of its teams were absorbed into the National Basketball Association. In the latter case, the players fought hard to prevent the merger, realizing the deleterious effects on salaries.

Thus, the professional leagues have had mixed success in keeping out interlopers, but the leagues' failures have not been due to lack of effort.

Conclusion

What have we learned during our tour of the economics of professional team sports?

Scarcity drives economics. Even wealthy owners face scarcity. Scarcity means that using a resource for one purpose incurs an opportunity cost: the cost of the best foregone alternative use. Identifying opportunity costs is crucial in making good decisions. A person making a decision should weigh marginal benefit and marginal cost.

By using the concept of economic profits, a fan can get a better understanding of how decisions are made.

Basic economic principles, such as supply and demand, help explain why ticket prices and player salaries are higher today than in the past.

Knowledge of basic probability theory and statistics helps us understand whether events in sports are rare or not and how difficult it is to measure productivity in sports, even with a plethora of statistics. Although professional sports are not coin tosses, coin tosses can sometimes serve as a model for sports statistics.

The strategic interactions between teams within a league and between teams and players make sports a fruitful place to apply basic game theory tools. The Prisoner's Dilemma concept helps illuminate why price fixing is difficult without outside enforcement. Principal/agent tools demonstrate how owners might create incentives for players to do their best. Game theory also shows why an astute coach might buy a random number generator to create predictable unpredictability.

While professional team sports receive much publicity, their actual impact on a local economy tends to be limited. There's little evidence that building new stadiums and enticing teams to relocate really helps a local economy. Usually, expenditures on stadiums and teams are a re-shuffling of spending in the local economy.

The demand for sporting events depends upon a number of factors. Because owners have territorial protection, they have some discretion over prices. By measuring the demand, owners can calculate the most profitable prices to charge for admission. In general, the demand for sports has grown throughout the past century. Under such an environment and coupled with the advantages of the reserve clause, favorable depreciation allowances, and frequent public financing of stadiums, it is difficult to see how owners can incur economic losses. The rising values of franchises and fees charged for expansion franchises may prove better clues as to profitability.

Part of the demand for sporting events results from the uncertainty of the outcome. Fans appear to like uncertainty, although they also value seeing the best teams, even if the presence of the best team means a high probability that the weaker home team will lose. Too much dominance by a superior team, though, squelches the competitive balance and may prove disastrous to a league. Ascertaining and achieving the optimal competitive balance has proven elusive. On average, leagues may desire that teams in the larger cities win more frequently, but just how much more frequently remains obscure.

Attempts to redress competitive imbalance have often been an illusion. Owners, as a group, may feel that such ultimately futile attempts appease fans while disguising other benefits, which include reducing the demand for star players and salaries.

Economists believe that the primary result of switching from the reserve clause to free agency should be a shift of the economic rent associated with a player's productivity from the owners to the players. The effect upon competitive balance may be minimal. Other nostrums, such as revenue sharing, reverse-order drafts, and salary caps, may not significantly affect competitive balance.

Ultimately, moving teams to larger cities, including placing more teams in the largest cities, or preventing the movement of players (coupled with a reverse-order draft) appear to be more effective in creating parity. However, complete parity may not be optimal in terms of collective profits.

Revenue sharing may not really be about reducing disparities in revenues and creating competitive balance. Instead, revenue sharing may be initiated at the behest of strong teams in large cities. Owners of these teams may desire a system where they are rewarded for bringing their teams into smaller cities and generating large gates. Because Major League Baseball had long exhibited a strong connection between a team's win-loss record and its ability to draw on the road, its revenue-sharing plan was not particularly effective in helping the teams in smaller cities. Baseball's less "generous" plans were not really the culprits for the modest transfers to weak teams; it was the structure of attendance that mattered. Even in the reputedly generous National Football League, owners often paid lip service to revenue sharing while plotting to evade its effects, as witness the growth of luxury boxes.

Professional athletes make big money because they are supremely talented. They represent the apex of a huge pyramid of performers. In addition, because of growing demand for the games they play, thanks in part to network and cable television, they enjoy a wide but shallow demand for their services. While an individual might be willing to pay more for their child to have a capable teacher than to watch some ball games, the teacher can accommodate only a limited number of students. Thanks to technology, a player can entertain and thrill billions of fans.

The reserve clause created single-buyer bidding for a player's services, thereby depressing his earnings. Free agency pushed player salaries closer to the respective marginal revenue products. Instead of being some of the most exploited workers in America, professional athletes are now free to earn market wages after a number of years of playing. The switch from the reserve clause to free agency may have had small effect on competitive balance.

Players have frequently discriminated or have been discriminated against throughout sports history. Owners, fans, and players, at times, discriminated against black players, among others. Economists identify the costs of discrimination. In a competitive market, owners who wish to exercise a personal preference have to pay for their preferences. Of course, the group that is not favored receives lower salaries. However, this group has a measure of protection under the market, if other owners are willing to exploit the arbitrage opportunity created by owners with strong preferences.

Because professional sports teams are generally economically profitable, as witnessed by their increasing franchise values, other wealthy people desire to own teams. If they can't buy an existing team, they may be tempted by the economic profits to create a new team and a new league. The incumbent leagues have shown ruthlessness in preventing such entry, just as economic theory predicts.

The games on the playing field, then, are games-within-a-game. There are other, equally competitive, games being played in the front offices and the legislative arenas. An understanding of economics makes such activities easier to understand.

Chapter Notes

Chapter 1

1. The author's geometry teacher, who was also the head football coach, once pointed out that one should never make assumptions. He wrote, a-s-s u m-e on the board. "When you assume, you make an ass out of you and out of me." This was football wisdom par excellence. I sometimes wonder what he would think, if he knew I make my living by making assumptions.

2. Hazlitt 1946, pp. 23–24.

3. We're assuming the values are in present values: They are adjusted for the fact that a dollar received today is more valuable than a dollar received in the future, as you can invest the dollar received today. We'll discuss present value later in the chapter.

4. Recall that total revenue increases as you decrease the price in the region of elastic demand; total revenue also increases as you increase the price in the region of inelastic demand. Once you reach the point of unitary elasticity, there's no way to further increase total revenue.

5. Since the tax affected all ticket prices by the same 9.1 percent or 10 percent proportion, there shouldn't be any substitution between seat classes.

6. Burton Folsom, Jr.'s *The Myth of the Robber Barons* makes this distinction clear. James H. Hill built his railroad with private funds, while the builders of the transcontinental railroad relied upon government land grants (they also built shoddy railroads). Rockefeller and Carnegie concentrated upon containing costs. It is interesting to note that many of the alleged Robber Barons endowed some of America's finest universities: University of Chicago, Vanderbilt, Stanford, Carnegie-Mellon, and Duke. Years ago, Stanford's student body voted to change the school's mascot from Indians to Robber Barons. The university's trustees were not amused. This august board also stymied the students' second choice: Thunder Chickens.

Chapter 2

1. Almost forty years ago, the UCLA Bruins thoroughly dominated men's basketball. The team came to Eugene, Oregon, to play the Oregon Ducks. Apparently, one Los Angeles fan was so confident of the Bruins' superiority that he told his daughter he would buy her a new bike if Oregon won. The Ducks won, and I presume he honored his promise. Note, though, that he did not bet his life.

2. Noll 1998, no page numbers.

3. Now that "boy-wonder" Theo Epstein has left and returned to the Red Sox, perhaps he should have uttered a curse, thereby generating future fan and pundit interest: "The Curse of the Boy Wonder."

4. Tversky and Gilovich 1989.

5. For a quick explanation of baseball's Pythagorean Theorem, see *http://www.sciencedaily.com/releases/2004/03/0403300902 59.html* (viewed March 21, 2010).

6. St. John 2005, p. W6.

7. As an historical aside, economist

Roger Babson kept warning throughout the late 1920s that the stock market was destined to crash. In his account of the Great Crash, John Kenneth Galbraith immortalized Babson (Galbraith, *Great Crash*). Yet what was Babson's real record? As month after month went by and the market continued to rise, what credence was there to Babson's babbling? After all, with enough people making predictions, someone is bound to be right. Just recall those supermarket tabloid psychics who predict that someone famous will die in the coming year. More recently, Ravi Batra wrote a book entitled *The Great Depression of 1990*. You may have slept through said Depression. Subsequently, Batra wrote some other diatribe against contemporary economic policy. The blurb on the back cover said, "By the author of *The Great Depression of 1990*." That blurb should have squelched any credibility the author had.

8. Using 1998–2000 American League data, I ran regression equations. Using "Runs per At-Bat" as the dependent variable (the variable being affected by the independent variables), and On-Base Percentage and Slugging Average as the independent variables yielded:

Runs/At-Bat = -0.189 + 0.757(On-Base Pct.) + 0.171(Slugging Average). Both independent variables were statistically significant at the 0.1 percent level. The equation explained 90 percent of the variance. An equation using Runs had a similar four-to-one ratio: Runs = -1,121 + 4,260(On-Base Pact.) + 1,084(Slugging Average).

Again the variables were statistically significant and the R-Square was over 90 percent. Using data from 1975–78 yielded a three-to-one ratio.

9. This brings up the *Sports Illustrated* cover jinx. You make the cover by performing some feat that is out of the ordinary, your shining moment so to speak. The reader should not be surprised that your subsequent performances pale in comparison.

10. Boyle 1961, p. 17.

11. Thorn, Palmer, and Gershman 2001, pp. 539–542.

Chapter 3

1. Sullivan 1900–25, Vol. II, p. 322.

2. C.C. Spink, 12 December 1964, p. 4.

3. U.S. Senate 1965, p. 117.

4. U.S. Senate 1964, p. 358.

5. Smith [1776] 1976, p. 145.

6. One rather medieval approach would be for both parties to exchange hostages. If one of the participants reneged on the deal, bodily harm will happen to his friends or relatives held hostage. While this tactic seems barbaric, if it kept the peace the practice might have been seen as a blessing.

7. Smith [1776] 1976, p. 123.

8. Smith [1776] 1976, p. 126.

9. Noll 1998, no page numbers.

10. *Wall Street Journal*, editorial, March 5, 2010, p. A20.

11. Labor unions are usually vociferous advocates of raising the minimum wage. While union leaders will testify that such legislation will helping the working man and woman, what they should be saying is that the minimum wage shields unions from competition from unskilled workers. This assumes that skilled and unskilled workers are interchangeable. Professional sports athletes have mastered the knack of pursuing self-interest at the expense of unrepresented people via their player unions. By trading enhanced rights for incumbent players for limitations on the rights of amateur players, such as salary caps for draft picks, incumbent players are pursuing a variation on "taxation without representation."

12. Wikipediaquote.org.

13. Akerlof and Yellen 1970.

14. Brandenburger and Nalebuff 1997, p. 204.

15. I always wondered about the implications of giving 110 percent: Wouldn't the excessive strain lead to injury or death?

16. McManus 1975, pp. 334–50.

17. Halberstam 1989, p. 305.

18. Mickey Mantle and his teammates apparently ruminated about how much fun it might have been to play for the Washington Senators, where there was no pressure to win. They eventually decided that playing for a losing team would be demoralizing.

19. Then again, baseball and hockey owners can plausibly argue that players received a lot of training in the minor leagues at company expense.

20. Edgar Allan Poe, "The Purloined Letter," quoted in Davis 1997, pp. 27–28.

21. Cook 1966, pp. 87–95.

22. *Sporting News Complete Super Bowl Book 1994*, 69.

Chapter 4

1. U.S. Department of Commerce 1975, p. 317; U.S. Department of Commerce 2008, pp. 432 and 745.

2. *Barron's*, 26 August 1957, p. 1.

3. Frank, 16 April 1960, p. 133. A few years later, Mr. Weiss would be the General Manager of the New York Mets, who occupied (rode?) the white elephant known as Shea Stadium. Irony is in abundant supply in professional sports.

4. Baade 1994, p. 15.

5. Baade 1994, p. 21.

6. Yes, I'm overdoing the George Steinbrenner motif, but he is one of the best-known owners.

7. Veeck 1965, pp. 20–22.

8. During the postwar era, owners often did not raise ticket prices after winning a pennant (Surdam 2008, p. 319). This era was marked by small changes in the Consumer Price Index, but the rarity of ticket-price hikes after pennant wins remains a surprise, at least to this researcher.

9. During the 1930s, even fans of the woebegone Phillies preferred games with league-leading teams, rather than with fellow bottom feeders (Surdam 2009, p. 46; Surdam forthcoming).

10. During the 1950s, this could also be a code for "too many blacks." Owners openly eschewed some cities because they had a greater than average proportion of blacks. Since black people had lower incomes, the owners assumed they would be less likely to attend games. Baseball owners in the late 1940s practiced cognitive dissonance, accusing black fans of refusing to attend games while they, the owners, refused to hire black players.

11. Quinn and Surdam 2010.

12. Creamer 1963, pp. 61–62; Veeck 1962, pp. 125–127.

13. Football coaches apparently agree. I recall hearing one coach respond to a reporter's question about how well his team played with "I won't know until I look at the film."

14. Couglan, 27 February 1956, pp. 22–23.

15. The alert reader will notice the similarity between this example and the free-lunch example in Chapter One.

16. Now, I realize that some arbitrageurs don't play fair in the eyes of the fans, having some inside influence to get tickets without standing in line or, as one of my graduate business students claimed, hiring homeless people to stand in line. These are possibly regrettable actions, although paying homeless people to stand in line seems to me a mutually advantageous outcome.

17. Kahneman, Knetsch, and Thaler 1986.

18. Surdam 2008, pp. 118–121.

19. Surdam 2008, pp. 132–134.

20. Miller 1991, pp. 167–168.

21. Veeck 1965, p. 33.

22. Quirk and Fort 1992, p. 124.

23. U.S. Congress 1957, p. 2,934; Surdam 2010.

24. Pluto 1992, p. 208.

25. Adams, 15 August 1964, p. 14.

26. Surdam 2008, p. 294; Rutter, 15 August 1964, p. 14; Smith, 28 November 1964, p. 11.

27. Durso, 16 August 1964, Sec. 5, p. 2; Durso, 15 August 1964, pp. 1 and 14.

28. Surdam 2008, p. 177–178; Leggett, 9 September 1963, p. 21.

29. Quirk and Fort 1992, p. 406.

Chapter 5

1. Ironically, in the fifteen seasons Ruth played for the Yankees, they only won seven pennants. The debut of Joe DiMaggio triggered a more sustained burst of winning: seven pennants in his first eight years. Yogi Berra had a string of fifteen pennants in eighteen years.

2. Baseball teams tend to cycle. A team playing well today tends to continue

playing well for a couple more seasons. Using sophisticated statistical analysis, sports economist Gerald Scully concluded that because teams tend to keep the core of their roster intact from year to year, there are patterns to team winning percentages over time. He calls these patterns "momentum" (Scully 1995, p. 89–96).

3. Surdam 2006, p. 208.

4. Surdam 2008, p. 57.

5. Surdam 2006, pp. 215–219.

6. Coase 1960.

7. Rottenberg 1956.

8. U.S. Senate 1958, p. 101.

9. U.S. Senate 1958, p. 183.

10. U.S. Senate 1958, p. 188.

11. U.S. Senate 1958, p. 315.

12. Surdam 2010.

13. Surdam 2008, pp. 11–31.

14. Weiss and Shaplen, 13 March 1961, pp. 31–32.

15. Surdam 2006, p. 209.

16. At a 12 percent rate of interest, $10 would be worth almost $34,000,000 in the 134 years between 1876 and 2010. Since the New York Yankees' franchise is worth in the hundreds of millions of dollars, $10 paid in 1876 would have had to increase at a faster than 12 percent rate of interest.

Chapter 6

1. Vrooman 1995, pp. 977–979.

2. Seymour 1971, p. 8.

3. Surdam 2007, p. 934.

4. Surdam 2002, p. 281.

5. Surdam 2007, p. 939–940.

6. Surdam 2007, p. 942.

7. Stann 1951, pp. 35–36.

8. I admit that this idea is not completely original. Along with polyester double-knit plaid pants and disco, the 1970s provided us with televised "sporting events" where celebrities and professional athletes competed.

9. Surdam 2008, p. 132.

Chapter 7

1. For my younger readers, a 1970s-style mystery.

2. If I don't quote Adams Smith in a book discussing economics, one of my former professors, who was purportedly on a first-name basis with the eighteenth-century thinker, will turn over in his grave.

3. Smith [1976] 1976, p. 124.

4. Don't Senators realize how creepy their hair styles (that don't occur in nature) appear?

5. Mix 1987, p. 55.

6. Harp and Hecht 2005, p. 1,062.

7. George, Kab, and Levy 2003, p. 367.

8. A few, sadly, fall short. There's a story from the 1980s about a seven-foot kid who did not finish college or make the pros. Without any marketable skills, he tried a life of crime. One day he donned a brown paper bag, presumably with eye slits but the news story didn't specify, and entered the local grocery store brandishing a gun. "Earl, what are you doing?" asked the bemused grocer. "How'd you know it was me?" replied Earl. The story is funny yet sad.

9. Miller 1991, pp. 266–267.

10. A one-third share, according to Voigt 1966, pp. 23–34.

11. Most teams were named White or Red Stockings, perhaps suggesting a postbellum foot fetish; the author has found no team nicknamed the Blue Stockings.

12. Surdam 2008, pp. 68–69.

13. Levin, Mitchell, Volcker, and Will 2000, pp. 61, 65, 69, 73, and 77.

14. Actually, as much as I've found Steinbrenner's antics deplorable, I have to admit, he'd be the perfect owner for my favorite team (if I had a favorite team). Aside from the late 1980s, when he didn't have as much direct involvement with the team, he has spent freely, if not always wisely — "Calling Oscar Gamble. Where are you?" He hasn't pocketed the profits but has plowed much of them back into the club. Fans of other franchises should be so fortunate.

Chapter 8

1. Herrnstein and Murray 1994, p. 275.

2. For a good economics treatise on discrimination, see Becker (1971).

3. After all, until the 1940s, even elite universities had quotas pertaining to the number of Jewish faculty members. Today, of course, such quotas would be disastrous to a school's reputation. In fields such as economics, Jewish professors are disproportionately represented relative to the population.

4. Fort 2006, pp. 242–243.

5. Surdam 2010.

Chapter 9

1. Scherer and Ross 1990, p. 392.

2. Smiley 1988, pp. 167–180.

3. Cashman 1991, p. 39.

4. Voigt 1966, p. 136.

5. Craig 1950, p. vii. This is Mr. Craig's bachelor's degree thesis. For an undergraduate thesis, his is first rate.

6. Seymour 1960, pp. 192–93.

7. Okkonen 1989, pp. 50–63.

8. Lowry 1992, various pages; Seymour 1971, pp. 50 and 52.

9. Riess 1995, p. 170.

10. Pietrusza 1991, pp. 213–214 and 229.

11. Salzberg 1987, pp. 93–94.

12. Levine 1985, pp. 44–45.

13. Seymour 1960, p. 196.

14. Wright and House 1989, p. 137.

15. Riess 1995, pp. 167–168; see also Vincent [1981] 1994.

16. Vincent [1981] 1994, pp. 98–99; Riess 1980, pp. 69 and 71.

17. White 1996, p. 21.

18. Pietrusza 1991, pp. 84–85.

19. Pietrusza 1991, p. 232.

20. Surdam 2008, pp. 209–243. The Continental League's appeal to Congress to thwart the American and National Leagues duopoly was ironic. The Republican and Democratic parties presented a classic duopoly. They acted similarly to our hypothetical grocery stores in setting the requirements for third parties to get campaign funds from taxpayers and to get on the ballot.

21. The whole topic of whether the American League, especially, did a good job with relocation and expansion is interesting. After bumbling an opportunity to shift the Browns and Athletics to San Francisco and Los Angeles, the American League continued to bumble. When the original Senators wanted to transfer to Minneapolis-St. Paul, the league immediately used one of its two expansion slots to place a new club in the capital. After the Athletics vacated Kansas City, the league again replaced it with an expansion club. The Kansas City Royals' sister expansion team, the Seattle Pilots, lasted just one year before transferring to Milwaukee (after the Braves left). Finally, the league put another expansion team in Seattle. The league's credo appeared to be, "Make no mistake just once."

Bibliography

Adams, Val. 1964. "Big Pitch at Networks Still in Nielsen Curve." *New York Times* (August 15), p. 15.

Akerlof, George, and Janet Yellen. 1970. "The Market for Lemons: Quality Uncertainty and the Market Mechanism." *Quarterly Journal of Economics* 84(3), pp. 488–500.

Baade, Robert. 1994. "Stadiums, Professional Sports, and Economic Development: Assessing the Reality." *Heartland Policy Study*. No. 62 (April 4).

Barron's. 1957. "Giant Subsidy: It Points Up a Dangerous Trend in Municipal Finance." (August 26), p. 1. No author.

Batra, Ravi. 1988. *The Great Depression of 1990*. New York: Dell.

Becker, Gary S. 1971. *The Economics of Discrimination*, 2nd ed. Chicago: University of Chicago Press.

Boyle, Robert H. 1961. "Yes, It's Livelier — and Here Is the Proof." *Sports Illustrated* (August 28), pp. 14, 16–17.

Brandenburger, Adam M., and Barry J. Nalebuff. 1997. *Co-Opetition*. New York: Doubleday.

Cashman, Sean Dennis. 1993. *America in the Gilded Age: From the Death of Lincoln to the Rise of Theodore Roosevelt*. New York: New York University Press.

Coase, Ronald. 1960. "The Problem of Social Cost." *Journal of Law and Economics* 3 (October), pp. 1–44.

Cook, Earnshaw. 1966. *Percentage Baseball*. Cambridge, MA: MIT Press.

Coughlan, Robert. 1956. "Baseball: Nine Men, A Diamond and $10 Million."

Sports Illustrated (February 27), pp. 20–23 and 55–58.

Craig, Peter S. 1950. "Organized Baseball: An Industry Study of $100 Million Spectator Sport." BA thesis: Oberlin College.

Creamer, Robert. 1963. "Quaint Cult of the Mets." *Sports Illustrated* (May 6), pp. 61–62.

Davis, Morton. 1997. *Game Theory: A Nontechnical Introduction*. New York: Dover.

Dienhart, Tom, Joe Hoppel, and Dave Sloan., eds. 1994. *The Sporting News Complete Super Bowl Book*. St. Louis: Sporting News.

Durso, Joseph, 1964. "Yanks' Sale to CBS Stirs Senate Moves for Inquiry." *New York Times* (August 15), p. 1.

———. 1964. "All Eyes in Sports Seek the Why for New Gleam in CBS's Eye." *New York Times* (August 16), Sec. 5, p. 2.

Folsom, Burton W., Jr. 1987. *The Myth of the Robber Barons*. Herndon, VA: Young America's Foundation.

Fort, Rodney D. 2006. *Sports Economics*, 2nd ed. Upper Saddle River, NJ: Pearson Prentice Hall.

Frank, Robert H., and Philip J. Cook. 1995. *The Winner-Take-All Society*. New York: Free.

Frank, Stanley. 1960. "Boss of the Yankees." *Saturday Evening Post* (April 16), pp. 31 and 111–13.

Galbraith, John Kenneth. 1988. *The Great Crash, 1929*. Boston, MA: Houghton Mifflin.

George, Charles F.P., M.D., Vyto Kab, and Allen M. Levy, M.D. 2003. "Increased Prevalence of Sleep-Disordered Breathing among Professional Football Players." *New England Journal of Medicine* 348 (No. 4, January 23), pp. 367–68.

Halberstam, David. 1989. *Summer of '49.* New York: William Morrow.

Harp, Joyce B., M.D., and Lindsay Hecht. 2005. "Obesity in the National Football League." *Journal of the American Medical Association* 293 (No. 9, March 2), pp. 1061–1062.

Harris, Mark. 1956. *Bang the Drum Slowly.* New York: Dell.

Hazlitt, Henry. [1946] 1979. "The Broken Window." *Economics in One Lesson .* Westport, CT: Arlington House.

Herrnstein, Richard J., and Charles Murray. 1994. *The Bell Curve: Intelligence and Class Structure in American Life.* New York: Free.

Kahneman, Daniel, Jack L. Knetsch, and Richard Thaler. 1986. "Fairness as a Constraint on Profit Seeking: Entitlements in the Market." *American Economic Review* 76 (No. 4, September), pp. 728–41.

Leggett, William. 1963. "Success Is Killing the AL." *Sports Illustrated* (September 9), p. 21.

Levin, Richard C., George J. Mitchell, Paul A. Volcker, and George F. Will. 2000. *The Report of the Independent Members of the Commissioner's Blue Ribbon Panel on Baseball Economics* (222.mlb.com/mlb/downloads/blue_ribbon.pdf).

Levine, Peter. 1985. *A.G. Spalding and the Rise of Baseball: The Promise of American Sport.* New York: Oxford University Press.

Lowry, Philip J. 1992. *Green Cathedrals: The Ultimate Celebration of All 271 Major League and Negro League Ballparks Past and Present.* Reading, MA: Addison-Wesley.

McManus, John C. 1975. "The Cost of Alternative Economic Organizations." *Canadian Journal of Economics.* Vol. 8, pp. 334–50.

Miller, Marvin. 1991. *A Whole Different Ball Game: The Sport and Business of Baseball.* New York: Birch Lane.

Mix, Ron. 1987. "So Little Gain for the Pain." *Sports Illustrated* 67 (No. 2, October 19), pp. 54–56 and 69.

Noll, Roger. 1998. "Economic Perspectives on the Athlete's Body." *Stanford Humanities Review* 62(2). www.stanford.edu/group/SHR/6–2. No page numbers.

Okkonen, Marc. 1989. *The Federal League of 1914–1915: Baseball's Third Major League.* Garrett Park, MD: Society for American Baseball Research.

Pietrusza, David. 1991. *Major Leagues: The Formation, Sometimes Absorption and Mostly Inevitable Demise of 18 Professional Baseball Organizations, 1871 to Present.* Jefferson, NC: McFarland.

Pluto, Terry. 1992. *Tall Tales: The Glory Years of the NBA, In the Words of the Men Who Played, Coached, and Built Pro Basketball.* New York: Fireside.

Quinn, Kevin G., and David G. Surdam. 2010. "The Case of the Missing Fans: Did Major League Baseball Owners Act Opportunistically?" Unpublished paper.

Quirk, James, and Rodney Fort. 1992. *Pay Dirt: The Business of Professional Team Sports.* Princeton, NJ: Princeton University Press.

Riess, Steven A. 1980. *Touching Base: Professional Baseball and American Culture in the Progressive Age.* Westport, CT: Greenwood.

_____. 1995. *Sport in Industrial America, 1850–1920.* Wheeling, IL: Harlan Davidson.

Rottenberg, Simon. 1956. "The Baseball Players' Labor Market." *Journal of Political Economy* 64(3), pp. 242–258.

Rutter, Richard. 1964. "Big-League Deal Is Minor to CBS." *New York Times* (August 15), p. 14.

St. John, Allen. 2005. "Totally Torre." *New York Times* (September 2), p. W6.

Salzberg, Charles. 1987. *From Set Shot to Slam Dunk: The Glory Days of Basketball in the Words of Those Who Played It.* Lincoln, NE: University of Nebraska Press.

Scherer, F.M., and David Ross. 1990. *Industrial Market Structure and Economic Performance,* 3rd ed. Boston: Houghton Mifflin.

Scully, Gerald. 1995. *The Market Structure*

of Sports. Chicago: University of Chicago Press.

Seymour, Harold. 1960. *Baseball: The Early Years.* New York: Oxford University Press.

Seymour, Harold. 1971. *Baseball: The Golden Age.* New York: Oxford University Press.

Smiley, Robert. 1988. "Empirical Evidence on Strategic Entry Deterrence." *International Journal of Industrial Organization* 6(2), pp. 167–180.

Smith, Adam. [1776] 1976. *An Inquiry into the Nature and Causes of the Wealth of Nations.* Indianapolis: Liberty Classics reprint.

Smith, Lester. 1964. "CBS Deal Pinpoints Soaring Price Tag on Big-Time Clubs." *New York Times* (November 28), p. 11.

Spink, C.C. 1964. "'Free-Agent Draft Legal'—Antitrust Expert." *The Sporting News* (December 12), p. 4.

Stann, Francis. 1951. "'Buy the Browns' Time." *Baseball Digest* (March), pp. 35–36.

Sullivan, Mark. 1900–25. *Our Times,* "Vol. II: America Finding Herself." New York: Charles Scribner's Sons.

Surdam, David. 2002. "The American 'Not-So-Socialist' League in the Postwar Era." *Journal of Sports Economics* 3(3), pp. 264–290.

_____. 2006. "The Coase Theorem and Player Movement in Major League Baseball." *Journal of Sports Economics* 6(2), pp. 201–21.

_____. 2007. "A Tale of Two Gate-sharing Plans: The National Football League and the National League, 1952–56." *Southern Economic Journal* 73(4), pp. 931–46.

_____. 2008. *The Postwar New York Yankees: A Revisionist View of Baseball's Golden Age.* Lincoln: University of Nebraska Press.

_____. 2009. "What Brings Fans to the Ball Park? Evidence from New York Yankees' and Philadelphia Phillies' Financial Records." *The Journal of Economics* 35(1), pp. 35–48.

_____. 2010. "The NBA: An Economic History." Unpublished manuscript.

_____. Forthcoming. *Wins, Losses, and Empty Seats: How Baseball Outlasted the Great Depression.* Lincoln: University of Nebraska Press.

Thorn, John, Pete Palmer, Michael Gershman, eds. 2001. *Total Baseball: The Official Encyclopedia of Major League Baseball,* 7th ed. New York: Viking.

Tversky, Amos, and Thomas Gilovich. 1989. "The Cold Facts About the 'Hot Hand' in Basketball." *Chance: New Directions for Statistics and Computing* 2(1), pp. 16–21.

United States. Congress. House of Representatives. 1957. *Organized Professional Team Sports: Hearings before the Antitrust Subcommittee of the Committee on the Judiciary.* Serial No. 8, 85th Cong., 1st sess. Washington, D.C.: Government Printing Office.

_____. _____. Senate. 1958. "Organized Professional Team Sports." *Hearings before the Subcommittee on Antitrust and Monopoly of the Committee on the Judiciary.* 85th Cong., 2nd Sess. Washington, D.C.: Government Printing Office.

_____. _____. _____. 1964. "Professional Sports Antitrust Bill—1964." *Hearings before the Subcommittee on Antitrust and Monopoly of the Committee on the Judiciary.* 88th Cong., 2nd Sess. Washington, D.C.: Government Printing Office.

_____. _____. _____. 1965. "Professional Sports Antitrust Bill—1965." *Hearings before the Subcommittee on Antitrust and Monopoly of the Committee on the Judiciary.* 89th Cong., 1st Sess. Washington, D.C.: Government Printing Office.

_____. Department of Commerce. Bureau of the Census. 1975. *Historical Statistics of the United States: Colonial Times to 1970.* 2 vols. Washington, D.C.: Government Printing Office.

_____. _____. _____. 2008. *Statistical Abstract of the United States: 2009.* Washington, D.C.: Government Printing Office.

Veeck, Bill. 1962. *Veeck as in Wreck.* New York: Putnam.

_____. 1965. *The Hustler's Handbook.* New York: Putnam.

Vincent, Ted. [1981] 1994. *The Rise and Fall of American Sport: Mudville's Revenge.* Lincoln: Bison.

Voigt, David. 1966. *American Baseball: From Gentleman's Sport to the Commissioner System*. Norman, OK: University of Oklahoma Press.

Vrooman, John. 1995. "A General Theory of Sports Leagues." *Southern Journal of Economics* 61(4), pp. 971–990.

Wall Street Journal. 2010. "Lost Wages of Youth." Editorial. March 5, p. A20.

Weiss, George, and Robert Shaplen. 1961. "The Best Decision I Ever Made." *Sports Illustrated* (March 13), pp. 28–32 and 37–39.

White, G. Edward. 1996. *Creating the National Pastime: Baseball Transforms Itself, 1903–1953*. Princeton, NJ: Princeton University Press.

Wright, Craig R., and Tom House. 1989. *The Diamond Appraised*. New York: Fireside.

Index

Abdul-Jabbar, Kareem 48, 77, 122, 171
African American athletes 113, 153–154, 156, 157–158, 160–161, 181; *see also* athletes
Akerlof, George 70
Alcindor, Lew *see* Abdul-Jabbar, Kareem
All-American Football Conference 159, 162
Allen, George 81–82
American Association 162, 170–171, 172, 175; competitive balance in 125; innovations of 163, 167; *see also* leagues
American Basketball Association 35, 163, 171, 178
American Basketball League 162
American Football League 162–163, 178
American League 123, 172, 173; competitive balance in 110, 111–112, 114, 125; and National League 162, 174, 175–177, 187; and reserve clause 120; and revenue sharing 132–133, 134, 138; *see also* baseball; leagues; National League
American League Championship Series (2004) 37–39, 49
American Professional Football Association 124
arbitrage opportunities 50, 52–53, 156; and ticket prices 97–99, 101, 185
arbitration, salary 71–72, 77, 145–146, 150; *see also* salaries, player
Arizona Diamondbacks 43–44
athletes 142; and blacklisting between leagues 170–171; "busts" 70–71; exploitation of 102, 145; and labor rights 119, 121–122; and local economies 85–86; movement of, between teams 114–117, 121–122, 127–128; and productivity 5, 72, 73–77, 152; and racial discrimination 113, 152–154, 156, 157–158, 160–161, 181; skill of 139–143, 181; and steroids 143–144; *see also* salaries, player
Atlanta Braves 44, 103–104, 114
Auerbach, Red 47–48, 161

Baade, Rob 87
Babson, Roger 184
Baltimore Colts 100
Baltimore Orioles 126
Bando, Sal 115
Bang the Drum Slowly (Harris) 77
Banks, Ernie 113
Barksdale, Don 161
Barrow, Ed 50
baseball: and antitrust legislation 60, 63, 82, 120, 176; and competitive balance 110–112, 113–114, 128–129; and curses 39–40; and discrimination 153–155, 156–158, 159; and the draft 60–61; and fan attendance 91, 92–93, 94–95; and farm systems 116, 126–127; and free agency 59–60, 72, 77, 92, 105, 117–118, 119, 121–123, 145–146, 150; and league competition 165, 167–178; and pension fund 76; and player movement 114–117; and politics 173–174; and revenue sharing 132–138, 180–181; and salaries of players 144–146, 147–148, 149–150; and salary arbitration 71–72, 77; and schedule strength 125; and scheduling 43–44; and statistics 45–46, 48–53, 54, 55–56; and taxes 19, 22–23, 127; and television 101, 103–104; and ticket prices 22–23, 151–152, 167; *see also* leagues; stadiums
basketball 139, 162, 178; and antitrust legislation 82; and competitive balance 112–113; and discrimination 153, 159–161; and the draft 77–78, 109–110; and fan attendance 94; and league competition 165, 173; and player blacklisting 170; and profits 104, 168; and revenue sharing 133; and rule changes 54, 163; and salaries of players 129, 146; and schedule strength 124–125; and statistics 47–48, 54
Basketball Association of America 133, 160
Batra, Ravi 184
batting averages 49–51; *see also* statistics
BCS rankings 55

Beane, Billy 49, 50
Becker, Gary 155
Berra, Yogi 116, 125, 144, 185
binding salary arbitration *see* arbitration, salary
Bing, Dave 112
black athletes *see* African American athletes
Blue, Vida 115
Bonds, Barry 112, 130
Bonilla, Bobby 112
Boston Braves 116
Boston Celtics 47–48
Boston Red Sox 113, 115, 122, 127, 156; American League Championship Series (2004) 37–39, 49; and salaries of players 75, 150; and win-loss records 111–112
Boston Red Stockings 111, 148
Bowie, Sam 113
Boyer, Clete 116
Brady, Tom 54
Brooklyn Dodgers 116, 128, 135, 157; and fan attendance 93, 134; move of, to Los Angeles 94, 138, 176; and star players 115; and World Series appearances 39
Brush, John 174
Buffalo Bills 40
Burke, Mike 108

Campaneris, Bert 115
cash costs 13, 15; *see also* opportunity costs
CBS 104, 106–107, 108
Celler, Emanuel 107
Cepeda, Orlando 117
Chamberlain, Wilt 48, 105, 122, 160, 161, 165
Chandler, Happy 157
Cheung, Steven 73
Chicago Bears 124
Chicago Bulls 83–84, 94
Chicago Cardinals 112, 124, 133, 135
Chicago Cubs 94, 103–104, 112, 169; and the "Curse of the Billy Goat" 39–40
Chicago White Sox 77, 91, 94, 103, 116
Chicago White Stockings 132, 172
Cicotte, Eddie 77
Cincinnati Red Stockings 109, 132, 147–148
Cincinnati Reds 101, 127, 174
city economies *see* local economies
Cleveland Browns 112, 132
Cleveland Indians 91, 122, 150
Clifton, Nat ("Sweetwater") 160
Coase, Ronald 117–118, 119, 120–121
Cochrane, Mickey 115
collusive agreements 59, 62–63, 66; *see also* price-fixing
commodities: and market demand 20; normal and inferior goods 18
competitive balance 110–113, 125; and free agency 117–123; measurement of 113–114;

and remedies for imbalance 126–130, 180; and revenue sharing 131–138; and salary caps 129; and schedule strength 123–126
competitive imbalance *see* competitive balance
Consumer Price Index 92–93, 94–95, 185
Continental League 76, 162, 176–177; *see also* leagues
Cook, Earnshaw 81
Cook, Philip 67
Cooper, Chuck 160
costs *see* opportunity costs
Cousy, Bob 107–108, 146, 161
Cuban, Mark 33
"Curse of the Bambino" 39
"Curse of the Billy Goat" 39–40
cushioning 17; *see also* price determination

Daley, Bud 116
DeBusschere, Dave 112
demand 17–25, 26–29, 32; elasticity 20–24, 183; and ticket prices 91–93, 94, 98–100, 180; *see also* price determination
Denver Broncos 40
Detroit Pistons 112
Detroit Tigers 150
DiMaggio, Joe 125, 126, 185
diminishing marginal productivity 123
discrimination 152, 181; and fans 157; and managerial staff 156; racial 113, 153–155, 156–161, 181, 185; statistical 153–154
Dixon, Paul 119–120
Doby, Larry 113
Doerr, Bobby 75
draft 126–127; baseball 60–61; basketball 77–78, 109–110; football 61–62, 112
Dunn, Jack 164–165, 171
Durocher, Leo 46, 112

Earnshaw, George 171
Eckersley, Dennis 49
economic models: definition of 8
elasticity of demand *see* demand
Elway, John 40
Embry, Wayne 160
Epstein, Theo 49, 50, 183
equilibrium price 26; *see also* price determination
Ewing, Patrick 62, 110
externalities 32, 118; *see also* price determination

fan attendance 90–95, 123, 134, 167–168; and goodwill 100; and television 96–97
farm systems 116, 126–127
Federal League 125, 162, 168, 169, 173, 175–176; *see also* leagues
Felix, Ray 161
Fingers, Rollie 49

Finley, Charlie 61, 115, 116
Flood, Curt 161
Folsom, Burton, Jr. 183
football 139, 162–163; and antitrust legislation 82; and competitive balance 112, 114;
   and the draft 61–62, 112; and integration
   159; and player movement 117; and revenue sharing 133, 135, 137, 138, 181; and
   rule changes 54–55; and salary caps 129;
   and schedule strength 123–124, 126; and
   statistics 53–54, 55; and television 138,
   178
Ford, Henry 75–76
Ford, Whitey 116, 126
Fort, Rodney 103
Foxx, Jimmie 115
franchise value 104–107, 151; see also profits
Frank, Robert 67
Frazee, Harry 106
free agency 59–60, 77, 92, 105, 145–146,
   149–151, 180, 181; and competitive balance
   117–123; and game theory 66, 72; see also
   reserve clause; salaries, player
Freedman, Andrew 174
Frick, Ford 119–120
Friedman, Milton 8

Gaedel, Eddie 137
Galbraith, John Kenneth 184
gambling 83
game theory 5; and arbitration 71–72; and
   asymmetric information 69–71; definition
   of 57; and principal-agent problems 73–
   78; Prisoners' Dilemma 57–58, 64–66,
   69, 179; and strategy mixing 78–82
Garvey, Steve 49–51
Gates, William ("Pop") 159–160
Gehrig, Lou 50, 154
Gomez, Lefty 126
Goodrich, Gail 48
Gottlieb, Eddie 105, 160
The Great Depression of 1990 (Batra) 184
Green, Pumpsie 156
Green Bay Packers 135
Greene, Bob 149
Gresham's Law 70
Grich, Bobby 56
Griffey, Ken, Jr. 115
Griffith, Calvin 119
Griffith, Clark 25
Grove, Lefty 115, 171

Halberstam, David 75
Harlem Globetrotters 160, 165
Harris, Mark 77
Hart, Basil Liddell 78
Hazlitt, Henry 11
Hebner, Richie 146
Henrich, Tommy 75

Hill, James H. 183
hitting statistics 49–51, 52; see also statistics
Hodges, Gil 39, 144
home advantage 124–125, 173
"hot hand" theory 40–41; see also probabil-
   ity theory
Houk, Ralph 117
Howard, Elston 116
Hulburt, William 132
Hunter, Jim ("Catfish") 115, 117, 150
Huntley, Chet 106

inelasticity of demand see demand
integration 159–160; see also racial discrimination
International League 164–165
Irsay, Robert 100

Jackson, Reggie 115, 117
James, Bill 45–46, 47, 49
Johnson, Ban 174, 175
Johnson, Magic 48
Johnson, Randy 43–44, 115
Johnson, Vinnie ("Microwave") 41
Jones, Sam 47–48, 122
Jordan, Michael 54, 83–84, 113

Kansas City Athletics 111, 115–116, 187
Kansas City Royals 115, 187
Keane, Johnny 116–117
Kennedy, John F. 146–147
Keynes, John Maynard 8
Killebrew, Harmon 54
Kinder, Ellis 116
Kramer, Jack 116
Kuhn, Bowie 115
Kurland, Bob 146

Laimbeer, Bill 145
Landis, Kenesaw Mountain 61, 154–155, 157
Landry, Tom 82
leagues: and advertising 172; and barriers to
   entry 29, 163–177, 181; and championship
   series 172–173; competition between 162–
   163, 167, 170–171, 172, 174–177; and competitive balance 110–112, 125, 127, 128–
   129; and expansion teams 176–178, 187;
   and minor league teams 171; and player
   blacklisting 170–171; and politics 173–174;
   and price wars 165–168; reputations of
   172; and stadium building 168–170; and
   territorial rights 25, 29, 129; see also
   American League; National League
Lloyd, Earl 160
local economies 83–87, 179; and stadiums
   86–90
Los Angeles Clippers 112
Los Angeles Dodgers 128, 138, 176
Los Angeles Lakers 40, 48, 122

Lucas, Henry 167
Lucas, Robert 6

Macauley, Ed 170
Mack, Connie 25, 115
MacPhail, Larry 108
Major League Baseball (MLB) *see* baseball
Malone, Karl 113
Malone, Moses 165
manager ratings 46–47
Mantle, Mickey 116, 126, 144, 145, 184
marginal analysis 16
marginal benefits 16–17, 23, 28, 131
marginal costs 16–17, 23, 25, 28
Marino, Dan 54
Maris, Roger 54, 116, 117
market demand 20; *see also* demand
Marshall, George Preston 159
Marx, Groucho 69
Mayberry, John 49–51
Mays, Willie 46, 113
McGraw, John 154
McLendon, John 160
media markets: and competitive balance
    110–111, 113, 114, 128, 129–130; and rev-
    enue sharing 131; and star player retention
    115, 117; *see also* television
Mexican League 162, 171, 176
Mikan, George 40, 146, 160, 161
Miller, Marvin 102, 130, 145–146
Milwaukee Braves 106, 134, 135, 157
Milwaukee Bucks 77, 122, 160
Milwaukee Hawks 124
Minneapolis Lakers 160
Minnesota Vikings 40
Mix, Ron 143
Motley, Marion 159
multiplier concept 85
Mundt, Karl 120
Munson, Thurman 127
The Myth of the Robber Barons (Folsom)
    183

National Association 111, 132, 148, 165
National Association of Base Ball Players
    29, 132
National Basketball Association (NBA) *see*
    basketball
National Football League (NFL) *see* foot-
    ball
National Hockey League 111, 133
National League 114, 125, 129, 138, 163, 167,
    170–171; and American League 162, 174,
    175–177, 187; and barriers to entry 165;
    competitive balance in 110–112; reputation
    of 172; and revenue sharing 132, 133, 134;
    see also American League; leagues
Negro League 165
New Orleans Saints 112

New York Giants (baseball) 94, 128, 134,
    174, 176
New York Giants (football) 106
New York Knicks 104, 109–110, 112
New York Mets 125, 128, 150
New York Yankees 50, 111, 113, 115–116, 125,
    128; American League Championship Se-
    ries (2004) 37–39, 49; and CBS owner-
    ship 104, 106–107, 108; and the draft 60;
    and fan attendance 91, 93, 94, 123, 134;
    and farm system 126–127; and player
    movement 115, 116–117; and racial dis-
    crimination 113, 156; and revenue sharing
    134–135; and salaries of players 75, 149–
    150; and star players 115; and television
    revenue 138; and ticket prices 22–23, 151;
    win-loss records 112, 114, 116–117, 125; *see
    also* baseball
Nixon, Richard 81–82, 166
Noll, Roger 67–68

Oakland Athletics 115
O'Conner, Leslie 61
Okkonen, Marc 169
Olajuwon, Hakeem 113
Oliver, Al 51
O'Malley, Walter 95–96, 97, 99–100, 101,
    135, 138
on-base percentage 49–51; *see also* statistics
opportunity costs 11–13, 34, 179; and stadi-
    ums 86, 87; and ticket prices 98–99;
    types 13–16
optimal competitive balance *see* competitive
    balance
owners, team: conglomerates 103–104; and
    discrimination 152, 154, 156–158; and fan
    attendance 90–91; and free agency 59–60,
    66, 119–120; and player depreciation 103,
    105, 146; and player pension fund 76, 171;
    and political connections 173–174; and
    profit maximization 25, 63–64, 97, 100;
    and profits 102–103, 105, 108, 167–168,
    180; and public funding 86–90, 103; and
    reserve clause 119–122; and rule changes 6;
    and salaries of players 145, 146

Pacific Coast League 162, 171, 176
parity *see* competitive balance
Phelps, Edmund 8
Philadelphia Athletics 93, 115, 174
Philadelphia Phillies 112
Philadelphia 76ers 41, 122
Philadelphia Warriors 105, 160
Phoenix Suns 77
pitching statistics 48–49, 51–52; *see also*
    statistics
Pittsburgh Pirates 112
play-calling 78–82
Players' Association 145–146

Players' League 125, 162, 175
Podoloff, Maurice 170
points-to-points-allowed ratios 45–46; *see also* statistics
Pollard, Fritz 159
Pollard, Jim 146
Portland Trailblazers 94, 113
present value 35–36; *see also* salaries, player
prestige costs 14–15; *see also* opportunity costs
price determination: and efficiency 27–29, 32; and equilibrium price 26; and externalities 32; and preference changes 20; and price discrimination 29–32; and price mechanism 26–27; and supply and demand 17–29, 32; and variable pricing 31; *see also* ticket prices
price elasticity of demand 20–24, 183; *see also* demand
price-fixing 58–59; and drafts 60–63; and free agency 59–60; *see also* profits
Prisoners' Dilemma 57–58, 64–66, 69, 179; *see also* game theory
probability theory 37–39, 40–42; and batting averages 44; and series lengths 42–44; and standard deviations 42–43, 44; *see also* statistics
productivity 73–77, 152; and player salaries 5, 142; and statistics 48
profits 102–104, 167–168, 180; and franchise value 104–107, 151; maximization 25–26, 58–59, 97, 100; and opportunity costs 33–34; and salaries of players 60, 63–64; and synergy 106–108; *see also* ticket prices

Quirk, James 103

racial discrimination 113, 153–155, 156–161, 181, 185; *see also* discrimination
Ramirez, Manny 130
Reichardt, Richard 60
"relegation and promotion" process 164–165; *see also* leagues
reserve clause 59–60, 77, 144–145, 181; and competitive balance 119–122; and owner profits 102, 105, 151, 180; *see also* free agency; salaries, player
revenue sharing 131, 133–138, 180–181; history 132–133; *see also* competitive balance
reverse-order draft *see* draft
Rickey, Branch 157, 177
Riess, Steven 169, 173–174
Rivera, Mariano 49
Robertson, Oscar 54, 160, 161, 165
Robeson, Paul 159
Robinson, Frank 117
Robinson, Jackie 113, 134, 156, 157, 159
Rockefeller, John D. 27, 29, 183
Rodman, Dennis 54

Rodriguez, Alex 72, 115
Ross, David 163
Rottenberg, Simon 117–118, 119, 120–121
Rudi, Joe 115
Ruppert, Jacob 23, 154
Russell, Bill 107–108, 160, 161
Ruth, Babe 50, 106, 111, 122, 125, 185; and the "Curse of the Bambino" 39; and discrimination 154–155

St. Louis Browns 40, 93, 112, 115–116, 135
St. Louis Cardinals 116
salaries, player 66–69, 139–144; and arbitration 71–72, 77, 145–146, 150; and bargaining power 142; and bonuses 60–61, 76–77; and depreciation 103, 105, 146; and discrimination 158; and free agency 59–60, 77, 92, 105, 145–146, 149–151, 180, 181; and present value 35; and productivity 5, 142; and reservation salaries 144–145; and the reserve clause 59–60, 77, 102, 105, 144–145, 151, 180, 181; and salary caps 66, 102, 129–130; and technology 147–149; and ticket prices 92, 150–151; *see also* athletes
San Francisco Giants 86, 176
Santo, Ron 56
Saperstein, Abe 160
scarcity: and allocation 16–17; definition 9–11, 17, 179; and opportunity costs 11; and price determination 22; and supply and demand 17
schedule strength 123–126
Scherer, F.M. 163
Schilling, Curt 43–44
Scott, Bryon 48
Scully, Gerald 186
Seattle Mariners 115
series length 42–44
Seymour, Harold 132
Shibe, Ben 174
Shula, Don 82
Simmons, Al 115
slugging average 49–51; *see also* statistics
Smiley, Robert 163–164
Smith, Adam 58, 63, 67, 142
Spalding, Albert 172
Speaker, Tris 122
stadiums 95–96, 148; as barriers to league entry 168–170; and player statistics 52–53; and present value 36; and public funding 86–90
Stanton, Frank 106–107
statistics 44–45, 47, 179; and baseball 45–46, 48–53, 54, 55–56; and basketball 47–48, 54; and computer models 55; and discrimination 153–154; and football 53–54, 55; and player productivity 48; *see also* probability theory

Steinbrenner, George 10, 90, 117, 128–129, 160, 186; and purchase of the Yankees 108, 151
Stengel, Casey 156
Stephens, Vern 116
Stern, David 109
steroid use 54, 143, 144
Stockton, John 113
Stokes, Maurice 161
Stoneham, Charles 95–96, 101
Stottlemyre, Mel 116, 126
Summer of '49 (Halberstam) 75
supply 17–18, 25–29, 32, 33; shifters 25–26; see also price determination
Syracuse Nationals 124–125

taxes: amusement (post–World War I) 22–23; corporate 19; paid by athletes 85–86; payroll 127; and player depreciation 103, 105; rates of (1950s) 146–147
TBS 103–104
television 101; and baseball 101, 103–104, 107; and fan attendance 96–97; and football 138; and opportunity costs 15, 107; and revenue sharing 101, 135, 137–138; and salaries of players 148–149; see also media markets
Terry, Ralph 116
ticket prices 91–95; and arbitrage opportunities 97–99, 101; and league competition 165–167; and local economies 83; owners' power over setting 102, 180, 185; and player salaries 92, 150–151; and price elasticity of demand 22–23; and revenue sharing 132, 133–134; and territorial rights 29; and variable pricing 31, 101; see also price determination
time costs 13–14, 98, 99; see also opportunity costs
Topping, Dan 108
Total Baseball Rating (TBR) 55–56
tourism 84–85
transaction costs 121–122

Union Association 111, 125, 162, 167, 170–171, 172, 175; see also leagues
Utah Jazz 113

Vandeweghe, Ernie 146
Vandeweghe, Kiki 146
variable pricing 31, 101; see also price determination
Veeck, Bill, Jr. 90–91, 94–95, 103, 137
Veeck, William 90
Vincent, Ted 173–174
voluntary trade 27–28, 69
von der Ahe, Chris 172
von Neuman, John 5
Vrooman, John 131

Walk, Neal 77
Washington Senators 150, 154, 184
The Wealth of Nations (Smith) 63
Webb, Del 108
Weiss, George 86, 126, 185
West, Jerry 48, 54
WGN 103–104
White, Maurice 161
A Whole Different Game (Miller) 102
Wilhelm, Hoyt 49
Williams, Ted 146, 148–149
Willis, Bill 159
The Winner-Take-All Society (Frank and Cook) 67
World Series 39–40, 43–44, 172
Worthy, James 48
Wright, Craig 173
Wright, Harry 109, 132, 147–148

Yankees see New York Yankees
Yao Ming 140, 153
Yardley, George 146
Yawkey, Tom 75–76
Yellen, Janet 70